DINNER IN THE DINER

ILLUSTRATION: THE BETTMANN ARCHIVE, INC.

THE BETTMANN ARCHIVE, INC.

GREAT RAILROAD RECIPES OF ALL TIME

Pictures-Maps-Recipes From Famous Railways

Dinner in the Diner

★

by WILL C. HOLLISTER

Introduction by Spencer Crump

BOOK DESIGN: HANK JOHNSTON

TRANS-ANGLO BOOKS

DINNER IN THE DINER

Great Railroad Recipes of All Time

BY WILL C. HOLLISTER

FOURTH EDITION

Printed and Bound in the United States of America

Library of Congress Catalog Card Number: 77-154318

ISBN: 87046-011-0

Twelfth Printing: Summer 1989

Published by

Trans-Anglo Books

a Division of

Interurban Press

P.O. Box 6444 • Glendale, California 91205

INTRODUCTION

Until recently, the American passenger train seemed headed for oblivion, despite its healthy state in Europe and elsewhere. Now, Amtrak and skyrocketing gasoline prices have combined to foster at least a mild revival of the rail mode of travel. Alas, the railroad dining car, once the most notable feature of the great and not-so-great passenger train, may not fare so well.

Dinner in the Diner, once upon a time, was the high point of the trip. Railroads took great pride in serving meals on wheels and the condition of the car, with its shining interior and spotless napery, reflected this. The crews were courteous, the service usually excellent. And, ah . . . the food.

The great trains usually served great food. It helped make their reputations. Each railroad had its culinary specialty. The famed Northern Pacific Big Baked Potato. Oyster Bisque on the Chesapeake & Ohio. Fred Harvey Service on the Santa Fe, featuring fresh mountain trout caught the same day along the right-of-way.

Never mind that dining cars invariably lost money. In the day of the great trains it was cheap advertising, money well spent to lure the traveler who had a choice of competing roads. There was prestige in operating first-class dining cars, and in those days American railroads were after passengers very much like today's airlines.

Will Hollister has collected typical recipes from representative railroads throughout the U.S. and Canada, the roads which featured outstanding meal service. We have put them together in this volume which will appeal at once to the railfan, model builder—and the cook at home anxious to savor the type of meal which made the reputation of many a big railroad.

Since the recipes were gathered from railroads serving areas with distinctive regional food tastes, they are diverse and cosmopolitan in their offerings. The dishes also range from those developed for the demanding gourmet to the simpler ones for the hungry business traveler whose chief goal is satisfaction of an appetite.

This writer has, over the years, traveled on many of the railroads whose recipes are featured in this book. Until comparatively late in the era of privately owned passenger trains, the old standards were maintained.

But as the 1960s wore on, more and more of the main-line passenger trains vanished. On the trains remaining, dining service was sometimes downgraded, perhaps to a lunch-counter diner or even an automat car. A few kept the flags flying to the end, of course, as witness the Santa Fe's Super Chief and its famed "Turquoise Room" dining.

Written meal orders became a tradition to assure clarity on most railway diners. Here Spencer Crump prepares an order during a trip eastward on the Southern Pacific.

Alas, the Super Chief is no more. Amfleet is here. And Amtrak has done pretty well under trying circumstances. Some of Amtrak's main trains, such as the Broadway Limited, Empire Builder, San Francisco Zephyr, have offered full-length dining cars with good food and good service, with the traditional white linen tablecloths, napkins and the fresh rose in the bud vase. And, wonder of wonders, prices have been reduced.

More recent developments have not been so encouraging. In an effort to cut costs in an era of governmental belt-tightening, Amtrak has taken to offering airline-style meals heated in a microwave oven. The reviews have not been good, but improvements have been promised. The instant meals are still served in a dining car, though, and perhaps even if things are no longer done in the grand old manner, the opportunity will remain for the hungry rail traveler to step into the restaurant car, be ushered to a table by the steward, and be served dinner in the diner.

December 1981
SPENCER CRUMP

The sound of chimes traditionally became "First Call for Dinner" in the diner.

Dining on the Southern Pacific, with Mount Shasta in the distance.

☆ CONTENTS ☆

L and N dining cars in the 1900's featured leaded glass doors, ornate chandeliers, and gaily decorated ceilings.

PREFACE

Traveling across the nation aboard a train became an exciting and informative experience as soon as the first transcontinental link was completed in 1869. Even in the twentieth century, a journey by train retained much of the excitement and adventure that it did when the Iron Horse initially began its treks across the continent.

Only railways could present the fun and excitement of views from rights-of-way cut from rugged mountains or in primitive mountains, of Pullman sleepers, of comfortable lounge cars, and of the other rail cars adding up to a train.

Of all the fine cars in a train's consist, travelers long ago pronounced the dining car as the most exciting, dramatic, and luxurious.

Train trips always were exciting, but for most travelers a most memorable part of the journey was dinner in the diner.

Almost as soon as they were introduced, diners became centers of trains' activities. The hum of conversation combined with the rich, mixed aromas of fine cooking in an atmosphere pervaded with an aura of elegance.

The diner was the place where the passenger was made to feel like royalty, where his ego could be expanded, and his appetite for piquant foods rewarded.

Railroads developed a pride in the contents of their dining car menus, which in turn attracted travelers from rival lines. Many railways produced dishes related, in many ways, to the territories served--adding to the pleasure of the journeys as well as appeasing the hungry appetites of travelers.

The mid-twentieth century brought an apparent waning in rail traffic, following which railroad companies began to merge in efforts to meet the changing economic conditions. Mergers and the reduction in rail traffic resulted, unfortunately, in fewer passenger trains and fewer diners.

Unless there is a change in the trend, the railway diner will eventually take its place with the stagecoach, bi-winged airplane, and electrically-powered auto.

And with the railway diner will disappear the fabulously delicious recipes that became famous on the various lines.

This book is designed to preserve representative recipes served on railways throughout America.

The appetizing recipes served on dining cars were evolved through years of experience with travelers' appetites as well as the technical development of the dining car to the point in the twentieth century where it became in many ways a swank restaurant on railway wheels.

Early day rail travelers encountered a considerable number of problems when they sought to satisfy their hunger during trips. The diner familiar during the twentieth century--with heating, air conditioning, vestibules, comfortable seating, pleasing decor, and colorful lighting, to say nothing of stainless steel cooking facilities and refrigeration--evolved during the years.

Travelers during the first part of the nineteenth century not only had to change cars (because most roads were relatively short during that pre-merger era) for a trip of any sizeable distance, but they also had to delay their trips to stop at depots to eat.

Credit for developing the first railway dining car generally has been given to George M. Pullman (1831-1897), although this distinction can be debated.

The famed inventor of the Palace Sleeping Car in 1867 introduced a "hotel car" which was a combination sleeping and eating facility. One end of the car contained a kitchen and tables that at meal time could be set between the seats. The crew for the car included a cook and a porter who served as waiter.

The initial hotel car, "The President," made its debut on the Great Western Railway (later part of the Canadian National) on a much publicized excursion between Chicago and New York.

Dinner cost a princely 50 cents and the menu consisted of oysters, cold and broiled meats, eggs, Welsh Rarebit, coffee, and tea.

The eating car drew wide praise and immediately two similar cars, "Western World" and "Kalamazoo," were constructed and placed in operation on the Michigan Central, a line later absorbed by the New York Central.

Mr. Pullman's next step was the construction of what he called a "restaurant car," eliminating the sleeping facilities and devoted exclusively to serving food. The car, introduced in 1868, was named "Delmonico" after the famous New York restaurateur, and placed in service on the Chicago, Alton and St. Louis Railroad (later absorbed by the Gulf, Mobile and Ohio) on runs between Chicago and St. Louis. The price for a meal was $1.00, a relatively substantial sum for a meal at the time.

Even before George Pullman's epoch-making inventions, however, meals were served on trains--albeit with less publicity and success.

The first known instance of meals being served on a train was January 10, 1853, aboard a Baltimore and Ohio Railroad train from Baltimore to Wheeling, Virginia (now West Virginia). Boards for tables and benches were erected the full length of the car and travelers ate food prepared by a caterer before the journey.

Still another case of serving food during a trip came in 1855 on an excursion between Alexandria and Culpepper Court House, Virginia, aboard the Orange and Alexandria Railroad, later absorbed by the Southern Railroad. A baggage car was converted into a lunch room for the trip.

In June, 1858, writers, artists, and photographers rode a Baltimore and Ohio excursion train from Baltimore into the Allegeny Mountains and return, enjoying, according to *Harper's Magazine,* a "dining saloon with a table running the whole length of the car."

Most of the early day experiments with serving food during rail trips were on excursions, but attempts were made to serve the appetites of the average passenger.

Apparently the first railway dining cars on regularly scheduled passenger trains were used in 1863 on the Philadelphia, Wilmington, and Baltimore Railroad, later consolidated into the Pennsylvania Railroad.

These cars were remodeled day coaches fitted with an "eating bar," a steam box, and "other fixtures usually found in a first-class restaurant," according to *Appleton's Railway and Steam Navigation Guide* for 1863.

The food was prepared, however, at terminal stations or restaurants near depots and loaded onto the cars just before the trains departed.

It remained for George Pullman to produce the diner that became a tradition with its fine foods prepared during the trips and served in impeccable style.

Pullman dining cars helped to add pleasure and comfort to a much heralded transcontinental excursion in May, 1870, from Boston to San Francisco under sponsorship of the Boston Board of Trade.

By 1872 the rail trek from New York to San Francisco--a seven day journey if one did not stop enroute--was becoming popular and the convenience of diners added to the attraction. Describing the trip in his book, *California for Health, Pleasure, and Residence,* (Boston: 1874) author Charles Nordhoff cited the diner as "a great convenience, as well as an attractive novelty.

"I expected to find this somewhat greasy, a little untidy, and with the smell of the kitchen," he wrote. "It might, we travelers thought, be a convenience, but it could hardly be a luxury. But in fact it is as neat, as nicely fitted, as trim and cleanly, as though Delmonico had furnished it.

"And though the kitchen may be in the forward end of the car," Nordhoff continued, "so perfect is the ventilation that there is not even the faintest odor of cooking.

"You sit at little tables which comfortably accommodate four persons; you order your breakfast, dinner, or supper, from a bill of fare which contains a quite surprising number of dishes, and you eat from snow-white linen and neat dishes, admirably cooked food and pay moderate price.

"It is now the custom to charge a dollar per meal on these cars," Nordhoff wrote, "and as the cooking is admirable, the service excellent, and the food various and abundant, this is not too much.

"You may have your choice in the wilderness--eating at the rate of twenty-two miles per hour--of buffalo, elk, antelope, beef steak, mutton chops, or grouse.

"Beyond Omaha," Nordhoff noted, "unless you have taken seats in a hotel-car, you eat at stations placed at proper distances apart, where abundant provision is made, and the food is, for the most part, both well cooked and well served."

The growing rate of travel across the continent soon brought dining car facilities for chair car travelers as well as those who could afford Pullman accommodations.

It was at this time that the name Harvey House emerged in association with good dining facilities.

Frederick H. Harvey (1835-1901) was operating a group of small hotels with restaurants in the mid-west in 1876 when he induced the Santa Fe Railroad to allow him to furnish all eating facilities along the line's route in the southwest.

Harvey's operations proved so successful that arrangements were made for him to manage the entire Santa Fe dining car department.

The mid-twentieth century found the Harvey organization still managing the Santa Fe dining service with Harvey Houses and dining cars maintaining a reputation for fine food and services.

Railroads continually sought to improve their dining car facilities as means to attract passengers from competing lines.

In 1878, the Rock Island Railroad proudly was advertising "the only line of dining and restaurant cars in the United States with an elegant smoking salon." These cars operated between Chicago and Omaha.

In 1883, the Southern Pacific moved to attract more passengers by placing in service an elaborate diner, "Del Monte," which cost $15,000--a large sum for a car at that time--and was 70 feet long, or approximately 40% longer than contemporary diners.

Dining cars of this era were decorated elaborately with gold leaf, veneer panels, heavy carpeting, and stained glass windows. Large potted plants frequently decorated the interiors, and at each end of the cars were mirrored mantel pieces. Highly polished brass oil lamps were suspended from heavy chandeliers.

Travelers expected--and received--increasingly ornate surroundings in which to enjoy their meals.

Dining cars were directly responsible for a major improvement in all railway passenger cars. Prior to the event of the diner, there were few reasons to walk from car to car on a train.

More and more passengers were patronizing dining cars, and since coaches were open ended, wooden conveyances it became extremely hazardous for a passenger to make his way to the diner from a coach.

Recognizing this difficulty, H. H. Sessions of the Pullman Company invented vestibuled cars with covered passageways on platforms of cars. Initially used in April, 1887, on the Pennsylvania Railroad, the cars soon became standard equipment on all railways.

What apparently was the first reference to a "buffet car" is found in *The Railroad Gazette* for April 27, 1883, in reference to operations of the Missouri Pacific Railroad line from St. Louis.

In 1898, the Illinois Central introduced cafe cars -- described as composite baggage, smoking, cafe, and parlor cars -- which were 72 feet, six inches long and equipped with 16 wheels. The cars, built by the Pullman Company, cost $11,386 each.

The cafe compartments in these cars measured approximately 12 by nine feet and were furnished with four tables and 12 wicker arm chairs. Light came from Pintsch gas lamps, which by this time had replaced oil lamps.

In 1900, the Burlington Railroad placed buffet, smoking and library cars on trains between Denver and Chicago.

Buffet cars used extensively by railroads in the 1950's and 1960's appeared as innovations to many, but actually they had predecessors in the nineteenth century.

The Pere Marquette Railroad in 1904 revived

the practice of serving meals in the baggage car as an accommodation to summer vacationists taking excursions from Chicago. Lunch counter cars were introduced on the Southern Pacific in 1912 and on the Pennsylvania Railroad in 1913.

The passing years found the ornate finery of dining cars giving way to more simpler furnishings and decor. There was more emphasis on seating capacity and efficiency of operation.

Diners also became larger as the years passed.

Standard diners during the 1920's were 77 feet long and accommodated 36 passengers. The chef, with two assistants and a dish washer, worked in a kitchen containing approximately 30 square feet.

By 1950, diners had reached a length of 85 feet and contained a galley of approximately 130 square feet plus a pantry with 91 square feet.

Diners of the 1960's had developed into three-car complexes comprised of a kitchen car flanked by two dining cars, each of which also contained a lounge. Typical units measured 204 feet long and would accommodate 84 passengers in lavish surroundings.

The price tag, to the railroads, of these deluxe dining car units, had risen to approximately $250,000.

The staff of eleven manning such units included a steward, the chef, three assistant cooks, and six waiters.

While diners for major trips grew larger, single cars were developed for shorter trips. Snack cars with limited menus and automatic cars selling food from machines were placed on many trains formerly featuring complete dining service.

Passengers long have wondered why prices for meals aboard a standard dining car are substantially higher than similar food in a restaurant. (Dining car food prices on most railroads averaged two to three times the cost of similar meals in conventional restaurants during the 1960's) Diners must depend, unfortunately, on the limited number of patrons riding the trains and do not have access to the constant flow of traffic available to a restaurant on a public street.

Railroads began losing money on dining car operations shortly after World War I and in 1954, for example, spent an average of $1.44 for every dollar paid by a patron. Railways have attempted innovations to reduce costs. Among these experiments have been pre-cooked meals for short runs, meal coupons, meal tickets, and vending machines.

Some railroads chalk up losses to maintaining good public relations.

"There is no way that you can lose or pick up freight customers so fast as by the quality of the meal or the cup of coffee that you provide the traveler," Harry A. De Butts, president of the Southern Railway, once said.

The crews of modern dining cars received assistance in that a great deal of work is performed "off-train" in what became known as commissaries. Although most railroads found it preferable to do all cooking and baking in dining car kitchens, many lines utilized commissaries to prepare special items such as plum pudding, fancy cakes, and pies--all of which require extra attention and larger facilities.

Commissaries were developed to store meat and other perishables as well as staples; in addition, they became the headquarters of the supervising chef or dining car manager. They also provided the place for accounting, purchasing, and planning of menus.

Most commissaries were situated at terminal points of the road's system so that after each trip dining cars could be cleaned, loaded with provisions, and furnished with fresh linen.

The passing years called for the supervising chef to be aware of the varying popularity of dishes featured on the menus. Travelers' eating habits change with the years and recipes come and go like fashions. Chicken pie, sweetbreads, and the mixed grill, in demand during one period, become obsolete the next. Patrons periodically become calorie-conscious, and this must be reckoned with in planning menus.

Railroad chefs developed an understandable pride in their menus and recipes. Some chefs joined railroads after earning outstanding reputations and enviable backgrounds in leading European and American hotels.

Uniformity of service and quality in food preparation became important early in the dining car era, and railroads went to elaborate lengths to train personnel. Similarly, safety and sanitation standards were given careful attention and new recipes were tested in experimental kitchens before being offered to the public.

Railroads of the late twentieth century were finding themselves competing not only with themselves but also with air lines (which prided themselves on the food served en flight) and buses.

When railroads merge, some trains carrying diners generally are discontinued. Quite often a merger results in better passenger service and development of new types of dining equipment and service.

But the increasing competition of airplanes, buses, and automobiles doomed many fine trains. Many that remained alive revived box lunch and news-butcher refreshment service to economize.

Even with the departure of the last dining car, dinner in the diner will remain a pleasant memory for those who have enjoyed the pleasure.

Many times it occurred to the author that there should be a cookbook devoted to railroad recipes associated with dining car facilities. Searches of libraries and book stores through the volumes devoted to cooking and railways brought no record of railway recipes and very little about dining cars.

It is the author's hope that readers and users of the recipes will welcome this materialization of the idea.

The recipes described in this book have been provided by the railroads as featured as the most prominent trains operated by the lines. The railroads represented service virtually every section of the continent with the result, as would be expected, many of the recipes have regional flavor.

The past tense has been used in discussing the railroads' dining car operations because of mergers that will change the identity of many lines as well as trends away from rail travel that may doom the diner.

It is hoped that home users of these food formulas will be reminded of a time when they responded to the pleasant invitation, "First Call for Dinner" as the waiter marched down the rail car's aisles with his magical chimes, and will be able, in some measure, to recapture the pleasure of eating aboard our fabulous, luxury dining rooms on wheels.

●

It was a pleasant task to compile the work, chiefly because of the generous response and encouragement given by the railroads and related agencies. Indeed, without their cooperation this book would not exist.

Specifically, the author is indebted to the following organizations and individuals:

Association of American Railroads; David A. Swit, public relations department special representative, and his secretary, Aspasia Neophytos.

Atchison, Topeka and Santa Fe Railway: Bill Burk, manager of the public relations department, and D. Ross Sullivan, coast lines public relations department special assistant.

Baltimore and Ohio Railroad: J. B. Martin, manager for dining car and commissary facilities.

Canadian National Railways: D. S. Law, news editor.

Chesapeake and Ohio Railway: Howard Skidmore, director of public relations and passenger traffic.

Chicago, Burlington and Quincy Railroad: H. C. Murphy, president.

Chicago, Rock Island and Pacific Railroad: M. H. Bonesteel, general superintendent for dining and sleeping cars.

Fred Harvey Service: Byron Harvey, Jr.

Great Northern Railway: Frank Perrin, public relations assistant.

Illinois Central Railroad: Arthur C. Carlson, manager of press relations.

Louisville and Nashville Railroad: Clifford J. Haury, superintendent of dining cars.

Missouri-Kansas-Texas Railroad: M. R. Cring, vice president.

Missouri Pacific Railroad: Harry E. Hammer, assistant to the president for press relations.

Monon Railroad: William C. Coleman, Jr., vice president for traffic and marketing.

New York Central Railroad: Ann Kuss, public relations staff assistant.

Northern Pacific Railway: F. L. Steinbright, vice president.

Pennsylvania Railroad: Sidney N. Phelps, manager of dining car service.

Pullman Company: Ralph C. Buckingham, passenger traffic manager.

Seaboard Air Line Railroad: J. R. Getty, general passenger traffic manager.

Southern Pacific Lines: T. B. Lochhead, manager of dining car operations.

Texas and Pacific Railway: R. A. Malone, assistant director of public relations.

Western Pacific: Bernard E. Pedersen, director of advertising and public relations.

In addition, the author thanks Felisa Romero for her typing and Edwin R. Spencer for many suggestions.

Gratitude also is expressed to others who have made illustrations available and who have been credited elsewhere in this book.

WILL HOLLISTER

SPENCER CRUMP COLLECTION

The interior of a Pullman dining car — at the time an innovation in railroading — was depicted in this 1872 illustration in author Charles Nordhoff's "California for Health, Pleasure, and Residence."

ATCHISON, TOPEKA and the SANTA FE

ALL PICTURES THIS CHAPTER: SANTA FE RAILROAD

The Atchison, Topeka and Santa Fe Railroad was founded in 1858 in the frontier town of Atchison, Kansas. The line initially was intended to be a 50-mile route, but through acquisitions--largely the franchise of the Atlantic and Pacific Railroad--the Santa Fe developed into a system reaching from Chicago to the Pacific Ocean and into key areas of Texas.

It was the Santa Fe's completion to Los Angeles in 1885 that launched a rate war that helped bring many settlers westward. The price of a ticket from Missouri to Los Angeles via the Southern Pacific was $125 in 1885. Fighting the Southern Pacific, the Santa Fe cut rates until a year later the fare dropped to only $1.00. This low rate was in effect for only a day, but fares generally were reduced for many months.

Operating over approximately 13,000 miles of tracks, the Santa Fe network developed to serve 12 states and became one of the giants of the rail industry.

The name of Fred Harvey helped bring fame to the Santa Fe dining facilities. An operator of restaurants, Harvey in 1876 began furnishing restaurant facilities at the line's depots and subsequently took over management of Santa Fe's dining cars in the southwest.

The names Harvey House and Santa Fe became equally famous with travelers.

After beginning operation of its own dining cars in 1888, Santa Fe became noted for such celebrated trains as *The California Limited, The Navajo,* and *The Scout.*

Well-known Santa Fe passenger trains of the mid-twentieth century included *The Texas Chief, The San Francisco Chief, The Super Chief,* and *El Capitan.*

The Super Chief earned fame not only for a splendid dining car but also for a Pleasure-Dome-Lounge car where cocktails were offered in an attractive lower-level room. A special glamor facility was the Turquoise Room, a private dining room.

El Capitan starting in 1956 was featured as an all-coach high level train. Its high level dining car provided seating for 80 persons to dine in pent-house style--receiving food sent up by elevator from the galley below.

The lower level galley, 36 feet long, was rated as one of the largest kitchens in railroad service.

In addition to the penthouse dining room, *El Capitan* also carried a coffee shop-cocktail lounge car.

Santa Fe commissaries, in Chicago and Los Angeles as well as Richmond, California, and Clovis, New Mexico, were designed to serve as storehouses rather than kitchens.

In the 1960's, the Santa Fe fleet of diners employed 96 regular crews consisting of a total of approximately 800 men.

The recipes offered here have been featured on the noted Santa Fe trains as well as in the Fred Harvey restaurants in hotels and depots along the railroad's lines.

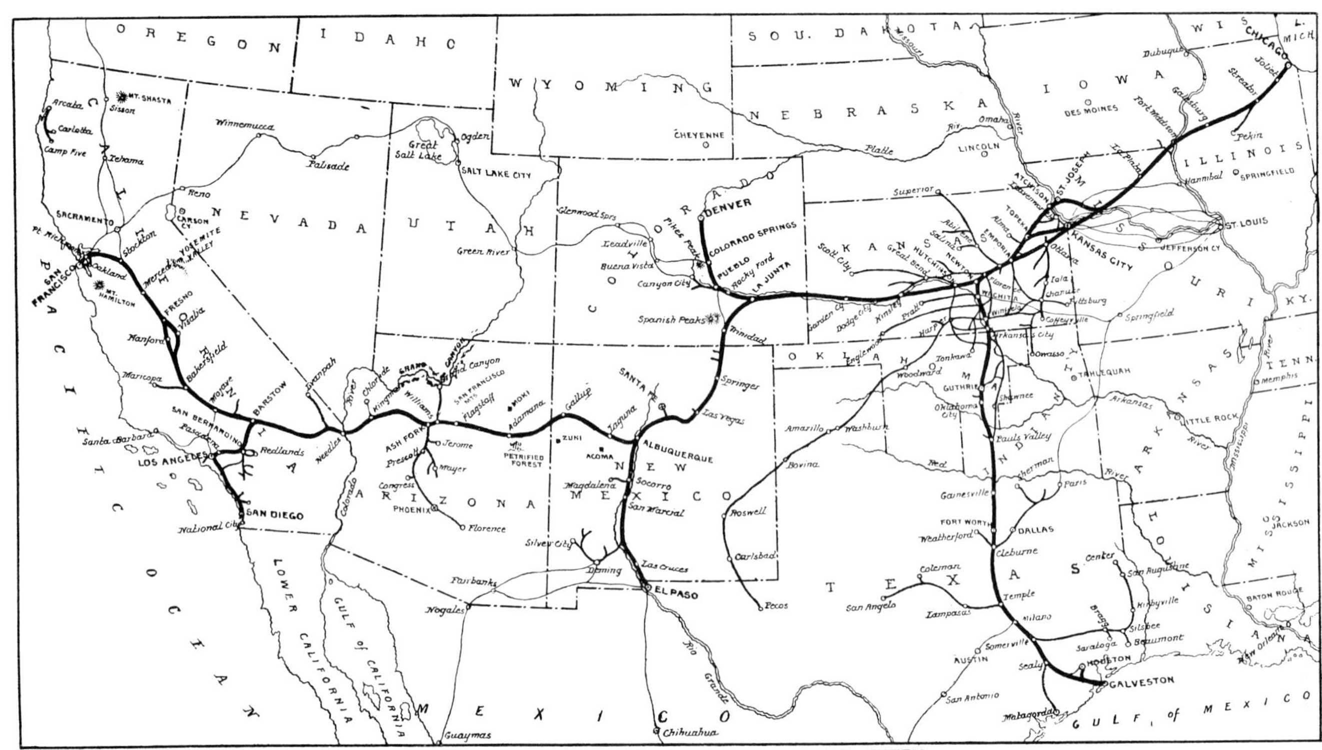

THE ATCHISON, TOPEKA AND SANTA FE RAILWAY SYSTEM.

Not only did the Fred Harvey operation manage Santa Fe's on-board dining car service until the last years before Amtrak, but it ran a large number of Harvey House hotels, restaurants and cafeterias both on line and in areas not served by the railroad. This is the dining room at the La Posada Hotel in Winslow, Arizona, decorated in southwest architecture with Indian designs. —*Donald Duke Collection*

Above, "The California Limited" rolls on its inaugural run from Los Angeles to Chicago in 1892.

STUFFED ZUCCHINI ANDALOUSE

Here's an unusual recipe you might like to try on some leftover beef and ham. Chef Carlos Gardini reported his patrons on *The Super Chief* have found it different and delicious. Most of the patrons, connoisseurs of good food, said they liked simple dishes well prepared with the special touches that a good chef gives to fine food.

6 small zucchini
2 tablespoons chopped onion
3 tablespoons chopped mushrooms
3 tablespoons chopped green pepper
1/3 cup chopped tomato
1/4 cup chopped cooked ham
1/2 clove garlic, minced
1/2 cup chopped cooked beef
1 1/3 cup soft bread crumbs, piled lightly
2 tablespoons broth, if needed
Dash salt
Dash pepper

Cook zucchini in salted water 5 minutes; cut in half lengthwise; remove pulp. Combine pulp with remaining ingredients; pile this into zucchini and bake in moderate oven (350 degrees F.) 30 minutes. Yield: 6 servings.

CHICKEN CACCIATORE

This hearty chicken dish shows the fine Italian hand of Chef Louie Sogno and was first served in the Fred Harvey Dining Room at the Los Angeles Union Station. Sogno had his training in his native Italy. His cooking has added flavor to Fred Harvey menus for many years. His Chicken Cacciatore has been enjoyed by Santa Fe passengers from Los Angeles to Chicago, and by visitors to the Grand Canyon and Chicago Union Station.

2 broiling chickens (1 1/2 lbs. each, ready-to-eat weight)
1/2 cup flour
1 teaspoon salt
1/8 teaspoon pepper
1/4 cup butter or olive oil
1 medium onion, sliced
1/2 lb. fresh mushrooms, sliced
1 clove garlic, minced
12 ripe olives, whole
1 can tomato puree (or 1 cup canned tomatoes)
1/2 cup claret or sherry

Cut chicken in quarters, and dust with flour which has been well mixed with salt and pepper. Saute in butter or olive oil until golden brown. Add remaining ingredients, cover, and simmer over low heat 20 to 30 minutes. Yield: 4 servings.

Passengers in the Roaring 20's enjoyed dining on the Santa Fe "Scout," crack train on the Los Angeles route.

RAGOUT OF LAMB KIDNEYS PIQUANTE

Originated by Erich Walther, the results of this recipe have been enjoyed by many Santa Fe passengers as they are whisked across the country. We hope it will taste as good served in your own home.

12 lamb kidneys
1/4 cup butter
4 teaspoons all-purpose flour
1 1/2 teaspoons dry mustard
2 cups beef bouillon (or 2 teaspoons concentrated meat extract dissolved in 2 cups boiling water)
3 tablespoons vinegar
Dash pepper
Chopped parsley

Wash kidneys well and remove membranous covering. Split in half and remove white center. Slice thinly. Melt butter in frying pan. Add sliced kidneys and brown over high heat 3 or 4 minutes; remove kidneys. Cook onions in butter until tender but not browned. Combine flour and mustard. Add onions. Add bouillon and vinegar and cook until thickened. Remove from heat. Add kidneys and heat but do not boil. Add seasoning if needed. Sprinkle with chopped parsley just before serving. Yield: 4 servings.

RISOTTO, PIEMONTAISE

Chef Louis Sogno's Risotto is one of many interesting recipes devised for dressing up rice and is as cosmopolitan as Los Angeles Union Station itself, where it has been served.

1 small onion, chopped fine
4 tablespoons butter
1 cup rice
1/2 teaspoon salt (approximately)
2 1/2 cups chicken broth, heating to boiling
Grated Parmesan cheese

Saute minced onion in butter to a golden brown. Add uncooked rice and continue heating until rice is browned slightly, about 10 minutes, stirring constantly. Add salt and boiling chicken broth, cover, reduce heat to low and cook slowly for 18 to 20 minutes or until rice is tender and excess liquid has evaporated. Serve hot, topped or mixed with grated Parmesan cheese. Yield: 4 servings.

BRAISED DUCK CUMBERLAND

Few pleasures could match that of enjoying this dish as the landscape flows rhythmically past the train's windows. First prepared by Chef Joseph Stoesser, Braised Duck Cumberland will make your guests feel as expansive as they would if they were dining on *The Super Chief*. The sauce alone should win you kudos as an epicure.

1 (5- or 6-lb.) duck
Salt and pepper
1/4 cup chopped onion
3 tablespoons butter
1 cup rice
2 1/2 cups boiling chicken broth
1/4 cup butter
1/2 teaspoon salt
1 large stalk celery
1 large carrot
1 small onion
1 cup water

Sauce:
1 teaspoon all-purpose flour
1 cup bouillon
1 large orange
1/3 cup Burgundy wine
1/4 teaspoon English mustard
1 teaspoon Worcestershire sauce
1 tablespoon currant jelly
Dash cayenne pepper

Season cavity of duck with salt and pepper. To make stuffing: Cook chopped onion in butter until tender; add rice and cook until rice turns yellow. Add chicken broth, butter, and salt. Cover and simmer 20 minutes. Stuff duck with mixture and truss. Place duck on trivet in roasting pan, breast up. Add celery stalk, whole carrot, onion, and water. Cook in slow oven (325-degrees F.) 25 minutes per pound (about 2 1/2 hours), basting duck occasionally. Remove duck from pan; drain off excess fat. Sprinkle flour in pan, add bouillon and simmer about 20 minutes, stirring occasionally; strain. Peel orange, remove white membrane and cut peel into thin strips. Boil 5 minutes, drain and add to hot mixture with wine, mustard, Worcestershire sauce, jelly, and cayenne pepper. Separate orange into sections, removing white membrane. Place duck on serving platter; arrange orange sections in two rows over duck. Pour a few spoonfuls of sauce over all. Serve remaining sauce with duck.

ROULADE OF BEEF

This dish was developed by Erich Walther, in charge of the modern brick and glass Santa Fe commissary in Chicago, where meats are cut, trimmed and prepared "oven-ready" before being taken aboard the dining car.

4 8-oz. pieces sirloin butt
2 teaspoons salt
1/4 teaspoon pepper
4 slices bacon
4 thick slices onion, cut in half
1 large dill pickle, cut lengthwise into fourths
1/4 cup all-purpose flour
4 teaspoons butter
1 tablespoon all-purpose flour
2 cups beef broth
2 tablespoons catsup

Flatten steaks with meat cleaver until very thin; season with salt and pepper. On each steak, place a slice of bacon, 1/2 onion slice, and 1 pickle stick. Roll up steak and tie with string. Roll in 1/4 cup flour and saute in butter until well browned. Add 1 tablespoon flour to butter. Add broth and catsup, cover pan and cook slowly for 30 minutes. Remove string before serving. Yield: 4 servings.

QUICK (or Ersatz) DOBOS TORTE

R. T. Hillyard, Superintendent of Dining Cars, recalled that this dish was suggested by the dining car staff in response to requests from travelers who have enjoyed the wonderfully rich and difficult-to-make Hungarian Dobos Torte served occasionally (1100 pounds a year) on *The Super Chief*. The special type of chocolate and ingredients necessary for the authentic version are not always available even to professional cooks, and baking of the thin cake layers is almost impossible without professional baking ovens and thick cake pans.

1 (10 oz.) pound cake
2/3 cup whipping cream
1 1/3 package (1 1/3 cups) semi-sweet chocolate bits
2 (1/4 pound) packages German's sweet chocolate

Trim crusts from cake. Cut cake in half lengthwise. Slice each half into eight slices, lengthwise and parallel with top. Melt the chocolate bits over hot water, remove from hot water and let cool while whipping the cream stiff but not dry. Fold chocolate into whipped cream. Spread between layers of each half cake. Melt German's chocolate over warm water. Pour over top and sides of cake to make a thin coating. Chill cake until firm. Slice and serve. Yield: 2 cakes, each 4 3/4x2x2 1/2 inches, or 16 servings, 5/8-inch thick.

Above, dining on "The Super Chief" became a memorable part of the trip in the 1960's on the Santa Fe streamliner from Chicago. Below, a Santa Fe train rolls through Cajon Pass during the steam era.

The El Capitan *Hi-Level train included this two-level diner (ABOVE) in which the galley was beneath the restaurant level. (BELOW) The dining room was the largest on any railroad with facilities to serve 80 persons. Food was sent up to the top deck on two electric "Subveyers."*

—Donald Duke Collection

FINNAN HADDIE, DEARBORN

This dish became popular with Fred Harvey patrons as soon as it was first placed on the menu at Dearborn Station, Chicago, in about 1900, by Louis Feichtmann, who was manager for many years of the Fred Harvey restaurants in the station. Feichtmann, remembered with love and affection by Dearborn Station old timers, was a Hungarian and a half-brother of Willie Pogany, famous artist and designer of theatrical settings. Before associating himself with Fred Harvey, he worked at the Richelieu Hotel, once renowned among fine Chicago hostelries for its excellent cuisine. His original recipe for Finnan Haddie Dearborn, has been treasured through the years by Fred Harvey chefs as it is enjoyed by patrons.

1 pound finnan haddie	Melted butter
1 1/2 cups milk	Salt
2 medium potatoes, cooked and cut in thick slices	1 cup cream
	Paprika

Simmer fish in milk for 10 minutes. Place in two individual shallow casseroles or shirred egg dishes. Arrange potato slices at one end of casserole. Brush potatoes with butter; sprinkle with salt. Pour cream over fish and potatoes, sprinkle with paprika. Bake in moderate oven (350 degrees F.) 15 minutes. Sprinkle with parsley if desired. Cover casserole to retain the wonderful aroma, and serve immediately, hot and bubbly. Yield: 2 servings.

LOBSTER AMERICAINE

Here is a gourmet dish as served on Santa Fe's crack *Super Chief* Originated by Chef Carlos Gardini, the dish held its popularity long after his retirement--frequently appearing on the gargantuan menus of the train's Turquoise Room. Fred Harvey food buyers achieved distinction by canvassing many markets for the best in meats, seafoods, poultry, fruits, and vegetables to prepare this and other appetizing selections.

1 (2-lb.) lobster, boiled	2 tablespoons flour
3 tablespoons butter	1/4 cup broth
1 tablespoon minced celery	2 tablespoons white wine
1 teaspoon minced carrots	2 tomatoes, peeled and chopped
1 teaspoon minced leeks	Dash salt
1 teaspoon minced shallots	Dash pepper
1/2 garlic clove, minced	Dash cayenne pepper
2 tablespoons cognac	1 tablespoon butter

Remove meat from shell (saving the brain) and cut in pieces an inch thick. Melt butter, add minced vegetables, and saute several minutes without browning. Add lobster meat and garlic, and continue sauteing for five minutes. Add cognac and set aflame. Blend in the flour, add broth and stir until smooth and slightly thickened. Add wine and chopped tomatoes, season to taste and cook slowly for 20 minutes. Mix brain with softened butter, add to lobster mixture and serve at once. Yield: 1 serving.

The Santa Fe "Chief" crosses the Colorado River into California as it nears end of its trip from Chicago.

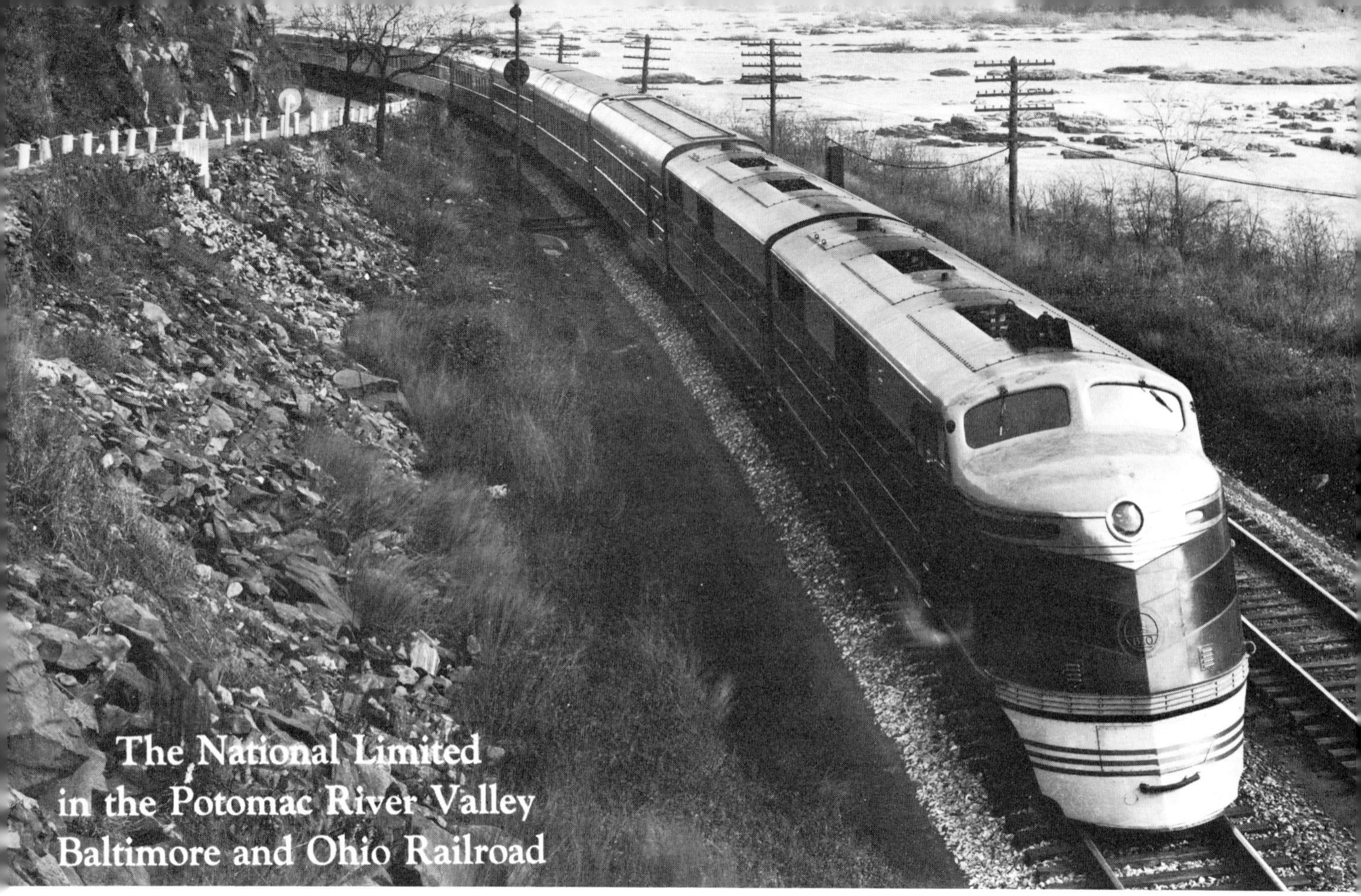

The National Limited in the Potomac River Valley Baltimore and Ohio Railroad

Above, the B and O crack passenger train, "The National Limited," speeds alongside the Potomac River.

Below, self-propelled rail diesel cars carry commuters over historic Thomas Viaduct at Relay, Maryland.

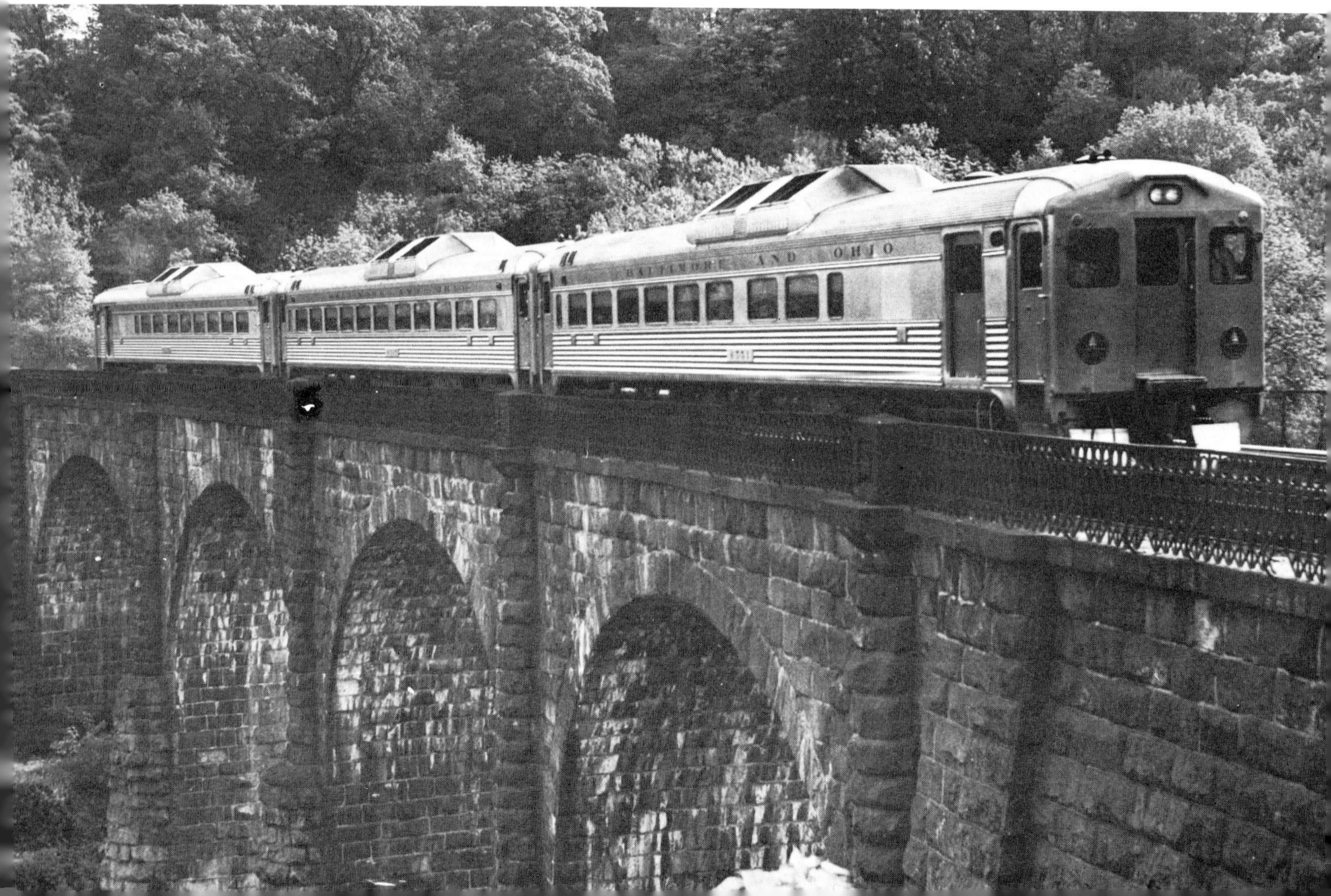

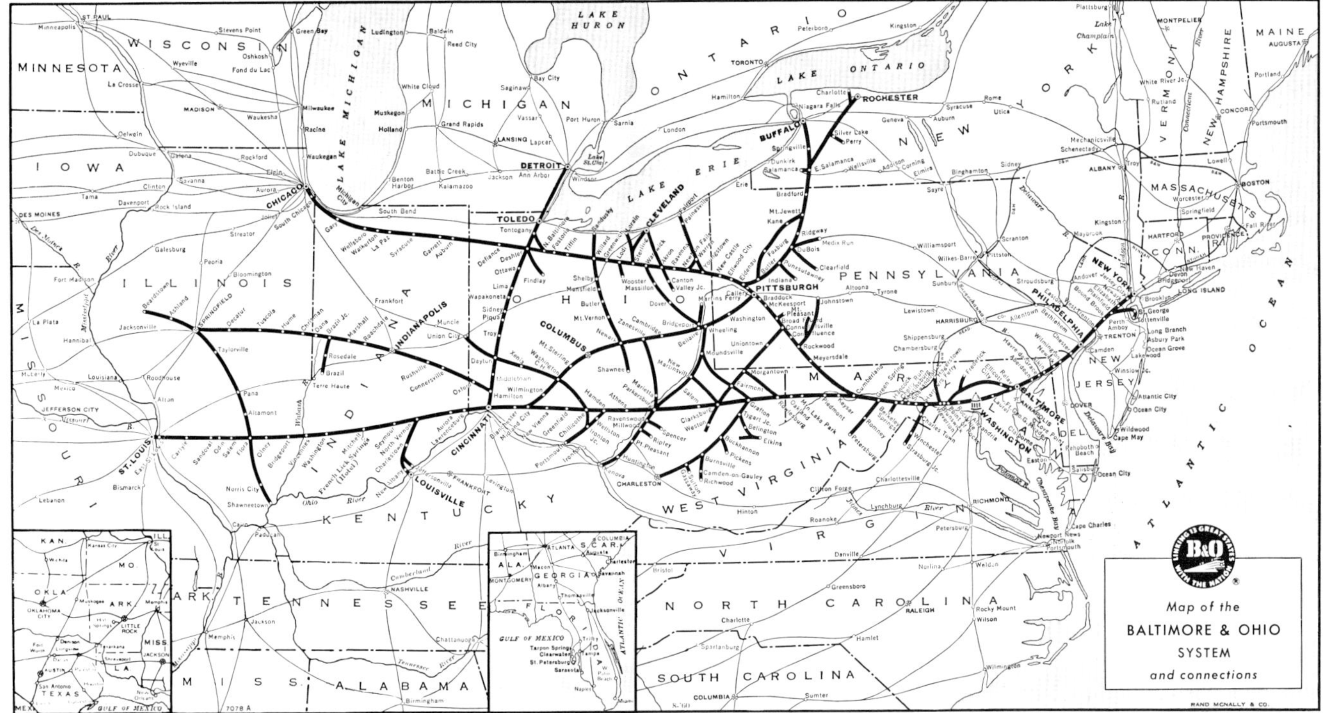

BALTIMORE and OHIO

The first stone for the Baltimore and Ohio Railroad was laid ceremoniously on July 4, 1828, by Charles Carroll (1737-1832), one of the signers of the Declaration of Independence. Two years later the line began service, initially using horses to draw cars over its 13 miles of track.

Baltimore business interests immediately gave support to the railroad, recognizing the Iron Horse as a means to help their city achieve leadership in the trade rivalry between cities on the Atlantic Coast.

Vigorous leadership stretched the Baltimore and Ohio to key areas in New York, Pennsylvania, West Virginia, Ohio, Indiana, and Illinois as well as to St. Louis for connections to the west. The system developed so that the B and O operated approximately 6,000 miles of track in 11 states.

The Baltimore and Ohio's company-owned dining car service was inaugurated at an undetermined time prior to 1900. The line's commissaries, in Baltimore, Chicago, and Cincinnati, were designed primarily as service accessories since the policy was to prepare food on the trains.

Two of the Baltimore and Ohio's most celebrated trains, *The Capitol Limited* and *The National Limited,* became noted for "Help Yourself Salad"--made up in 15-inch bowls and offered free to dining car patrons. The chef, by keeping the bowls heaped high with salad at all times, helped to emphasize that a full bowl is more attractive and conducive to eating than a half empty one.

Since the railroad began in Baltimore, dining cars of the B and O have been partial to Maryland cookery. Typical of the state's dishes are Crab Imperial, Maryland Crab Cakes, Hush Puppies, and Oyster Pie.

Recipes for these fine eating items are reproduced here.

ALL PICTURES THIS CHAPTER: BALTIMORE AND OHIO RAILROAD

HUSH PUPPIES

They call these "Hush" puppies, but your family won't be quiet waiting for you to dip down in the deep fat and dredge up these hot golden nuggets of pure eating pleasure. A succulent substitute for potatoes, they're perfect with fish.

2 cups cornmeal
1 cup flour
2 eggs
3 teaspoons baking powder
1 finely chopped onion
1 teaspoon salt
Some milk

Mix all these ingredients, drop in the eggs, then add enough milk to make a medium batter and stir well. Drop the mixture into hot deep fat a spoonful at a time. Remove when outside is crisp and golden.

CURRY OF CHICKEN

Here's a chicken feast for "chicken feed." You have all the ingredients right in your pantry except the chicken and perhaps the curry powder, which can be obtained quickly at your grocer's.

2 lbs. chicken
2 small onions
1/4 cup butter (or margarine)
2 teaspoons curry powder
1 tablespoon flour
1 egg yolk

Have your butcher cut up the chicken as for fricassee. Wash it well and place in stew pan with enough water to cover it. Cover pan and let boil slowly until chicken is tender. Now add a heaping teaspoon of salt and boil a few minutes longer. Remove chicken from pot, but save the liquid. Now cut up the onions and fry them in the butter. Whenthe onions are brown, remove them from the frying pan and put in the chicken. Fry the chicken for 3 or 4 minutes, then sprinkle it with the curry powder, and pour over it the liquid in which the chicken was boiled. Add the brown onions, stir thoroughly and stew for five more minutes. Now mix in a tablespoon of flour which you have thinned with a little water and stir in the beaten egg yolk. Remove from the fire and that's it!

OMELETTE

The secret of light omelettes is beating. Beat eggs until they are fluffy and your omelette won't fall. The pan should be fairly hot, but not hot enough to burn the edges of the omelette. Remember to stir a little when you pour the omelette into pan--until it begins to rise. Turn it over once. Then roll when done. Serve immediately on warm plate. All hot foods taste better on warm plates.

HOGS HIPS AND CACKLEBERRIES

Bacon and eggs! Many people fry eggs too fast. That makes the eggs leathery--and burns the edges off the bacon. Cook slowly and you'll always have delicious eggs, bacon and sausage.

COFFEE

One good tablespoon for each cup and one for the pot. If you use a percolator, don't overperk, or you'll have bitter coffee.

GOURMET SAUCE

Here is the Baltimore and Ohio's aristocratic concoction for baked ham, baked spareribs and barbecued dishes. You can use this sauce on leftover beef, pork, or ham.

1/3 cup minced onion
1 cup catsup
2 tablespoons brown sugar
2 teaspoons prepared mustard
1/8 teaspoon salt
3 tablespoons butter or margarine
1/3 cup vinegar or lemon juice
1/2 cup water
2 tablespoons Worcestershire sauce

Saute the onions in butter in a saucepan until they are tender but not brown. Add all other ingredients, cover with saucepan lid, and let simmer for about 10 minutes. That's all. You'll now have two full cups of one of the world's great sauces.

BREAKFAST DISHES . . . hints from Baltimore and Ohio chefs on how to make them tasty.

WHEAT CAKES

You'll get light fluffy cakes instead of tough, leathery ones if you beat the batter thoroughly. And don't overheat the griddle. It should be hot enough to make the cakes rise, but no hotter. Turning the cakes more than once makes them tough. Wheat cakes, by the way, need even heat. That's why the old-fashioned iron skillet is the best griddle.

OATMEAL

Plenty of stirring is the secret of good, lumpless oatmeal. Stir lightly while the oatmeal is cooking.

SCRAMBLED EGGS

It's still the same story: beat well! Your pan should be hot, but not quite smoking hot. Keep stirring eggs as you pour them into the pan and until they have reached the degree of dryness you like. Then remove and serve immediately.

EGG PLANT CREOLE

Here is a B & O dish that is economical to make. It is also a favorite among the highways and bayous of old New Orleans.

1 egg plant
3 tablespoons butter or margarine
3 tablespoons flour
3 large tomatoes, peeled and sliced (you can use canned tomatoes, in a pinch)
1/2 cup thinly sliced peppers
1 small onion, sliced thin
1 teaspoon salt
1 small bay leaf
2 whole cloves
1 cup buttered bread crumbs

Slice the egg plant crosswise, peel and cut into one-inch cubes. Cook in boiling salted water for ten minutes. Then drain and put the egg plant into a buttered (or margarined) casserole. In another dish, melt the butter, add the flour and mix until blended. Then add the tomatoes, the peppers, the onion, salt, pepper, bay leaf, and cloves. Cook for five minutes, then pour this over the egg plant and cover with a thin layer of buttered bread crumbs. Bake this in a 350 degree oven for ten minutes and serve hot.

CORN BREAD PIE

B & O passengers have been known to continue past their stations in order to have a second helping of this corn creation. It takes a little making, but it's worth it.

1 lb. ground beef
1 large onion, chopped
1 can tomato soup
2 cups water
1 teaspoon salt
3/4 teaspoon pepper
1 tablespoon chili powder
1/2 cup green peppers
1 cup whole kernel corn (drained)

Brown the beef and onion in a skillet. Add the soup, water, seasonings, corn, and green pepper. Mix well and allow to simmer for 15 minutes. Then fill a greased pie dish or casserole 3/4 full, leaving room for the corn bread topping. To make the corn bread top, sift together the following:

3/4 cup cornmeal
1 tablespoon sugar
1 tablespoon flour
1/2 teaspoon salt
1 1/2 teaspoon baking powder

After they are sifted together, add one beaten egg and 1/2 cup milk. Stir lightly and fold in 1 tablespoon of melted fat. Cover the meat mixture with this topping and bake in a medium oven at 350 degrees for 18 to 20 minutes. Don't be surprised when the topping disappears into the meat mixture. It will rise during the baking and form a good layer of corn bread. Don't be surprised when the whole dish disappears after you put it on the table, because it has been one of the most popular items--with both men and women--served on the Baltimore and Ohio.

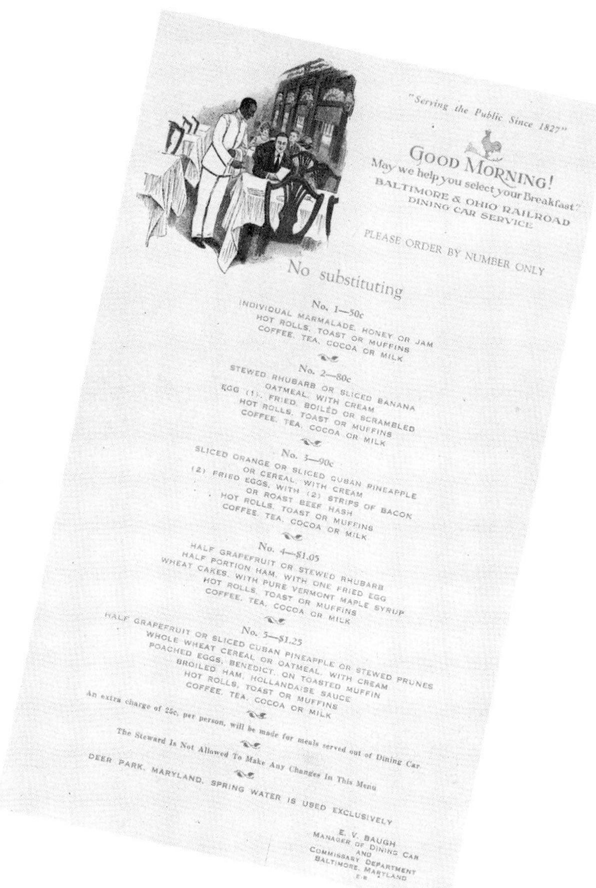

"Serving the Public Since 1827"

GOOD MORNING!
May we help you select your Breakfast?
BALTIMORE & OHIO RAILROAD
DINING CAR SERVICE

PLEASE ORDER BY NUMBER ONLY

No substituting

No. 1—50c
INDIVIDUAL MARMALADE, HONEY OR JAM
HOT ROLLS, TOAST OR MUFFINS
COFFEE, TEA, COCOA OR MILK

No. 2—80c
STEWED RHUBARB OR SLICED BANANA
OATMEAL, WITH CREAM
EGG (1), FRIED, BOILED OR SCRAMBLED
HOT ROLLS, TOAST OR MUFFINS
COFFEE, TEA, COCOA OR MILK

No. 3—90c
SLICED ORANGE OR SLICED CUBAN PINEAPPLE
OR CEREAL, WITH CREAM
(2) FRIED EGGS, WITH (2) STRIPS OF BACON
OR ROAST BEEF HASH
HOT ROLLS, TOAST OR MUFFINS
COFFEE, TEA, COCOA OR MILK

No. 4—$1.05
HALF GRAPEFRUIT OR STEWED RHUBARB
HALF PORTION HAM, WITH ONE FRIED EGG
WHEAT CAKES, WITH PURE VERMONT MAPLE SYRUP
HOT ROLLS, TOAST OR MUFFINS
COFFEE, TEA, COCOA OR MILK

No. 5—$1.25
HALF GRAPEFRUIT OR SLICED CUBAN PINEAPPLE OR STEWED PRUNES
WHOLE WHEAT CEREAL OR OATMEAL, WITH CREAM
POACHED EGGS, BENEDICT, ON TOASTED MUFFIN
BROILED HAM, HOLLANDAISE SAUCE
HOT ROLLS, TOAST OR MUFFINS
COFFEE, TEA, COCOA OR MILK

An extra charge of 25c, per person, will be made for meals served out of Dining Car

The Steward Is Not Allowed To Make Any Changes In This Menu

DEER PARK, MARYLAND, SPRING WATER IS USED EXCLUSIVELY

E. V. BAUGH
MANAGER OF DINING CAR
AND
COMMISSARY DEPARTMENT
BALTIMORE, MARYLAND

When built in 1875 the B and O's "J. C. Davis" was the world's largest and most powerful locomotive.

Chef Jim Watkins works in a B & O stainless steel kitchen typical of those on modern dining cars.

PORK CHOPS NORMANDY

If you want to create a stir with something new and catchy in cooking, here's a Baltimore and Ohio favorite that will have your friends secretly copying you. It's savory, satisfying and simple.

Pork chops (1 per person)	Brown sugar
Apple cider	Cinnamon
Cooking apples	Butter or margarine

Ask butcher to cut chops about one and three-quarters of an inch thick. Place chops in greased baking dish. Now add apple cider until it is level with top of chops. Put thin slices of apples on the chops, then sprinkle chop tops with brown sugar and cinnamon and dot with butter. Bake in medium oven (350 degrees) about 45 minutes.

BOILED EGGS

Eggs keep cooking in the shell when taken from boiling water. Unless you want your three-minute eggs to be four-minute eggs, dunk them in cold water immediately after taking them from the pot.

CRAB IMPERIAL

Here's a fish-day feast that will fascinate even finicky folk who fiddle with their food. In these days of fast transportation and modern methods of preserving foods, obtaining crab is no problem, regardless of how far you live from the water. This dish is easy to make--and only two bowls to wash.

1 lb. crab meat	1 egg, well-beaten
3 teaspoons mayonnaise	

Mix these ingredients together, and salt and pepper to suit your taste--or your company's taste, if you know what it is. Fill crab shells with the mixture, dot with melted butter or margarine and brown in a hot oven. It'll take from six to ten minutes in a 400 degree oven. One pound of crab meat will make three Imperial Crabs--which probably won't be enough, they are so delicious.

HUNGARIAN GOULASH

Here's a dish that makes happy Hungarians or happy husbands. It'll stick to his ribs and make him hug yours.

1 lb. beef, cut into half-inch cubes	Flour
1 1/2 oz. ham fat, chopped fine	1 large potato, cubed
1 large onion, chopped	Paprika

Brown the onions lightly in a frying pan with the chopped ham fat, and add the paprika. Stir for a few minutes, letting meat simmer until it's brown. Then add enough flour to make a medium-thick gravy. Continue cooking until the gravy has thickened, then add enough water to cover the concoction. Cook for 60 minutes; then add the cubed potatoes. Season with salt and pepper and cook for 15 more minutes. When you call "come and get it," stand aside or you'll be trampled in the rush.

OYSTER PIE

A seafood recipe that is different, this dish became especially popular aboard the line's *National* and *Capitol* limiteds.

1 pint of oysters	2 teaspoons of finely chopped green pepper
4 carrots	Tabasco sauce
2 potatoes, diced	4 tablespoons of butter
4 tablespoons of grated onion	8 tablespoons of flour
1 tablespoon of chopped parsley	Salt, pepper, milk, and oyster liquor

Melt butter in saucepan and add the flour. Then add oyster liquor and milk in equal amounts until you have a fairly thick cream sauce. Put the oysters in the sauce and cook them over a very low heat until their edges start to curl. Meanwhile, boil the carrots and onion until they're tender, then dice them and add them, the parsley, onion, green pepper, a dash of Tabasco sauce and salt and pepper to the sauce. Put the "pie filling" in a deep casserole and top with a thin flaky crust, made from your favorite pie-crust mix. The casserole should be baked in the oven for about 20 minutes at 375 degrees, until the crust is brown and the filling is bubbling hot. Yield: 4 servings.

These Baltimore and Ohio passengers enjoy meals as the train speeds them to their destinations.

BAKED STRING BEANS WITH MUSHROOMS

A B & O recipe packed with vitamins, this dish is recommended to make men happy with a vegetarian touch.

1/2 lb. string beans, cut in slivers	1/2 tablespoon flour
1/2 lb. mushrooms	1 cup milk
1 tablespoon butter (or margarine)	2 oz. buttered bread crumbs

String the beans, if necessary. Sliver them, cook in boiling, salted water until tender. Then drain them well. Meanwhile, the mushrooms must be peeled and sliced, and sauteed in butter with the flour and milk added. Cook until thickened. Now add the beans and pour the combination in a baking dish. Over the top, sprinkle the bread crumbs. Bake in medium oven of 375 degrees just long enough to heat thoroughly and to brown the crumbs.

MARYLAND SPOON BREAD

1/2 cup fine yellow cornmeal	1/2 cup boiling water
1 teaspoon bacon drippings	1 egg
1 teaspoon sugar	1 cup sour milk or buttermilk
1/2 teaspoon salt	1/4 teaspoon soda

Put the cornmeal, bacon drippings, sugar and salt into a baking dish. Pour the boiling water over them gradually and beat well. When the mixture is cool, add the egg (beaten) and the milk and the soda and one teaspoon of cold water. Beat the whole mixture well. Bake in deep dish for 20 minutes in medium oven at 350 degrees. If you wish to use sweet milk, add one teaspoon of baking powder instead of the soda. This recipe will serve about eight hearty eaters.

MARYLAND CRAB CAKES

Here's another crab concoction that will captivate your company--or your husband. You can whip it up in less time than it takes to run to the grocer for a can of sardines.

1 lb. crab meat	1 tablespoon mayonnaise
1 level tablespoon dry mustard	1 egg, well-beaten
3/4 tablespoon salt	1 slice bread
1 teaspoon pepper	

Soak the bread in water and squeeze dry. Then break it into little pieces in a bowl, add the rest of the ingredients and mix. Pat the mixture into six or seven crab cakes, being careful not to break up the large lumps of crabmeat. Fry in deep fat for about five minutes, or until brown. (One nice thing about this dish: the more company you get, the smaller you can make the crab cakes.)

OLD FASHIONED NAVY BEANS

1 lb. navy beans	1 pinch dry mustard
4 oz. tomatoes (can be canned)	1 pinch baking soda
2 oz. molasses	1 very small onion, minced fine
	1/2 lb. salt pork

Soak the beans for 12 hours. Put all the ingredients in a big pot with salt and pepper to suit your taste. Let them simmer on the back of the range for 4 hours. Then bake them in a medium (325 degrees) oven for 60 minutes. Serves 10.

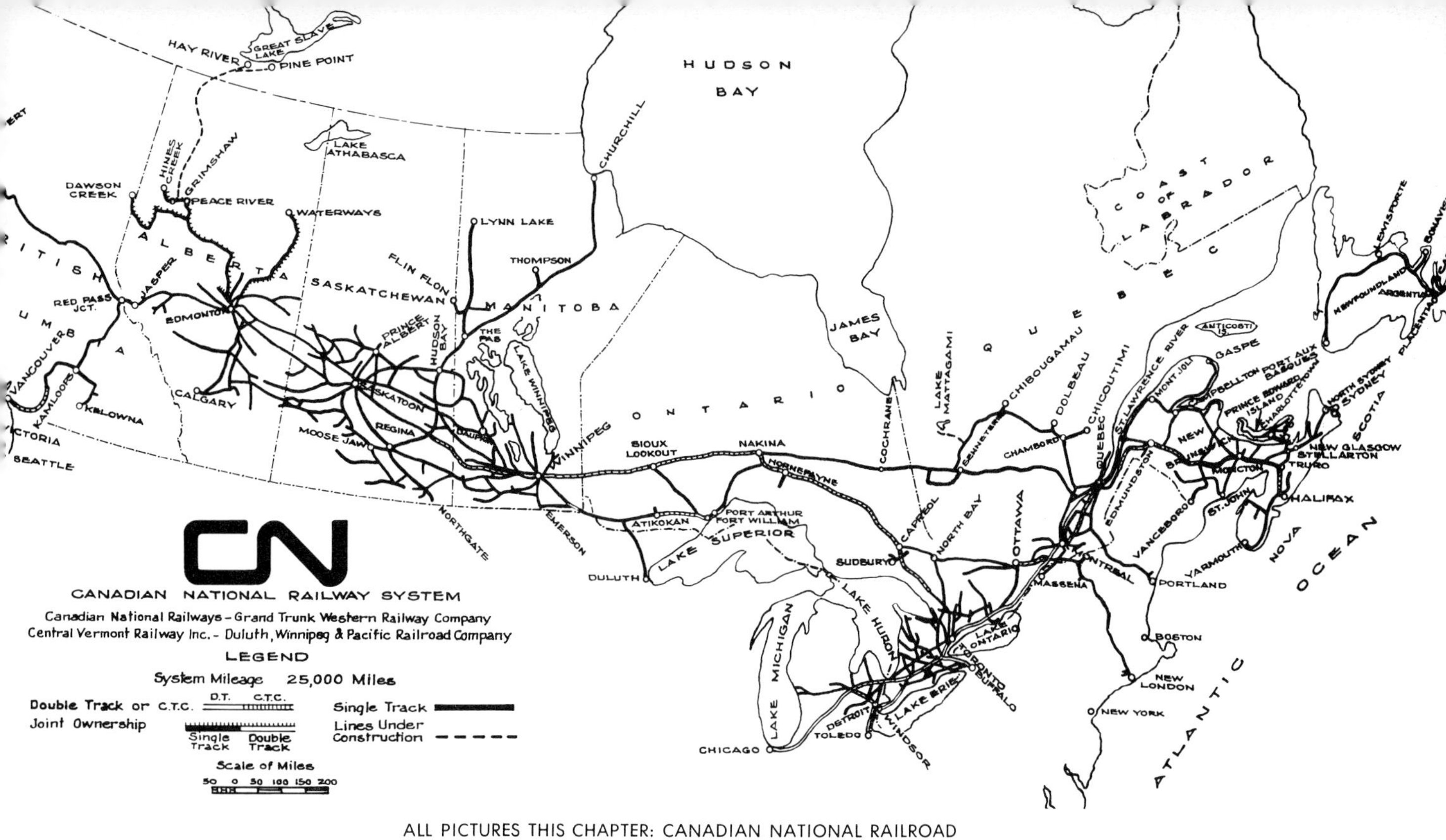

ALL PICTURES THIS CHAPTER: CANADIAN NATIONAL RAILROAD

CANADIAN NATIONAL

The government owned Canadian National Railways knitted a rail network stretching from New Foundland to British Columbia and up to Hudson's Bay when it was activated in 1923 as the unification of several railroads. The consolidated system proudly began serving all 10 provinces of Canada and, through subsidiaries, 12 states of the Union.

It was on the Great Western Railroad, later consolidated into the Canadian National, that George Pullman in 1867 introduced the first diner on the line between New York and Chicago.

The Canadian National evolved by stages, absorbing numerous railroads--including many financed primarily with government guaranteed bonds.

Among the lines consolidated into the Canadian National were the Intercolonial Railway, completed by the government in 1876 to link the Maritime provinces with the St. Lawrence River, and the privately constructed Grand Trunk Railway, Grand Trunk Pacific, Canadian Northern, and National Transcontinental systems.

The C.N.R.'s principal United States subsidiary is the Grand Trunk Western, with headquarters in Detroit. This railroad operates approximately 1,000 miles of track in Illinois, Indiana, and Michigan and connects with the Canadian National at Port Huron, Michigan.

The Canadian National began operating diners when it was formed. An unusual aspect of diner service is the menu in English and French, in keeping with the bi-lingual nature of Canada.

Regional dishes logically became favorites on the Canadian National diners. Dinner might include cod tongues for the passenger riding through the picturesque villages of Newfoundland, crab salad to be enjoyed as the lights of Vancouver, British Columbia, form a background on the train heading for the rugged Fraser Canyon on the trip across Canada to Montreal.

Left, the C.N.R.'s "Super Continental" of the 1960's is mirrored in a lake in the Canadian Rockies.

Canada's provinces contributed a variety of regional selections for the menu. Fish chowder came from British Columbia, while Canadian National chefs borrowed chicken pot pie, beef dishes, and steak and kidney pie from Alberta, Saskatchewan, and Manitoba. Lake trout came from Ontario, while lobster salad from Prince Edward Island became a favorite.

Canadian National's Red, White, and Blue fare plan providing complimentary meals to passengers with sleeping or parlor car accommodations were becoming increasingly popular during the 1960's. Under the sliding "color" plan, fares were graduated up or down according to busy days or seasons. The Red, or lowest fares, were applicable on slow days, White or medium fares were in effect on certain days, and the Blue or highest fares were charged during the busiest times of operations.

But regardless of the day, the C.N.R. made sure that delicious food was served to passengers--with the cost of meals included in the price of "color" tickets.

Canadian National established terminal kitchens or commissaries in St. John's, Newfoundland; Halifax, Nova Scotia, and Montreal. Designed to reduce the amount of work required of kitchen crews aboard trains, these centers were used to prepare meat and fruit pies, cakes, and pastries.

The pride of trains made for pride of food aboard the Canadian National. More than 6,000 pounds of prime ribs of beef were served monthly on *The Super Continental* and *The Panorama*--the system's crack transcontinental trains. Approximately 35,000 twenty-ounce cans of the C.N.R.'s famous plum pudding are prepared annually to meet the demands of passengers riding during the Christmas-New Year's season. Popular nationally on a seasonal basis, plum pudding became a staple for holiday menus on Canadian National dining cars across the nation.

The recipes offered were developed by Canadian National Railways supervisory personnel on the basis of practical experience and testing dating back to many years of catering to train passengers.

●

IRMA SALAD

1 cucumber
1 bunch asparagus
1 head lettuce
1 bunch water cress
1 can (No. 1) green beans
1/2 cup mayonnaise
1 cup cream
Sliced radishes
Capers

Mix mayonnaise and cream. Chop cucumber, asparagus, green beans and water cress. Add mayonnaise and cream, and mix together. Arrange on lettuce leaves, adding sliced radishes around the top, garnishing with capers.

CHICKEN SALAD

2 cups chopped cooked chicken
1 cup chopped celery
6 hard-boiled eggs, cut in quarters
Dash of paprika
6 teaspoons vinegar
12 teaspoons salad oil
6 small fresh tomatoes cut in quarters
2 tablespoons chopped parsley
2 tablespoons mayonnaise

Mix chicken, celery, vinegar, oil, mayonnaise, and paprika. Serve each portion unmolded on lettuce leaf. Garnish with quarters of egg and tomato around side and two pieces of chicken on top of salad.

LOBSTER SALAD

(Note: For Crab Salad the only change is the meat. An individual proportion is listed below.)

3 oz. meat with
Sufficient chopped celery to fill bouillon cup
1 hard-boiled egg cut in quarters
Dash of paprika
1 teaspoon vinegar
1 small tomato cut in quarters
Dash of chopped parsley
1 teaspoon mayonnaise
1 teaspoon lemon juice
Capers
2 teaspoons salad oil

Serve unmolded on lettuce leaf on dinner plate. Garnish with quarters of egg and tomato around side and two or three pieces of meat and a few capers on top of salad.

GRAHAM ROLLS

1 1/2 lbs. graham flour
2 lbs. wheat flour
1 yeast cake
3/4 oz. salt
1/5 pt. molasses
2 oz. butter
1 qt. water

Proceed as for ordinary rolls and allow to rise until the dough will recede to the touch. Fold over and let rise about one-half of its bulk. Give three-quarters proof when molded and bake. Sufficient for two dozen rolls.

BRAN MUFFINS

1/3 cup butter
1/2 cup sugar
2 tablespoons molasses
2 eggs
1 cup milk
2 cups flour
4 teaspoons baking powder
1/2 teaspoon salt
2 1/2 cups bran
1 cup raisins (optional)

Cream the butter and then add sugar--cream thoroughly together. Beat eggs, add molasses and milk and add to butter and sugar mixture. Add bran (also raisins if desired) then flour, baking powder and salt, sifted together. Bake in well-greased muffin pans in hot oven--about 425 degrees F. Reduce to 375 degrees after ten minutes.

CANADIAN PEA SOUP

1 lb. dry yellow whole peas
1 onion
1 carrot
1 bunch of celery
1/4 lb. salt pork
1/8 lb. lard
Salt and pepper

Soak peas overnight. Wash peas thoroughly then add carrot, celery, onion, salt pork, lard, salt and pepper. Cover with cold water and cook for 2 1/2 hours. Will serve 8 people.

CHICKEN GUMBO SOUP

1 cup rice
1 can (No. 1) tomatoes
1 can (No. 1) okra
1 qt. chicken stock
1 stalk celery
Salt and pepper

Cook rice and okra separately. Then add to chicken stock, with celery (cut in julienne shape) and tomatoes. Season with salt and pepper. Will serve 10 persons.

SWISS STEAK WITH MUSHROOMS

3 lbs. lean beef butt or hip
3 medium-sized onions
2 green peppers
1 lb. mushrooms
1/2 teaspoon salt
1/4 teaspoon pepper
1/2 cup flour
1 can (28 oz.) tomatoes
1 teaspoon steak sauce
2 cups cold water
2 bay leaves
Butter

Cut beef into 8 equal pieces, one-half inch thick. Season with salt and pepper, and sprinkle with flour. Saute in butter until brown and remove to roasting pan. Slice onions and green peppers thin, spreading over meat. Dredge remaining flour over meat and cover with mushrooms. Mix cold water with tomatoes, bay leaves and sauce and pour mixture over meat. Cook slowly in moderate oven for one hour. Serves eight.

A Canadian National train glides through the woodlands in the province of Quebec.

BAKED SCALLOPS

1 lb. fresh scallops
Butter
Flour
Fish stock or water
Seasoning
Cracker dust or bread crumbs
Dash of paprika

Scald scallops and drain. Butter casserole and place scallops therein. Melt piece of butter about the size of an egg, sift sufficient flour to make a smooth paste, and then add enough fish stock or water to make a cream sauce. Season to taste. Cover scallops with the cream sauce, sprinkle with cracker dust or bread crumbs. Add a few drops of melted butter and a dash of paprika. Cook until golden brown.

FILLET OF SOLE "FLORENTINE"

2 lbs. fillet of sole
Spinach
2 cups table cream
2 egg yolks
6 mushroom heads, sliced
Grated cheese
2 wine glasses white wine

Roll fillet of sole in finely chopped, cooked spinach in an individual baker with sauce as follows: Mix table cream and slightly beaten egg yolks, add sliced mushroom heads and white wine. Top with grated cheese and cook for approximately eight minutes in oven at 375 degrees F. Sufficient for four servings.

STEAK AND KIDNEY PIE

2 lbs. round steak
2 lbs. beef kidneys
1 lb. chopped onions
2 branches of celery, diced
2 carrots, diced
1/4 lb. lard
1/2 cup flour
1 teaspoon thyme
Salt and pepper to taste
10 oz. tomato juice

Saute until brown, beef, onions, celery, carrots and flour with lard in saucepan. Slice kidneys, removing white membrane, and blanch in salt water. Wash well and stew one hour. Add to other ingredients and cover with tomato juice and water. Cook until tender about 40 minutes. Put in casserole and cover with pie paste made from any standard one-crust pie recipe. Bake until brown. Will serve from six to eight persons.

CHICKEN PIE "FAMILY STYLE"

1 5- to 6-lb. chicken
2 carrots, diced
3 branches of celery, diced
2 onions, cliced
2 bay leaves
1/2 teaspoon pepper, white
Salt to taste
1/4 lb. butter
1/4 lb. shortening
1/2 cup flour

Put onions, celery, carrots and shortening in sauce pan and braise lightly. Add chicken, bay leaves and pepper. Cover with cold water and cook until very tender. Take chicken from pot and take meat from bones. Strain chicken stock to make sauce with flour and butter. Salt chicken to taste. Fill casserole and cover with pie paste made from any standard recipe for one-crust pie. Bake in moderate oven until brown. Diced carrots and peas may be added. Enough for four to six portions.

CODFISH TONGUES

Codfish tongues has been a popular dish served on the Canadian National dining cars in Newfoundland. Take six or eight codfish tongues, according to size, dip them in an egg batter, then in bread crumbs or cracker meal and fry until cooked and serve. This may be served with tartar sauce if desired.

"CHEF'S" RICE SALAD

First mix:
1 1/2 cups cooked rice (not too well cooked)
1 cup finely chopped celery
2 tablespoons finely chopped green onions
2 tablespoons finely chopped parsley
2 tablespoons olive oil
4 tablespoons vinegar
2 tablespoons mayonnaise
Salt and pepper to taste

Then add:
1 cup finely diced lettuce
1 cup finely chopped watercress

These amounts will make enough for six salads. Serve each salad unmolded on bed of lettuce and garnish with the following items:

1 hard-boiled egg cut in quarters
1/2 medium-sized tomato cut in thirds
4 asparagus (2 on each side)
2 slices of cucumber
2 half-rings of green pepper
1 dessert spoon mayonnaise
1 dash paprika and chopped parsley

PLUM PUDDING

10 oz. seedless raisins
12 oz. currants
10 oz. sultanas
8 oz. mixed peel
4 oz. almonds
4 oz. walnuts
8 oz. apples
1/2 lemon, peel and juice
1/2 orange, peel and juice
1/2 teaspoon vanilla extract
3 oz. rum
4 oz. stout
4 eggs
8 oz. flour
1/8 teaspoon baking soda
1/8 teaspoon baking powder
10 oz. bread crumbs
10 oz. ground beef suet
8 oz. brown sugar
1/4 teaspoon ground ginger
1/2 teaspoon cinnamon
1/4 teaspoon nutmeg
1/4 teaspoon allspice
1/4 teaspoon salt

These are ingredients for a six-pound pudding.

Thoroughly wash the raisins, currants, and sultanas. Then soak for approximately 12 hours in the rum, stout, orange and lemon juices, and the vanilla. If too dry after soaking, add a little water or fruit juice. Chop the apples, and the lemon and orange peels; add the mixed peel. Then whip and add the eggs. Add this mixture to the soaked fruit. Mix the dry ingredients and the chopped suet, well. Add the chopped almonds and walnuts. Then mix thoroughly with all ingredients. Fill a bowl or mold 3/4 full. Cover with a piece of waxed paper and a folded greased cloth and tie securely in place. Boil steadily for five hours.

PUMPKIN PIE

1 qt. strained pumpkin
3 tablespoons flour
1/2 pt. cream
1 pt. milk
10 eggs, slightly beaten
1 3/4 cups brown sugar
1 teaspoon ginger
1/2 teaspoon cinnamon
1/2 teaspoon mace
1/2 teaspoon nutmeg
1/2 teaspoon salt
1 dessert spoon lemon extract

Mix the above ingredients in large bowl and pour into pie pans lined with pie paste made from any standard two-crust pie recipe. Bake at 450 degrees for 10 minutes and at 325 degrees, 35 minutes. This recipe makes three pies.

FRENCH DRESSING

1 1/2 cups malt vinegar
2 teaspoons mustard (mixed with vinegar)
1 cup olive oil
1 teaspoon white pepper
2 teaspoons salt
6 teaspoons powdered sugar
1 teaspoon Worcestershire sauce
1 1/2 teaspoons paprika

Mix all these ingredients together and shake very well. If desired, a slice of onion may be added. This should be made in advance and allowed to ripen in refrigerator.

TARTARE SAUCE

1/2 pt. mayonnaise
1 teaspoon chopped parsley
1 tablespoon gherkins, chopped fine
1 tablespoon chopped onion
1 teaspoon chopped capers

Add gherkins, onion, parsley and capers to mayonnaise and stir thoroughly.

Mount Fitzwilliam soars spectacularly in the background as the Canadian National's streamline "Panorama" winds through Canada's Rockies.

This dinette car, like a lunch counter on wheels, supplements conventional Canadian National diners.

MEAT SAUCE FOR SPAGHETTI

1 lb. minced beef	1 green pepper, minced
1 lb. minced pork	1 head of garlic, minced
2 lbs. minced onions	

2 20-oz. cans of tomatoes	1 teaspoon ground cloves
4 oz. of tomato paste	6 bay leaves
1 oz. chili powder	1 pt. chicken stock
1/4 oz. basil leaves, ground	Salt, cayenne pepper to taste

Saute first five ingredients in olive oil and mix all together in saucepan. Bring to boil and simmer for two hours.

THOUSAND ISLAND DRESSING

1 hard-boiled egg, chopped	1 medium-sized beet
1/4 green pepper	1 dessert spoon parsley
1/2 red pepper	1/2 pt. mayonnaise
1/2 bunch chives	1/2 bottle chili sauce
1/2 medium-sized onion	1/2 pt. whipping cream

Mix all ingredients together. If dressing is to be kept, ingredients should be mixed without the whipped cream, which should be added to the preparation at the time of serving.

LOBSTER NEWBURG

2 lobsters	1/2 cup Madeira wine
Truffles	1 cup cream
6 tablespoons butter	5 egg yolks

Cut meat of two lobsters in inch pieces with some slices of truffles. Saute in butter for five minutes, add a half cup of Madeira wine and reduce to one half. Beat a cupful of cream with five egg holks, and add to the lobster. Shuffle about till thick. Serve in a chafing dish.

TOMATO SAUCE FOR SPAGHETTI

1 20-oz. can of tomatoes	6 whole cloves
4 oz. of tomato paste	1 teaspoon salt
4 bay leaves	Pinch of cayenne pepper

Stew for 20 minutes.

1 large onion, minced	6 mushrooms, minced
1 green pepper, minced	2 cloves garlic, minced
	3 oz. olive oil

Saute second group of ingredients and add to first group. Simmer until thick.

GOLDEN PUDDING

1/4 lb. butter
1 cup sugar
2 egg yolks
1 cup milk
2 cups flour
1 teaspoon baking powder
1/2 teaspoon vanilla
1/8 teaspoon salt

Cream butter and sugar well. Add yolks. Whip until creamy adding milk, well-sifted flour, salt, and vanilla, mixing until light and smooth. Stir in baking powder and bake in well-greased baking dish in moderate oven for 35 minutes. Serve with Rich Orange Sauce (see below). Serves eight.

RICH ORANGE SAUCE

1/2 pt. boiling water
1/4 cup sugar
1 orange
1 oz. butter
2 oz. cornstarch
1 pinch salt
1 bay leaf

Grate rind and squeeze juice from orange. Blend all ingredients except cornstarch, and simmer for 10 minutes. Remove bay leaf. Dissolve cornstarch in a little cold water and stir into mixture. Cook until creamy.

ORANGE CREAM PUDDING

Peel and remove seeds from five oranges. Cut into small pieces. Add one cup of sugar and let stand for two hours.

Make custard in double boiler with:

2 1/2 cups of milk
2 tablespoons cornstarch
1/2 cup of sugar
1 egg

Let cool. Fill custard cups 1/3 with orange and fill up with custard when cold. Turn out on fruit saucer. Serve with whipped cream. This is enough for eight portions.

FISH CHOWDER

1 medium haddock
1 qt. fish stock
1 pt. milk
3 large potatoes, diced
3 slices salt pork, diced
1 large onion, diced
1 clove of garlic, diced
4 tablespoons flour
2 tablespoons finely minced parsley
2 tablespoons butter
Pepper, salt, and Worcestershire sauce to taste.

Remove all white flesh from haddock and dice in inch squares. Remove eyes from head of haddock, washing latter thoroughly. Place diced haddock, head and bones, in one quart of water. Allow to simmer for one hour. Dice the potatoes and cook in salted water until soft. Braise together salt pork, onion, and garlic without browning. Put butter in saucepan, add flour and stir freely. Pour milk on fish stock and then strain into butter and flour, stirring briskly until smooth. Add fish squares, onion, pork, garlic and potatoes. Season to taste.

CANADIAN PORK PIES

3/4 lb. ground pork
1/4 lb. ground beef
1 onion
Salt and Pepper
Mixed spices, ground
1 cup water
Any recipe for a 2-crust pie

Bake in an oven like an ordinary pie for 1 1/2 hours, and allow to cool off before serving. This is enough for four persons.

TOURTIERES (PORK PIES)

1 lb. minced pork
1 small minced onion
1 clove garlic (optional)
1/2 teaspoon salt
1/4 teaspoon celery salt
1/4 teaspoon ground cloves
1/4 teaspoon cinnamon
1/2 cup water

Mix all together in saucepan and cook for 20 minutes. Bake for 30 minutes with two crusts in pie plate, like flat pie, in 450 degree oven. This is enough for four portions.

Diners in the era of steam power enjoyed meals as this C.N.R. train rolled over a river in Quebec.

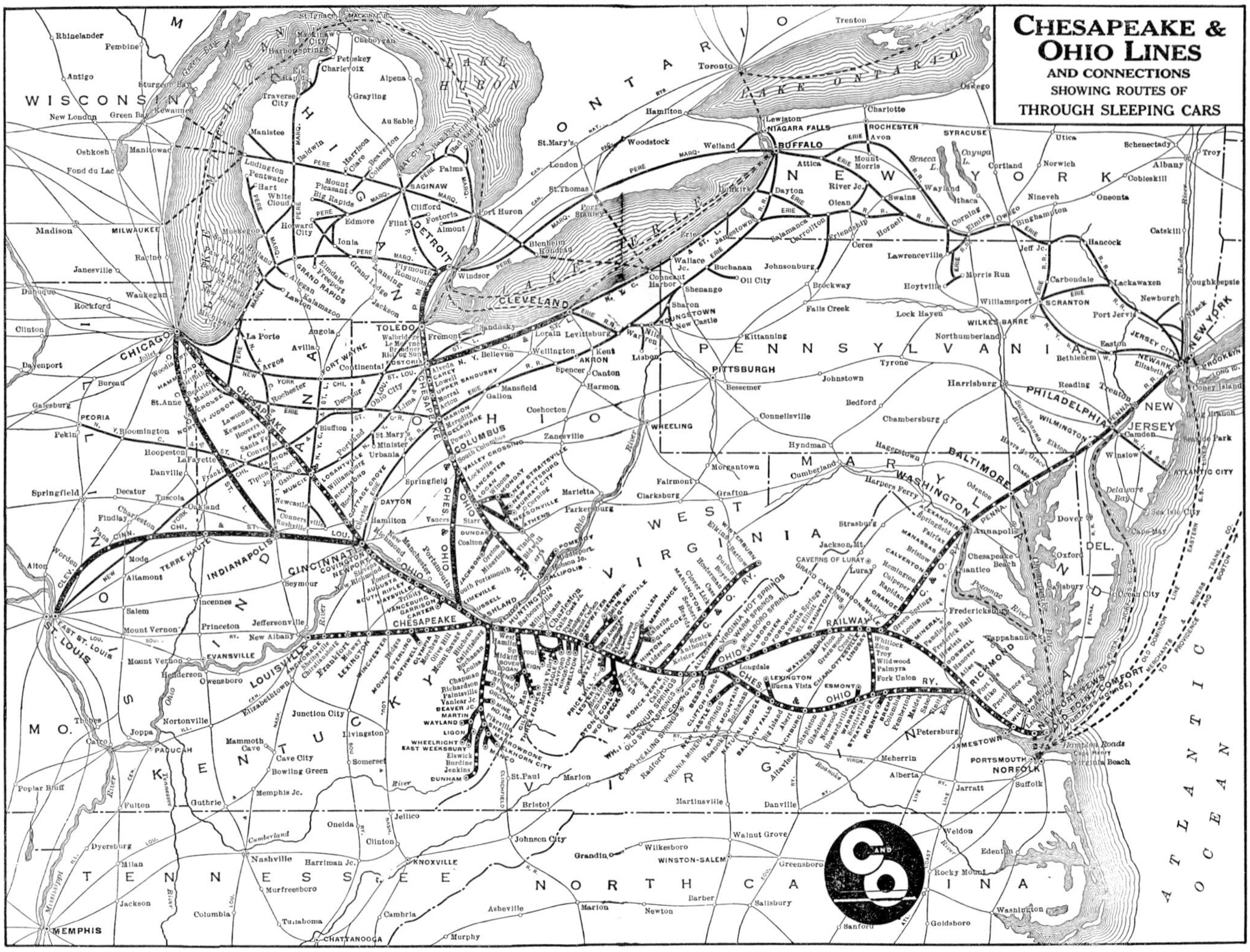

CHESAPEAKE & OHIO LINES
AND CONNECTIONS
SHOWING ROUTES OF
THROUGH SLEEPING CARS

"Chessie," below, symbolized the popular "sleep like a kitten" Chesapeake and Ohio advertising slogan.

This C and O train, pictured in approximately 1930 near Hinton, West Virginia, helped the railroad build a reputation for serving superb meals in its diners.

CHESAPEAKE and OHIO

The Chesapeake and Ohio, founded in 1878, originally was a part of the rail empire forged by Commodore Cornelius Vanderbilt (1794-1877) and his son, William Henry Vanderbilt (1821-85). The system's acquisition in 1947 of the Pere Marquette Railroad gave it approximately 5,000 miles of road linking Chicago, Detroit, and Buffalo with key cities in Indiana, Ohio, Kentucky, West Virginia, and Virginia as well as Washington, D. C.

While relatively unimportant as a passenger carrier (although a major freight line), the Chesapeake and Ohio sought the highest standards in its dining cars--perhaps partially through its ownership of "The Greenbrier," a resort hotel at White Sulphur Springs, West Virginia, world renown for its superb cuisine and the elegance of its service and appointments.

The C and O's ancestry was southern and its dining car menus naturally reflected many of the culinary traditions of the Old South when it began operating its own dining car service in 1888.

Acquisition of the Pere Marquette, which operated between Chicago and Buffalo, coincided with a major change in tradition. It was on this portion of the route that the first railway dining car waitresses were employed instead of the waiters that had become so familiar to passengers.

The Chesapeake and Ohio's famous passenger trains have included *The Kentuckian, The West Virginian, The F.F.V., The Sportsman,* and *The George Washington.*

In addition to trains, the Chesapeake and Ohio became an important maritime factor through operation of Lake Michigan train-ferries. While designed primarily for freight cars, these ships also carried passengers and their automobiles. Staterooms, lounges, and dining facilities were designed for the comfort of those using the lake route as a shortcut for automobile drivers.

The Chesapeake and Ohio's headquarters became an important maritime factor through operation of Lake Michigan train-ferries. While designed primarily for freight cars, these ships also carried passengers and their automobiles. Staterooms, lounges, and dining facilities were designed for the comfort of those using the lake route as a shortcut for automobile drivers.

The Chesapeake and Ohio's headquarters commissary was built at Ashland, Kentucky, while subsidiary commissaries were established at Charlottesville, Virginia, and Grand Rapids, Michigan. The system's marine division commissary was situated at Ludington, Michigan, home port of the Lake Michigan fleet. These facilities are used to assist in preparing food for the dining cars and ferries as well as for storing supplies and serving as purchasing offices.

Here are recipes a la the Old South.

ALL PICTURES THIS CHAPTER: CHESAPEAKE AND OHIO RAILROAD

The Chesapeake and Ohio's "Sportsman" rolls up during the steam era to White Sulphur Springs, bringing passengers to the resort owned by the railroad.

BEEF STEW, HOME STYLE

3 tablespoons lard
12 lbs. boiled beef chuck, cut in 1 1/2 inch cubes
6 medium-sized onions, sliced
10 medium-sized carrots, cut in 1-inch cubes
8 medium-sized potatoes, cut in 1-inch cubes
3 bay leaves
1/2 teaspoon ground thyme
2 cloves garlic, crushed
2 No. 2 1/2 cans whole tomatoes
5 cups water
1 tablespoon corn starch
1 No. 2 1/2 can fine peas
2 tablespoons freshly chopped parsley

Heat lard very hot in large pot and add meat. Let brown well, then add onions, bay leaves, thyme, and garlic, and simmer a couple of minutes. Add tomatoes, water, salt and pepper. Bring to a boil, cover and cook in oven for one hour. Add carrots which have been slightly browned in small quantity of lard. Add potatoes and cook until done, skim off all fat, checking seasoning, and sprinkle peas on top. When serving, sprinkle with chopped parsley. 24 portions.

The President's portrait was carried on the C and O's "George Washington" open-end observation car.

OYSTER BISQUE

60 oysters, chopped coarse
3 cups celery, chopped fine
1 cup onion, chopped fine
1 1/2 cups cooking butter
1 cup white flour
1/4 cup paprika
1 gallon boiling milk
Salt and ground white pepper to taste
Freshly chopped parsley

Place chopped oysters with their own juice in saucepan, on fire. As soon as oysters begin to curl, remove from fire and put away. In half the butter, simmer onion and celery until tender, then add paprika; simmer for two minutes, and put away. Make a roux with remaining butter and flour, *do not brown;* pour in boiling milk, add salt and pepper and cook for 15 minutes. Mix together oysters and juice, simmered onion, celery and paprika, and strain the light cream sauce over. Mix thoroughly; *do not boil;* correct seasoning. This makes 25 portions.

WELSH RAREBIT

3 tablespoons butter
1 lb. American cheese, sharp
1/2 cup ale
1 teaspoon Worcestershire sauce
2 eggs
1/2 teaspoon salt
1/2 teaspoon mustard

Melt butter in double boiler. Cut cheese in small pieces and add. Cook until cheese is melted. Add mustard, salt, Worcestershire sauce and pour the ale in gradually, stirring constantly. Then add the slightly beaten eggs and stir until it becomes thick. Serve while hot on crisp toast and piece of Canadian bacon.

SOUTHERN FRIED CHICKEN, CREAM GRAVY, CORN FRITTERS

Disjoint chicken to make four pieces out of a bird (two breasts and two legs). Season with salt and pepper, dredge in flour and fry until *thoroughly* done and golden brown.

CORN STICKS

2 cups yellow corn meal
1 egg
1 tablespoon butter
2 teaspoons baking powder
1/2 teaspoon salt
1 cup milk

Beat all ingredients together and bake in iron corn stick pan (oven 500 degrees F.) for ten minutes.

BREAD AND BUTTER PUDDING

1 qt. milk
1 cup granulated sugar
6 eggs
8 slices sandwich bread, 1/4-inch thick, well-buttered, trimmed and cut in 4, so it will result in 4 triangles
3/4 cup seeded raisins
1/4 cup currants
1/2 teaspoon vanilla extract

Put one-half the quantity of raisins and currants in the bottom of an oblong Pyrex utility dish, capacity about 2 3/4 quarts. Arrange sliced, buttered bread in systematic rows, the pointed ends up, to cover the entire bottom of dish. Put milk in a pan and bring to a boil. Mix raw eggs and sugar in a bowl until creamy. Pour boiling milk over eggs and sugar mixture, strain and add vanilla extract. Skim off all foam. Pour above strained mixture over bread with a ladle, taking care not to disturb the bread. Be sure that all bread has been covered with the mixture. Sprinkle balance of raisins and currants over mixture. Put the dish in a shallow pan with hot water and cook in oven as you would a custard. Average temperature 375 degrees. Increase the heat the last five minutes to give color to top of the pudding. Serve hot or cold, with cream, if desired. Cooking time--35 minutes; makes 10 portions.

The C and O "Sportsman" was pictured at the White Sulphur Springs station in the 1960's after diesel power took over the chore of hauling passengers.

DRESSINGS AND SAUCES

CHIFFONADE DRESSING (1 QT.)

Add to one qt. French dressing:
4 hard-boiled eggs, finely chopped
1/2 cup parsley, finely chopped
1/2 cup pimento, finely chopped
1 tablespoon onion, finely chopped

Chill thoroughly and mix well before serving. Sauce should not be too sharp.

COCKTAIL SAUCE (1 QT.)

1 pt. chili sauce
1 pt. catsup
1/2 cup horseradish
3 dashes Worcestershire sauce
Salt and pepper

TARTARE SAUCE (1 QT.)

1 qt. mayonnaise
1/4 cup chopped capers
1 cup onions, chopped fine
4 dill pickles, chopped fine
1 1/2 tablespoonsful chopped parsley
4 drops Worcestershire sauce
1 pinch ground white pepper

RUSSIAN DRESSING (1 QT.)

2 cups mayonnaise
1 cup chili sauce
3/4 cup chopped onions, fine
3 chopped boiled eggs
2 tablespoons parsley
1/2 teaspoon Worcestershire sauce

VINAIGRETTE DRESSING, PLAIN (1 PT.)

1 2/3 cups olive oil
1/3 cup tarragon vinegar
1 teaspoon salt
1 pinch pepper
1/4 clove garlic, crushed fine
1 teaspoon dry mustard

C & O BARBECUE SAUCE (1 PORTION)

2 tablespoons chili sauce
1/2 teaspoon dry mustard
1 patty butter
2 dashes Worcestershire sauce

Heat all ingredients together until hot.

VINAIGRETTE DRESSING, GARNISHED (1 PT.)

1 pt. plain vinaigrette
2 small onions, chopped fine
1 tablespoon chopped parsley
1 small dill pickle, chopped fine

To the plain vinaigrette, add: onion, parsley, and pickle. Check seasoning.

1,000-ISLAND DRESSING (1 QT.)

Use 3 cups Russian dressing and add:
1 cup chopped beets
1 1/2 cups whipped cream
1 dash Worcestershire sauce

ROQUEFORT DRESSING (1 PORTION)

1 portion French dressing
1 portion Roquefort Cheese

Blend together with a fork.

Above, this C and O Lake Michigan car ferry also carried passengers and served a variety of fine foods. —*Author*

Below, this ex-Pere Marquette diner had varied seating arrangements. —*Donald Duke Collection*

This photo was made at Lincoln, Nebraska, as "The California Zephyr," noted for its appetizing menus, paused during a transcontinental trip.

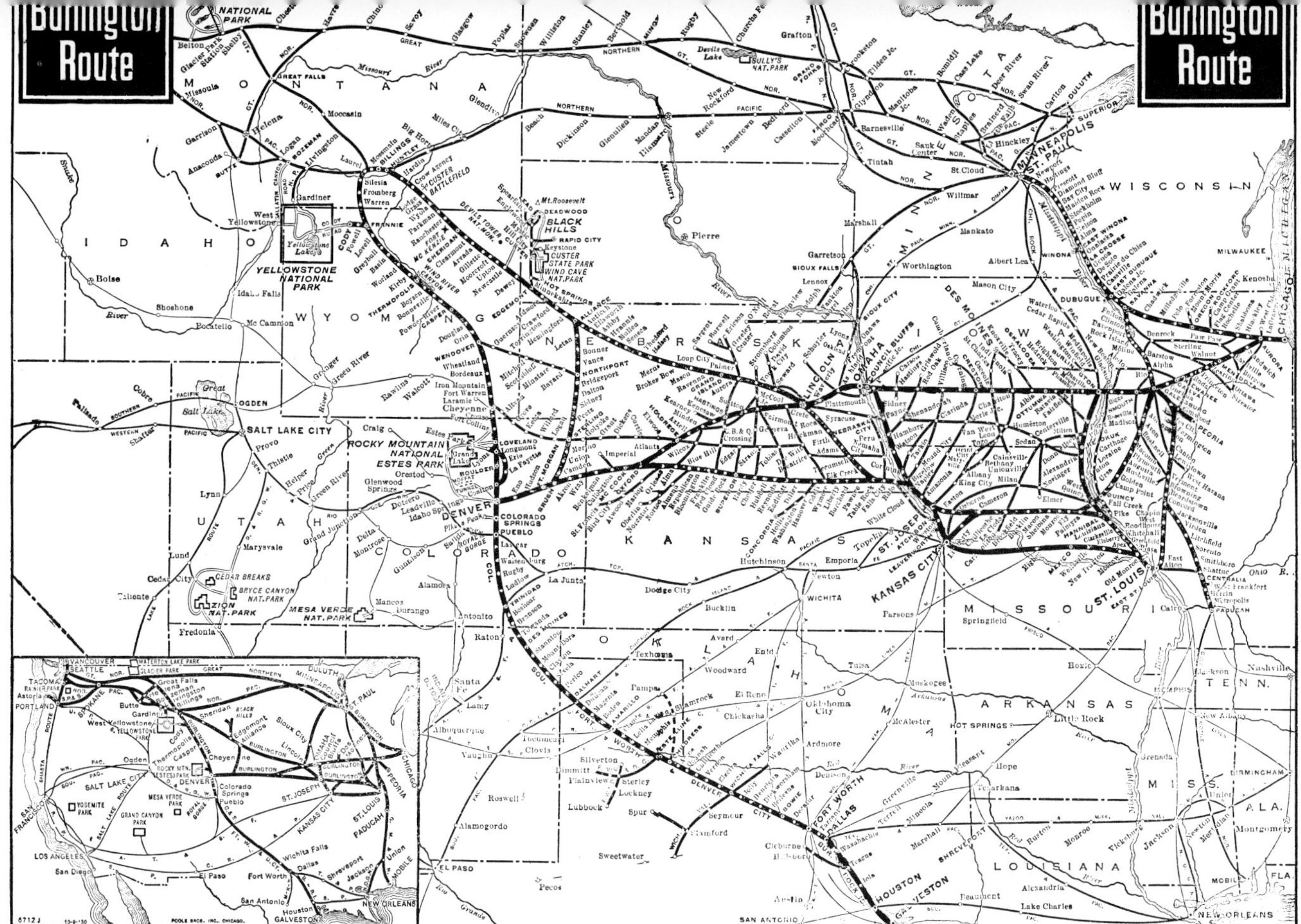

CHICAGO, BURLINGTON & QUINCY

Beginning as the Aurora Branch Railroad in 1849, the Chicago, Burlington and Quincy expanded during the ensuing half century to serve an important section of western America. The line helped shape railroading history with introduction in the mid-1930's of the *Burlington Zephyr,* the crack streamliner that paved the way for general use of diesel locomotives.

Growth of the Burlington system into an empire of 11,000 miles of tracks in 14 states carried the line to such key cities as St. Louis, Houston, Denver, Billings, Minneapolis, and Kansas City.

Pullman-operated dining cars first went into service in 1870 on the Burlington and by the early 1880's the railroad was operating its own diners. Burlington advertising of that era indicated a high standard of service, meals, and comfort.

Shortly after World War II, the line's best-known train became *The California Zephyr,* operated from Chicago to Oakland in conjunctionwith the Western Pacific and the Denver and Rio Grande Railroad.

Chicago, Burlington and Quincy commissaries, situated in Chicago and Denver, were designed to provide many services although chefs cook passengers' meals on the trains.

Covering a wide range of dishes, most Burlington menus were selected from well known cookbooks dating back many years. In some instances, dining car department managers added their own innovations to standard recipes.

The baked corn and tomatoes recipe included here was obtained by P. M. Scott, manager of the dining car department, from his mother, who resided in Illinois and Iowa. Since her parents came from England, the recipe could be traced either to the midwest or Great Britain. Scott also is responsible for the Hot Chicken Sandwich on Toast with Green Asparagus Spears. Asparagus was added, he explained, to give the sandwich greater eye-appeal.

ALL PICTURES THIS CHAPTER: BURLINGTON RAILROAD

NATIVE ROCKY MOUNTAIN TROUT SAUTE MEUNIERE

Individual trout (10 oz.)
Salt
Paprika

Meuniere butter (See recipe)
Wedge lemon, 1/8 piece
Butter

Clean trout, remove gills and wash. Season with salt and sprinkle with paprika. Saute in butter until golden brown on both sides. Serve with tablespoon of meuniere butter over each individual trout. Garnish with wedge of lemon and sprig of parsley.

BAKED LIMA BEANS

1 1/4 lbs. dry lima beans
1/4 lb. dry onions
3/4 lb. salt pork
1/8 jar prepared mustard

1/8 lb. brown sugar
1/2 lb. potatoes
Salt
Pepper

Soak lima beans overnight in cold water, drain and wash well. Cover with cold water and cook for about 30 minutes. Add salt pork and let simmer until about two-thirds done. Peel onions and potatoes and cut into small cubes; add to beans and continue cooking until beans are tender, seasoning with salt and pepper to taste. Remove the salt pork and cut it into small cubes. Saute in a little fat until golden brown. Mix and blend mustard and brown sugar in sufficient amount to give good flavor. Add salt pork and mix. Place in baking pan and bake in oven until a nice brown. This recipe serves approximately six portions.

OLD FASHIONED STRAWBERRY SHORTCAKE, WHIPPED CREAM

Strawberries
Whipped cream

Sugar
Shortcake biscuit

Strawberries should be cleaned, washed and drained. Place berries in stone jar and cover with one cup of granulated sugar to each quart of berries. Let berries marinate in this syrup. Split shortcake biscuit in half, place bottom half in baked apple dish, and one heaping tablespoon of berries over it. Place top half of shortcake biscuit on berries and another heaping tablespoon of berries over this. Using whipped cream in pastry bag, place large rosette of whipped cream on top of berries. Garnish with whole berry on top of whipped cream.

BAKED CORN AND TOMATOES

2 No. 2 canned kernel corn
2 med.-size onions, finely chopped
1 level teaspoon sugar
Cracker meal

2 No. 2 canned meat tomatoes
1/2 cup butter
Salt
Pepper

Saute the finely chopped onions in butter, do not brown. Drain the liquid from the corn and tomatoes, chop tomato meat, and mix whole kernel corn, tomatoes and sauted onions. Add teaspoon of sugar and season with salt and pepper. Place in stainless steel roll pan and bake in oven about 20 minutes. Remove from oven, sprinkle with cracker meal, dot with butter, and place back in oven and bake until golden brown. This serves about 20 portions.

CREAM GRAVY

Make a roux with some of the fat into which you fried the chicken, add equal amount of boiling milk and boiling water with some chicken base added, let boil for 15 minutes. Correct seasoning and strain through fine strainer. Sauce should have the consistency of light cream sauce and the color of ivory.

CORN FRITTERS

3 cups drained whole kernel corn
2 cups white flour
2 tablespoons granulated sugar
2 1/2 teaspoons salt

1 1/2 tablespoons baking powder
2 whole eggs
1/2 cup milk

Mix dry ingredients first, then add remaining. Pan fry in hot fat, dropping one tablespoonful of the mixture for one fritter. Service - place one bastingspoonful of cream gravy on hot dinner plate; 1/2 chicken (one leg, one breast) attractively arranged on top of gravy; two corn fritters on side of chicken and sprig of fresh parsley for garnish.

ROMAINE, AVOCADO, GRAPEFRUIT, FRESH PEAR SALAD

Romaine
Avocado
Green Pepper

Grapefruit
Fresh Pear
Pimento

Olive oil and vinegar French dressing

Dinner portion--Place three crisp leaves of romaine (on top of each other) on a leaf of lettuce in center of chilled six-inch salad plate. Peel avocado, fresh pear and grapefruit and cut in segments lengthwise. On the romaine place slice of avocado, pear and segment of grapefruit in alternate layers until two segments of each are used. Garnish with one thin-sliced ring of green pepper, crossing the ring of green pepper with two julienne-cut strips of pimento (forming a cross). Pour one oz. of olive oil and vinegar French dressing (Old Monk style) over salad just prior to service.

ORANGE JUICE WITH SHERBET FRAPPE

Fresh orange juice

Orange sherbet

Fill eight-oz. glass two-thirds full of chilled fresh orange juice. Add one small ice cream scoop of orange sherbet. Serve in shaved ice in combination bowl.

GRILLED VEAL CHOP, HUNTER STYLE

Veal chop
Onion
Mushrooms
Bacon

Toast
Oil or shortening
Salt
Pepper

Veal chop should be about one and one-half inches thick. Trim well and scrape bone clean. Season with salt and dip in oil or shortening. Broil as desired--rare, medium, or well done. Serve on slanted triangle of toast. Garnish with one thick slice of grilled onion, one sauted fresh mushroom, one slice of grilled bacon, a sprig of parsley. The onion, mushroom and bacon to be placed on the chop.

Crack streamliners in the Burlington's Chicago yards are, from left, the Burlington-Northern Pacific "North Coast Limited;" the Burlington-Great Northern "Empire Builder," and the Burlington "Denver Zephyr."

TOMATO SHRIMP CANAPE

Crisp lettuce
Fresh shrimp
Pimento
Ravigote sauce
Slice of large tomato
Lemon
Parsley

Arrange crisp bed of lettuce on chilled six-inch plate. Place large slice of tomato one-half inch thick in center of lettuce. Arrange four jumbo shrimps on tomato, cover with chilled ravigote sauce. Place strip of pimento one-fourth inch wide, one and one-half inches long across top of canape, and garnish with one-eighth lemon and sprig of parsley.

COCKTAIL SAUCE RAVIGORE

2 cups oil
1/4 cup vinegar
3 egg yolks
2 gherkins
2 pimentos
1 cup chili sauce
1/2 cup celery
1 oz. anchovy paste
1/2 teaspoonful sugar
1 teaspoonful dry mustard
1 bunch shallots or green onions
1 tablespoonful parsley
1 teaspoonful paprika
1/2 teaspoonful salt

All ingredients must be thoroughly chilled. Place egg yolks in mixing bowl along with the dry mustard, paprika, salt and sugar. Beat well, add oil slowly, beating constantly until sauce thickens, and part of vinegar slowly, then rest of oil blending it in well with wire whip. When finished it shoul have the consistency of mayonnaise. Add one cup of chili sauce, one ounce of anchovy paste, blending well. Add the finely chopped shallots, pimento, gherkins, parsley, celery, and season to taste. Serve cold.

SUPREME SAUCE

Chicken fat
Egg yolk
Seasoning
Chicken stock
Cream
Flour

Strain and remove fat from top of chicken broth. Reduce stock one-third, using the fat for roux. Place fat on fire in sauce pan and work flour into fat, cooking about 10 minutes. Add stock, and to each gallon of sauce, add whipped together yolk of two eggs and one cup of cream. Blend slowly into sauce and season to taste. Sauce should not be too thick.

HOT CHICKEN SANDWICH ON TOAST WITH GREEN ASPARAGUS SPEARS

Place slice of toasted bread, trimmed, on center of a 9-inch dinner plate. Cover toast with two oz. of sliced white chicken meat and two oz. of sliced dark chicken meat. Spoon thin chicken fricassee sauce lightly over the meat. Place triangles of toast (made from one-half slice of toast) on each side of sandwich with two green spears of asparagus on each triangle. Place one oz. of sauted carrots on inner side of plate equally spaced between triangle toast. Place small ramekin of jelly on outer side of plate equally spaced between triangle toast.

MEUNIERE BUTTER

Butter
Parsley
Lemon Juice

Brown butter and add lemon juice, placing small amount over each serving. Sprinkle with freshly-chopped parsley.

Here is the Burlington's Vista-Dome "Zephyr" on its overnight dash from Chicago to the Rocky Mountains.

NEW ENGLAND BOILED DINNER

Boiled cabbage
Boiled turnip
Boiled carrot
Boiled onion
Boiled beet
Boiled potato
1 slice boiled ham
1 slice boiled salt pork
1 slice boiled corned beef

Great care must be taken that all vegetables are kept bright during cooking and serving of entire meal. The cabbage must be boiled very fast in order that it may retain as much flavor and color as possible. Place cabbage in center of platter, surround with other vegetables and lay sliced ham, corned beef and pork across top of vegetables.

BAKED INDIVIDUAL CHICKEN PIE BURLINGTON

Boiled hen
Supreme sauce
Parisienne potatoes
Pie crust
Seasoning

After fowl has been cooked, place six balls of potatoes (cut with parisienne knife and boiled in salt water until tender) in chicken pie dish. Add equal amounts of light and dark meat of chicken cut in finger strips. Cover with supreme sauce, rich and well seasoned. Top with pie crust, and bake until golden brown.

FRESH MONTEREY ABALONE, SAUTE

Abalone
Egg
Shortening
Salt and pepper
Mixed flour
and
Cracker crumbs
Milk

Pound the abalone steak well. This is necessary to tenderize it. Mix salt and pepper with beaten egg to which a little milk is added. Dip the abalone in this mixture and then into the cracker crumb-flour mixture. Add shortening to saute pan, heat, and when quite hot, place abalone in pan and saute slowly until slightly brown on both sides. Care must be taken that the pan does not become too hot. When done remove and serve piping hot. Garnish with parsley and wedge of lemon. Service per menu, i.e. tartar sauce, etc.

PEACH MELBA

Chilled half melba peach
Tablespoon melba sauce
Small dipper ice cream

Place small dipper of ice cream in sauce dish (press against side of ice cream container to make it flat on bottom). Place half of chilled melba peach on top of ice cream and pour tablespoonful of chilled melba sauce over peach.

A mural on the theme of the Old West was an appropriate decoration for Burlington's Chuck Wagon car aboard the Vista-Dome Denver Zephyr. *—Donald Duke Collection*

SPRING SALAD BOWL

Lettuce	Celery
Tomatoes	Water cress
Cucumbers	Green peppers
Radishes	Hard-boiled egg

Into baked apple dish lined with lettuce, place pyramid of pulled lettuce, two slices of cucumber that has been peeled and stripped down side with fork, and two pieces of skinned tomato that is cut into about eight pieces. Sprinkle with sliced radishes, diced celery and green peppers. Pour small portions of French dressing over this. Garnish with sprig of water cress and slice of hard-boiled egg, cutting egg with egg slicer.

FRUIT COCKTAIL CHANTILLY

Fresh pineapple	Peaches (fresh or canned)
Oranges	Pears (fresh or canned)
Grapefruit	Banana
Apples	Maraschino cherry
Simple syrup	Whipped cream

Dice all fruit, except banana and cherry, in small cubes. Marinate in simple syrup, mixing fruit and syrup well. Chill thoroughly. When ready to serve dish up in cocktail glasses, top the center with a slice of banana and a rosette of whipped cream on banana. Garnish with half red maraschino cherry in center of top of whipped cream.

WHEAT CAKES

4 cups flour	1 oz. melted butter
1 oz. baking powder	Pinch of salt
3 eggs	1 pint milk
2 oz. sugar	(more or less)

Sift flour, salt and baking powder together twice. Beat eggs with wire whip until they are very light. Add the sugar and two-thirds of the milk and stir well; then add the flour, salt and baking powder to the milk and egg mixture. Beat well into a thin batter, adding what milk is necessary. At last stir slowly the melted butter into batter. This recipe will make one-half gallon of batter.

PUREE MONGOLE

Green split peas	Carrots
Puree of tomato	Pimento
Tongue	Seasoning
Stock	

Into a good puree of split pea soup add one-third puree of tomato, cut carrots, julienne and saute in butter. Add carrots and small julienne strips of boiled tongue with diced pimento and some cooked green peas. Season to taste. Be sure soup is not too thick when finished.

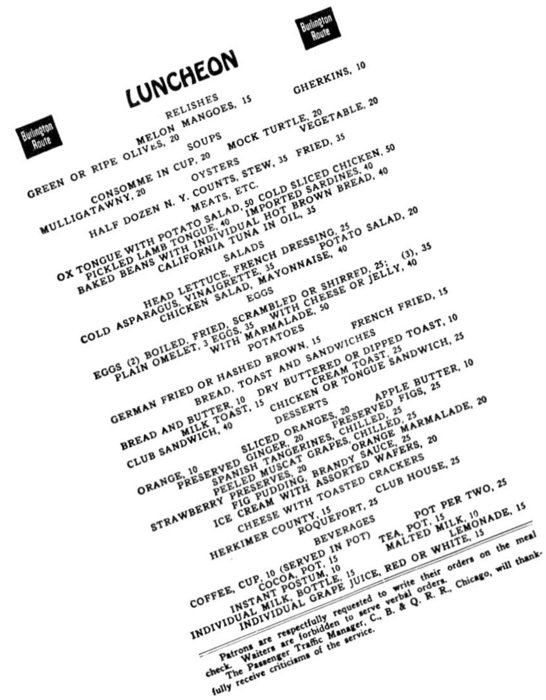

Burlington Route

LUNCHEON

Burlington Route

RELISHES

GREEN OR RIPE OLIVES, 20 MELON MANGOES, 15 GHERKINS, 10

SOUPS

CONSOMME IN CUP, 20 MOCK TURTLE, 20
MULLIGATAWNY, 20 VEGETABLE, 20

OYSTERS

HALF DOZEN N. Y. COUNTS, STEW, 35 FRIED, 35

MEATS, ETC.

OX TONGUE WITH POTATO SALAD, 50 COLD SLICED CHICKEN, 50
PICKLED LAMB TONGUE, 40 IMPORTED SARDINES, 40
BAKED BEANS WITH INDIVIDUAL HOT BROWN BREAD, 40
CALIFORNIA TUNA IN OIL, 35

SALADS

HEAD LETTUCE, FRENCH DRESSING, 25 POTATO SALAD, 20
COLD ASPARAGUS, VINAIGRETTE, 35
CHICKEN SALAD, MAYONNAISE, 40

EGGS

EGGS (2) BOILED, FRIED, SCRAMBLED OR SHIRRED, 25; (3), 35
PLAIN OMELET, 3 EGGS, 35 WITH CHEESE OR JELLY, 40
WITH MARMALADE, 50

POTATOES

GERMAN FRIED OR HASHED BROWN, 15 FRENCH FRIED, 15

BREAD, TOAST AND SANDWICHES

BREAD AND BUTTER, 10 DRY BUTTERED OR DIPPED TOAST, 10
MILK TOAST, 15 CREAM TOAST, 25
CLUB SANDWICH, 40 CHICKEN OR TONGUE SANDWICH, 25

DESSERTS

ORANGE, 10 SLICED ORANGES, 20 APPLE BUTTER, 10
PRESERVED GINGER, 20 PRESERVED FIGS, 25
SPANISH TANGERINES, CHILLED, 25
PEELED MUSCAT GRAPES, CHILLED, 25
STRAWBERRY PRESERVES, 20 ORANGE MARMALADE, 20
FIG PUDDING, BRANDY SAUCE, 25
ICE CREAM WITH ASSORTED WAFERS, 20
CHEESE WITH TOASTED CRACKERS
HERKIMER COUNTY, 15 CLUB HOUSE, 25
ROQUEFORT, 25

BEVERAGES

COFFEE, CUP, 10 (SERVED IN POT) POT PER TWO, 25
COCOA, POT, 15 TEA, POT, 15
INSTANT POSTUM, 10 MALTED MILK, 10
INDIVIDUAL MILK, BOTTLE, 15 LEMONADE, 15
INDIVIDUAL GRAPE JUICE, RED OR WHITE, 15

Patrons are respectfully requested to write their orders on the meal check. Waiters are forbidden to serve verbal orders.
The Passenger Traffic Manager, C., B. & Q. R. R., Chicago, will thankfully receive criticisms of the service.

SOUTHERN FRIED CHICKEN, CREAM GRAVY

Spring chicken (2 1/2 lbs. av. wt.)
Flour
Shortening
Milk
Chicken stock
Paprika
Salt
Pepper

Split chicken down back, remove neck, disjoint each half of chicken at each joint (drumstick, thigh, wing, breast, back). Clean and wash well and season the flour with salt and pepper, adding a little paprika. Then, while the chicken is wet, roll it in the flour mixture, leaving the chicken in the flour for a few minutes. Remove the chicken from flour and place in frying pan which contains enough hot clear fat to come up around the chicken. Fry fast for a few minutes, reduce the heat and cover; cook until brown; turn the chicken, recover and cook until both sides are brown. Remove the chicken and pour off excess fat. To the dripping add a little flour, stirring the flour and letting it brown lightly; slowly blend in equal amount of hot milk and chicken stock. Simmer slowly, stirring often, season with salt and pepper, and when done strain. Gravy should be hot and medium thick (about consistency of coffee cream).

CORN FRITTER

2 cups corn
1 1/4 cups flour
1 level teaspoon salt
2 eggs
1 teaspoon baking powder
Milk
Dash of paprika

Sift and mix dry ingredients. Add the drained corn; add two egg yolks, well beaten. Beat whites of eggs until stiff and add to fritter, a little milk to be added if needed to make stiff batter. Fry in deep hot fat until it is golden brown.

STUFFED BAKED INDIVIDUAL WALL-EYED PIKE

Wall-eyed pike (1 lb. ea.)
1 medium size onion
1 cup chopped celery
1 egg
Butter
8 cups bread crumbs
1/2 green pepper
1 tablespoon chopped parsley
1 pinch powdered thyme
Fish stock
Salt
Pepper

Remove the crust from one-day old bread and then crumb the bread. Place crumbs in a pan and toast in oven until slightly browned. Chop the onion, green pepper and celery very fine and saute in butter until they are tender, but do not brown. Add them along with the chopped parsley to the bread crumbs. Season with salt, pepper and powdered thyme. Blend together by mixing lightly with fork and sprinkle with sufficient fish stock to moisten. Scale, split open and clean each individual fish. Fill each fish with the stuffing and tie closed with string. Place stuffed fish in baking pan, sprinkle with a little butter, salt and pepper, and dust lightly with flour. Bake in hot oven until done (do not over-cook). In serving, remove string from fish and serve on platter. Garnish with wedge of lemon and sprig of parsley.

TOSSED SALAD LOUISIANA

Romaine
Lettuce
Celery
Green pepper
Garlic
Salt
White pepper
Shrimp (Fine cut 1/8 inch pieces)
Green onions
Pimento
Tomato (Skinned cut in 1/8 wedges)
Radishes
Olive oil and vinegar French dressing (Old Monk Style)

Use equal portions of romaine and lettuce pulled into small pieces. To each two quarts add one cup of thin julienne cut (1 1/2" length) celery, one cup of thin julienne (cut 1 1/2") length green peppers, one cup of thinly sliced radishes, one cup of finely cut fresh shrimp, one-half cup of finely chopped green onions, and one-half cup of small square cut pimento. All ingredients should be kept chilled and crisp. Just prior to service, rub large salad bowl with pod of crushed garlic. Place mixed salad items in bowl, add olive oil and vinegar (white) French dressing, and season lightly with salt and pepper. Toss salad lightly until all ingredients have slight dressing covering. Garnish salad with skinned tomatoes cut in 1/8 wedges. After salad is tossed in large wooden salad bowl, garnish the salad with skinned tomatoes cut in 1/8 wedges; place the tomatoes around the side of bowl until complete circle of tomatoes is placed around bowl. Place six or eight pieces of tomato on top center of salad in pin wheel pattern. Line chilled baked apple dish with leaf of crisp lettuce, fill with tossed salad, and garnish with two wedges of tomato.

FRENCH TOAST

Beat two eggs with a half cup of cream. Use bread at least one day old. Cut slices one inch thick, trim and cut in diamond shape. Soak bread well in cream and egg mixture on both sides and fry until golden brown. When done, dry the toast on a clean towel and dust over with powdered sugar and serve.

Above, the streamline Burlington "Twin Cities Zephyr" speeds with its diner over the countryside.

Below, recalling the glory of the steam era is Burlington locomotive 4002, built by Baldwin in 1930.

The interior of the Rock Island's "Golden State Limited" coffee shop diner of the 1960's was distinguished by attractive decorations and furnishings.

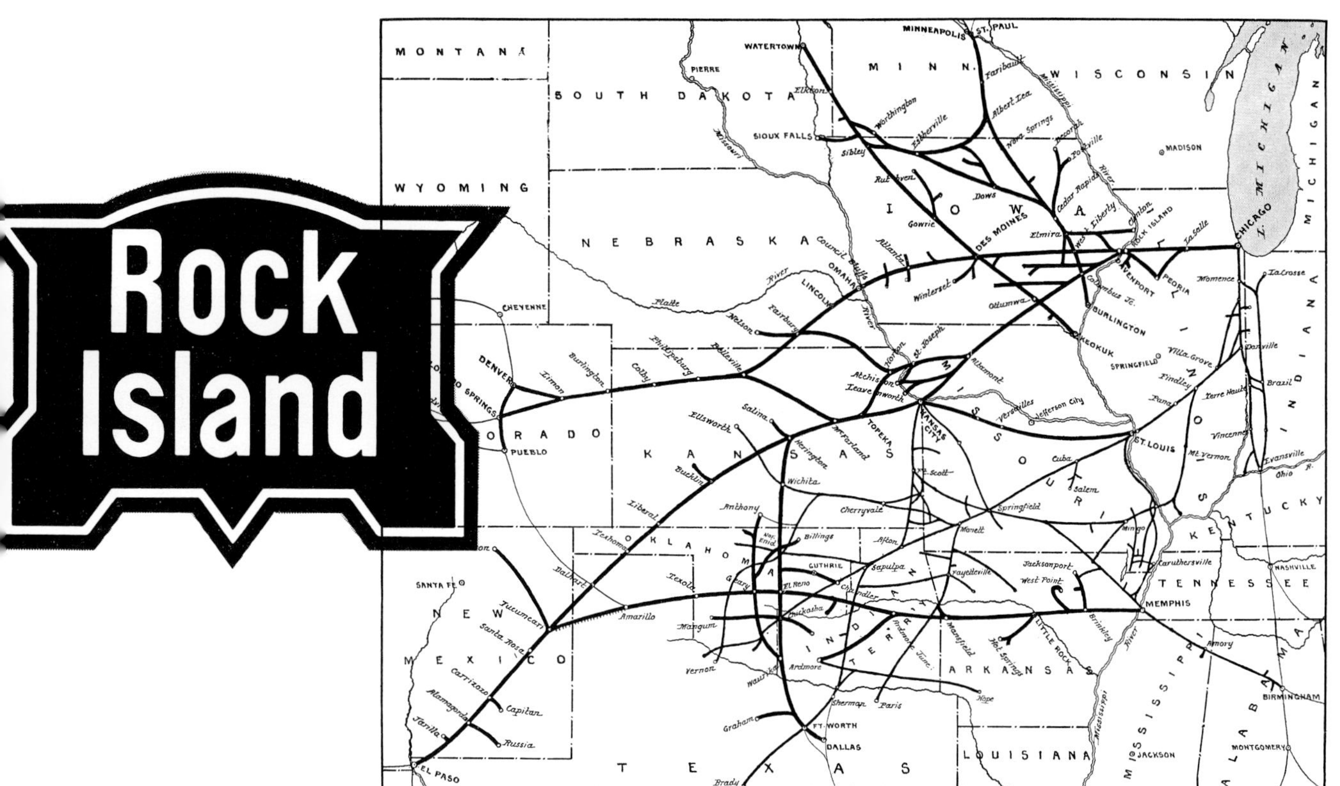

CHICAGO, ROCK ISLAND & PACIFIC

The Chicago, Rock Island and Pacific Railroad achieved fame early in its existence by building, in 1856, the first railway bridge across the Mississippi River. The bridge initially was regarded as an engineering impossibility and its construction was threatened by legal action launched by steamboat owners.

Among the attorneys who won the lawsuit for the Rock Island was Abraham Lincoln.

The Rock Island's approximately 7,500 miles of tracks carried it into 14 states, serving such cities as Chicago, Denver, Colorado Springs, Minneapolis, St. Louis, Kansas City, Memphis, Little Rock, Oklahoma City, Houston and Des Moines. Connections with the Southern Pacific at Tucumcari, New Mexico, gave connections via *The Golden State Limited* to Los Angeles.

The line's crack streamliners, appropriately called *Rockets* for their speed, have been known widely for their fine menus.

Rock Island commissaries, situated in Chicago (with facilities for making ice cream to be served on the trains) and Minneapolis, were designed primarily as storage facilities.

Among outstanding Rock Island dining car staff members have been two men of German extraction who helped to plan tasty menus. W. Heidenreich, who became general dining car supervisor, served his apprenticeship as a waiter in Hamburg before emigrating to the United States in 1929. He then served in key capacities at several outstanding American eating establishments before associating himself with the railroad.

Herbert Bannwolf began his career as a cook's apprentice in the Weihen Stafan Stafanie Restaurant of Cologne in 1928. He prepared food for numerous ocean liners as well as leading American hotels before joining the Rock Island, where he became traveling chef.

The Rock Island's *Rocky Mountain Rocket,* speeding between Chicago and Denver-Colorado Springs, achieved special praise from travelers for its serving of fresh Colorado Mountain Trout, Saute Meuniere, included in the recipes here.

ALL PICTURES THIS CHAPTER: ROCK ISLAND RAILROAD

CLAM JUICE COCKTAIL

1/2 pt. tomato catsup	1 teaspoon grated horseradish root
1/2 pt. chili sauce	Juice of one lemon
1 pt. clam juice	One dash Tabasco sauce
1 teaspoon salt	

Mix these ingredients together and place in refrigerator to chill. Serve in juice glasses. Very good for "hangover." May also be used as a luncheon appetizer. Serves six to eight portions.

STUFFED TOMATO, BRETONNE

Take six or eight medium sized tomatoes and blanch in boiling water to remove the skins. Scoop out tomatoes, leaving center free to be stuffed. Dice the scooped out tomato centers with finely chopped mixed greens such as lettuce, romaine, escarole, chicory, etc. Mix the above items in a dressing of 1/4 cup tarragon vinegar, 1/2 teaspoon sugar, 1/2 teaspoon dry mustard, 1 teaspoon freshly grated horeseradish, 1 teaspoon chopped capers. Now stuff in center of tomatoes with above mixture. On 7 1/2 inch salad plate underlined with lettuce leaf, place one stuffed tomato. Garnish with 1/4 hard boiled egg, ripe and green olives. Serve with cocktail fork. This is a good appetizer for six to eight persons.

CHESAPEAKE BAY OYSTER PEPPER POT

Saute one small finely chopped onion with 1/2 teaspoonful of crushed black pepper along with 1/8 lb. of finely chopped salt pork. Add 1/2 stalk of diced celery, 1/2 stalk diced leeks, one diced green pepper. Fill up with 1/2 gallon of beef stock. Add the juice of 1/2 pint blanched oysters. The oysters may be blanched in the same juice from the container in which they come. Remove the muscle and beard, cut oysters in three or four pieces and add to soup. Bring to a boil for a few minutes and add approximately 1 1/2 lbs. of diced raw potatoes, one diced peeled tomato, and 1/2 handful of raw rice. Also add one Bouquet Garni in a muslin bag and 1/4 cup finely chopped parsley. Let simmer until the raw potatoes are done. Remove the Bouquet Garni to keep the soup from becoming bitter. Dish up in a cup or tureen and sprinkle lightly with finely chopped parsley. Serves six to eight persons.

BOUQUET GARNI

Tie in bundle a very small piece of celery, of leek and of parsley in branches with a bay leaf and one clove, a sprig of thyme and, if desired, a small clove of garlic in the center. Should be enclosed in a muslin bag.

NEW ENGLAND BOILED DINNER

Boil three lbs. of fresh brisket of corned beef along with 1 1/2 lbs. of salt pork. Boil brisket of beef separately. Boil two heads of cabbage. Cut each head in four quarters. In juice of which corned beef was cooked, boil whole baby carrots and small boiling onions. When these are half done, add turnips. Whole peeled potatoes should be boiled separately. Dish up with cabbage in center of platter, with slice of corned beef, slice of fresh beef and slice of salt pork alternately. Arrange boiled potatoes around platter. Sprinkle with chopped parsley. Serves six to eight portions.

GOURMET BONELESS BREAST OF CHICKEN, SAUTE HAWAIIAN

Use boneless breast of chicken which weighs approximately 8 ounces. Season with salt and pepper, flour, saute in butter to golden brown. Remove from pan. Leave drippings. Fry in these drippings one thin slice of Smithfield ham. After this is done, saute in same pan, one slice pineapple ring. For dishing up, place one triangle of toast on dinner plate then place the slice of Smithfield ham onto the toast, then pineapple ring onto the ham, then place the breast of chicken onto the top of the pineapple ring. Now add two tablespoons butter to drippings left in pan after chicken, etc., is removed. Also, a small amount of cream and Sherry wine. Bring to boiling point and strain through fine sieve. Ladle this sauce over chicken on serving. Top with mushrooms. Garnish with parsley.

FRESH PINEAPPLE AND BANANA COCKTAIL

Use fresh pineapple cubes. Pour pineapple cubes in stainless-steel jar, then add 1/2 cup maraschino syrup to each quart of pineapple cubes. Let set for minimum of 2 hours under refrigeration. Just before meal period, add sliced bananas as desired to these contents. Serve in sundae glass. Garnish with maraschino cherry.

FRESH VEGETABLE DINNER WITH POACHED EGGS

Boil one head of cauliflower, 1 1/2 lbs. fresh string beans, six carrots (peeled and sliced), 1/2 lb. new peas, until firm (do not over-cook). Blanch and peel six medium-sized tomatoes. All to be sauted slightly in butter with dash of salt and sugar. Boil 1/2 lb. fresh spinach. Arrange around platter or dinner plate, alternately, for color effect. In center of platter place pieces of toast. On top of toast place one poached egg for each person. Serves six to eight portions.

SIRLOIN BUTT STEAK WITH BAKED POTATO AND NEW CORN SAUTE, O'BRIEN

Order from butcher six or eight sirloin butt steaks which should be cut from top rump. Dip both sides of steaks in corn oil or olive oil and season with salt and pepper. Broil or grill steaks rare, medium, or well done, as desired. When ready to serve, sprinkle with melted butter and finely chopped parsley. After steaks have been cooked, let rest for a minute so that drippings of blood from steak can dissolve with melted butter. Serve on very hot plate with Baked Potato and New Corn Saute O'Brien.

NEW CORN SAUTE O'BRIEN

Remove husks from six or eight ears of corn. For 10 minutes boil corn in unsalted water to which has been added a little milk. Take out of water and cut corn off the cob. Saute corn in butter with diced green peppers and small amount of diced pimiento. Season to taste.

BAKED POTATO

Use large, raw, unpeeled potatoes. Slice tip off of each end of potato. Bake in oven to make potato mealy. When ready to serve, split potato down the center, lengthwise, and place two pats of butter in each potato with a dash of paprika.

DINING CAR BREAKFAST ROLLS

1/2 qt. milk
3 oz. shortening (butter or lard)
3 oz. sugar
2 yolks of eggs
Pinch of salt
3/4 oz. compressed yeast

Warm the milk and take about a 1/4 pt. in which to dissolve the yeast and set aside.

Take the remainder of the milk and add sugar, eggs, and salt. Mix thoroughly. After this, add enough flour to make a thin paste of about the consistency of wheat cake batter. Add the dissolved yeast to this mixture and work it thoroughly. Now add enough flour to make a fairly firm dough and work in the shortening at the very last. Place the dough in a dishpan, cover with a cloth, and set aside until next morning to prove.

In the morning the dough is placed on a floured board and shaped into small rolls about the size of an egg. When proved, press the center with thin rolling pin, fold over and place on a greased baking tin. Set them in a warm place, glaze with a beaten egg and let rise again, after which they are baked in a moderately hot oven. This makes enough for six to eight persons.

FRESH FRUIT SALAD, CHATELAINE DRESSING

On a 7 1/2-inch chilled salad plate place a large lettuce leaf. On lettuce leaf arrange various fresh fruits in season such as sliced bananas, sliced and peeled apple, fresh pineapple, strawberries, pulped orange sections, pulped grapefruit sections, sliced peaches, etc. Top off with fresh blueberries if in season.

CHATELAINE DRESSING

Combine 1/2 pt. mayonnaise, 1/2 pt. whipped cream, and a small amount of lemon juice. Pour generous amount of dressing on top of salad and place in refrigerator to cool before serving.

SALAD BOWL OF SPRING MIXED GREENS

Cut roughly one head each of lettuce, romaine, and chicory or escarole. Mix this with one peeled and sliced cucumber and one bunch of radishes, finely sliced. Garnish top of salad bowl with julienne of ham or chicken and cheddar cheese. Arrange in alternation around top of bowl quartered pieces of hard boiled eggs and quartered tomatoes. Top off with small piece of watercress. Pour over top genuine French dressing which is made of 2/3 olive oil, 1/3 cider vinegar, salt, pepper and garlic.

WINE SAUCE

1 pt. Burgundy or claret wine
1 pt. water
1 cup sugar
1 oz. arrowroot powder
1/2 stick whole cinnamon
1 whole clove
3 inches lemon peel

Bring to a boil and stir in one oz. arrowroot powder which has been diluted with wine. This will thicken the sauce. Serve two fritters per person in your favorite dessert dish. Cover with wine sauce.

Here is appetizing Colorado Mountain Trout, Saute Meuniere, as served to Rock Island passengers.

FRESH ASPARAGUS, DELMONICO

Two lbs. of fresh asparagus should be cut into 1 1/2-inch pieces. Boil in salted water until tender after which, drain. Put in baking casserole, pour over very rich cream sauce, and sprinkle with white stale grated bread crumbs. Also sprinkle with diluted butter and bake in oven until brown.

APPLE FRITTERS WITH WINE SAUCE

Peel and core four or five apples and slice clear through, each piece being about 1/2-inch thick. Dip in flour and then in heavy wheatcake batter. Fry in hot grease to a golden brown.

COLORADO MOUNTAIN TROUT, SAUTE MEUNIERE

Use 10-inch fresh water trout. Remove entrails of fish, but leave head and tail on. Also do not wash slick film off of the fish, as this was partly formed by the water the fish swam in and adds to the flavor. Dip trout lightly in flour. Saute in corn oil or lard to a nice golden brown. Remove trout from pan and drain oil or lard from pan. Add butter to pan and bring it up to a foam. Add a few drops of Worcestershire sauce. Pour over top of fish when dishing up. Garnish with julienne potatoes. (These are like shoestring potatoes, French fried). Also add a quarter of a lemon with each fish. When trout is served, head and tail should be removed. Trout may also be split down the side, lengthwise, gently opened up, entire bone structure removed, and sides of trout laid back in shape.

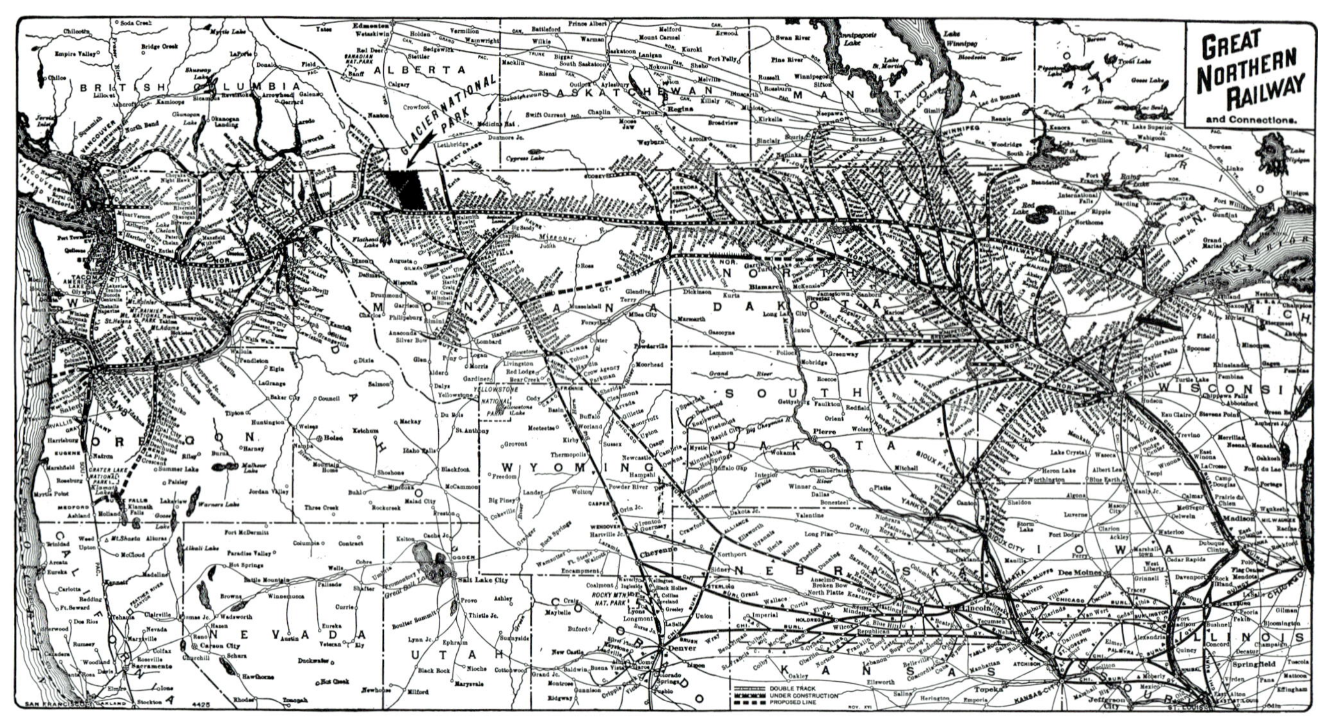

Swing over the skyline to the Old West—in

GLACIER PARK

A. J. Dickinson
Passenger Traffic Manager
St. Paul, Minn.

E. H. Wilde
General Passenger Agent
St. Paul, Minn.

C. W. Meldrum
Assistant General Passenger Agent
Seattle, Wash.

Come, climb to the very crest of America on the high-winding trails of Glacier Park —be lord of all you survey, mile-high Glaciers, mile-deep lakes, jagged peaks and sunshine! Adventure's waiting for you here—come west, young man, with all your informality. Low round-trip Summer Fares now in effect.

ROUTE OF THE RADIO EQUIPPED

EMPIRE BUILDER

Great Northern's "Empire Builder" rolls by Puget Sound after leaving Seattle on a transcontinental trek during which passengers will enjoy the diner.

GREAT NORTHERN

Dining car service on the Great Northern was launched in 1888, when the line was known as the St. Paul, Minneapolis and Manitoba Railway. Records indicate that George L. Bonney was the first superintendent of the system's dining and sleeping car department, a position that challenged him to provide all comforts possible for passengers on the pioneering line.

At the time, the railroad's main line extended westward only far enough to serve Great Falls, Helena, and Butte, Montana.

Even earlier efforts were made to accommodate passengers. An 1881 timetable advertised that the railroad boasted "first class eating houses at convenient points," although there was no indication as to whether these restaurants were operated by the railroad or individuals.

Six company owned dining cars went into service in 1889, the same year in which the line officially became known as the Great Northern.

Directed by rail tycoon James Hill, the Great Northern was completed to Seattle in July, 1893, and the additional travelers over the transcontinental route welcomed dining car service.

Great Northern's premier passenger train through the years has been *The Empire Builder,* operating between Chicago (via the Burlington), Minneapolis, St. Paul, Spokane, Seattle, and Portland--and serving meals that became famous. Other noted trains with diners have been *The Western Star,* also operating from Chicago to Portland; *The Winnipeg Limited,* rolling from Minneapolis and St. Paul, and *The Badger Express,* serving St. Paul and Minneapolis to Superior and Duluth.

Over the years the number of commissaries was reduced from four (St. Paul, Great Falls, Spokane, and Seattle) to two (St. Paul and Seattle). Increased speed of passenger trains, items requiring less storage space, better refrigeration, and frozen foods contributed to the efficiency of commissary service. These factors also were responsible for reducing the number of dining cars.

Modern dining car equipment was installed in 1947 on *The Western Star* and in 1951 on *The Empire Builder.* Highlights of the equipment included stainless steel kitchens with propane ranges and broilers, deep freeze units, and automatic dishwashers. Pies, rolls, and biscuits could be baked daily with ease.

The nature of the area served logically influenced the introduction into diner menus of such items as Washington apples, clams, salmon and other territory products.

ALL PICTURES THIS CHAPTER: GREAT NORTHERN RAILROAD

Here is Great Northern's "Empire Builder" alongside Puget Sound as it approached Seattle in 1930.

SPAGHETTI A LA GLACIER PARK

(As prepared by former Chef Steve Kogl of *The Empire Builder* -- 32 years of service.)

2 oz. bacon
2 oz. ham fat
4 oz. onion
1/2 oz. garlic
1 oz. green pepper
(All these ingredients to be chopped fine)

Braise all together with ham bone and one can of tomatoes. Cook for one hour. Strain and mix with hot spaghetti. Season to taste. Serve in casserole with Parmesan cheese and minced chicken.

MEAT LOAF

(As prepared by former Chef Dan Timm of *The Western Star* -- 45 years of service.)

1 lb. chopped round steak
1 cupful tomatoes
1 green pepper, chopped
1/4 cupful bread crumbs
2 tablespoons butter
1/2 cupful hot water

Season and bake an hour.

WENATCHEE APPLE CAKE

(As baked by former Chef Richard Rusnak of *The Western Star* -- 41 years of service.)

Make a dough with one lb. butter, one lb. flour, and one cupful milk. Roll thin and place in baking pan. Cover with sliced fresh apples. Mix ground cinnamon and powdered sugar, and dust over the apples, then bake. When nearly done add a custard made of one pint milk, 1/4 lb. sugar, and three eggs, mixed well. Bake again until custard sets.

CHICKEN PIE-GREAT NORTHERN STYLE

(As prepared by former Chef John Jurichko of *The Western Star* -- 36 years of service.)

Cover three large fat hens with cold water, and add one sliced onion, bunch of parsley, and sprig of sage. Boil over slow fire until meat is about ready to fall from bones. Separate meat from bones and cut up in fairly large pieces. Reduce stock by approximately one-third, then allow to cool off. Skim fat off top and mix with four heaping tablespoons of flour, and two tablespoonfuls butter. This is to be used as a binder; then add to the stock, while cold, yolks of three eggs, well beaten, with half cup rich cream.

Season to taste, then bring to a hot heat again, stirring continually, but do not boil. Add the binder and strain thoroughly.

Fill a chicken pie dish with layers of chicken, cold boiled potato, duchess shape. Sprinkle over all two tablespoons diced, crisp bacon, rendered out in frying pan, with some of the rendering.

Fill dish with roux described above, and cover all with top crust of pie dough, rolled moderately thick. Bake in a hot, quick oven.

G. N. LEMON PIE

(As baked by former Chef Fred Tobiska of *The Empire Builder* -- 47 years of service.)

Mix yolks of 20 eggs, one lb. sugar, juice and grated rind of eight lemons. Cook all over slow fire until it thickens. Remove from fire and stir in whites of 10 eggs beaten very hard. Pour into pie plates lined with pie dough and bake in a moderate oven for 25 minutes.

CHICKEN LOAF

(As prepared by former Chef Ben Roselle of *The Western Star* -- 39 years of service.)

2 cups cold cooked chicken
2 cups scalded milk
1/4 cup butter
3/4 cup shredded wheat biscuit crumbs
2 tablespoons chopped parsley
1 teaspoon salt
1/8 teaspoon white pepper
Yolks of 3 eggs
Whites of 3 eggs, beaten dry

Scald the milk, add butter, crumbs, salt and pepper; cook three minutes. Take from fire, add chicken, parsley and yolks of eggs beaten light. Last of all, fold in whites of eggs, turn into buttered dish and bake 45 minutes in moderate oven. Serve with sauce made from two cupfuls chickenstock, two tablespoons flour, two tablespoons butter, 1/2 teaspoon salt, 1/8 teaspoon paprika. Mushroom sauce may be used.

BAKED COLUMBIA RIVER SALMON

(As prepared by former Chef Homer Russell of *The Empire Builder* --38 years of service.)

Cut fish in desired pieces and place in well-buttered pan. Add salt and pepper, and a little flour to thicken; sprinkle with butter. Add a little stock, about 1/2 pint for two portions, prepared from bones and trimmings. Place in moderate oven and bake until done.

Streaking through the rugged Montana Rockies enroute from Chicago to Seattle and Portland is the Great Northern's streamline "Empire Builder."

Tableware and supplies for dining car service are stored at the Great Northern commissary in St. Paul, indicating the extensive preparations required to provide meals.

WENATCHEE APPLE PIE

(As baked by Chef Ervin Olson of *The Western Star* -- 38 years of service.)

Fine quality apples should not be boiled before making your pie. Line pie plate with pie paste rolled thin, and sliced good apples. Use 1/4 -lb. sugar to every two apples, juice of one lemon sprinkled over apples, and a slight dusting with powdered cinnamon. Wet edges and cover with paste rolled thin. Make cuts in top to allow steam to escape while baking, and cook in a moderate oven on bottom of oven first; finish on shelf of oven.

SWEET BREADS EN CASSEROLE

(As prepared by Chef Willford Krause of *The Western Star* -- 41 years of service.)

Soak sweetbreads in cold water with a little salt until all blood is out, then transfer to fresh water slightly salted, and bring to boil. Cool off in cold water and peel skin off. Put butter in frying pan, sweetbreads to saute in this. Add two or three tablespoons of good meat stock. Place all in casserole and cook in oven for 15 minutes.

G. N. COMBINATION GRILL

(As prepared by Chef Philo McCoy of *The Western Star* -- 42 years of service.)

Prepare small cut of beef tenderloin, one veal kidney split, one lamb chop, and one slice of ham or two of bacon. Serve hot. Garnish with watercress.

RANCH BEEF STEW

15 lbs. stew meat
3/4 cup oil
2 cups flour
1 gal. beef stock
1 1/4 cups salt
1 teaspoon pepper
4 cups celery, chopped
4 cups onions, chopped
2 tablespoons paprika
1 1/2 cups water
1 #2 can peas
1 #2 can beans

Place oil and cubed beef in saucepan, season with salt and pepper and paprika. Braise until brown. Dice celery, onions, cover with beef stock and cook until tender. Add to above, and simmer until meat is tender. Add stock, if needed. Combine flour and water to form a paste; add as much as needed. Season to taste with salt and pepper. Drain liquid from peas and beans, add to above. Serve in chicken pie baker.

BISQUE OF OYSTERS

1 pt. oysters
2 cups rice
3 qts. water
1 qt. cream
3/4 cup butter
1/2 cup flour
1/2 teaspoon mace
2 bay leaves
1/4 cup celery leaves
White pepper, salt, to taste

Place oysters, rice, water, bay leaves, celery in stock pot, cook until rice is done. Remove oysters and save, put remaining through sieve, melt butter, add flour to form a paste, add liquid stirring, add cream, chop oysters, add to soup, season with mace, salt and pepper to taste, serve hot.

SOUTHERN CORN MUFFINS

3 cups white cornmeal
3/4 teaspoon salt
1 1/2 cups buttermilk
3/4 teaspoon baking soda
2 eggs
3/4 teaspoon bacon grease
3/4 tablespoon melted butter

Sift cornmeal with soda and salt. Beat eggs, combine with buttermilk, bacon grease, and melted butter. Combine with cornmeal, beat well, fill greased muffin tin 2/3rds full.

Bake in a very hot oven at 450 degrees for 12 to 15 minutes. Serve hot. Two per portion. These can be frozen and reused. When taken out of freezer, place in oven at 350 degrees for 10 minutes. The recipe makes two dozen muffins.

MINCED BEEF TENDERLOIN WITH FRESH MUSHROOMS

(As prepared by former Chef Victor Warner of *The Western Star* -- 33 years of service.)

Shred two lbs. of lean tenderloin. Slice two onions, one green pepper, and six mushrooms, and saute all together until brown. Add one chopped tomato and cover with Espagnole sauce. Let simmer until meat is tender. Serve in casserole underlined with toast.

Espagnole sauce:

2 tablespoons butter
1/2 slice onion
2 tablespoons flour
1 cup stock
Salt
Paprika
Worcestershire sauce (optional)

Melt butter in small sauce pan. Add onion and saute until light brown. Remove onion. Cook and stir butter until it is light brown. Stir in flour and allow it to brown. Slowly stir in stock. Stir and cook sauce until it is smooth and boiling. Add seasoning to taste.

Above, this Great Northern dining car of the 1960's typifies equipment needed to accommodate passengers.

Below, peaks of Glacier National Park are among spectacular scenery enjoyed by Great Northern diners.

"The International Limited," Great Northern's train linking Seattle and Vancouver, was pictured in 1935 *along Puget Sound south of Everett, Washington.*

RICE MUSHROOM DRESSING

2 1/2 cups rice (raw)
2 green peppers
1 cup mushrooms
2 cups onions
4 ozs. butter
1 cup celery
Salt and pepper to taste

Cook rice in salted water until done, drain thoroughly. Dice onions and celery and green peppers fine. Saute in butter until tender. Just before taking off range, add mushrooms, add to rice and mix.

MAYONNAISE DRESSING

4 egg yolks
1 teaspoon dry mustard
1 pt. oil
1 teaspoon salt
1/4 teaspoon white pepper
1/4 cup vinegar

Mix mustard, salt, and paprika, add egg yolks; mix well. Add half of the vinegar and whip until smooth texture, then gradually add the oil, stirring constantly with whip, then add remaining vinegar, whip until smooth. Recipe makes one pint of dressing.

SOUTHERN RICE PUDDING

3 qts. milk
3 oranges
1 1/2 cups rice, raw
1 1/2 cups sugar
Cinnamon-Sugar
6 egg yolks
2 1/4 teaspoons salt
1 1/2 teaspoons vanilla
3 cups cream

Scald milk in double boiler. Peel orange, use peel only. To scalded milk add orange peel, rice, sugar, salt. Cook in double boiler until rice is tender, about 45 minutes. Stir often. Remove orange peel. Combine cream and egg yolks, stir in small amount of rice mixture; return to remainder of rice and mix, continue to cook until mixture thickens, stirring occasionally, and then add vanilla. Pour in custard cups and let cool. Sprinkle with one part cinnamon and two parts sugar. Garnish with whipped cream.

CLAM CHOWDER--GN STYLE

(As prepared by Chef Edwin Krey of *The Western Star* -- 46 years of service.)

1 lb. onions
1/2 lb. salt pork
8 lbs. fresh clams
1/4 lb. lard
1 gal. clam juice
1 gal. beef stock
1 qt. tomatoes
2 lbs. potatoes

Braise the onions and salt pork in the lard. When well-cooked add enough flour to absorb the moisture. Combine all in stock pot and bring slowly to boiling point.

1000 ISLAND DRESSING

1/2 green pepper
1 pimento (1/3 of 7-oz. can)
9 ozs. chili sauce
1/2 cup dry onions
2 tablespoons parsley, chopped
3 hard-cooked eggs
1 gal. mayonnaise

Chop green peppers, onions, pimentos, hard-boiled eggs very fine. Add mayonnaise and chili sauce and parsley; blend well. The recipe makes one gallon of dressing.

The Great Northern's "Empire Builder" was crossing the Crow River near Delano, Minnesota, when this 1929 photo was made. The line covers a scenic region.

FRENCH DRESSING

3 qts. oil
1/4 cup dry mustard
1/4 cup salt
1/4 teaspoon cayenne pepper
2 1/2 oz. paprika
1 cup sugar
1 clove garlic (or 1/2 teaspoon)
2 1/2 cups vinegar
5 eggs

Have oil and vinegar in icebox. Combine sugar, dry mustard, salt, cayenne pepper, paprika and garlic salt in mixing bowl, blend together, add eggs and whip 'til a smooth texture. Add oil and whip, alternate oil and vinegar, whip 'til smooth.

CREAM ROQUEFORT

1 1/2 bunches green onions
6 cloves garlic (or 1 oz garlic salt)
1 lb. Danish blue cheese
1 1/2 qts. buttermilk
1 gal. mayonnaise
Juice of 1 lemon
Salt and pepper to taste

Put green onions and bleu cheese through small grinder. Combine mayonnaise and buttermilk and lemon juice, garlic or garlic salt, salt and pepper. Whip until smooth. Add green onions and bleu cheese and stir.

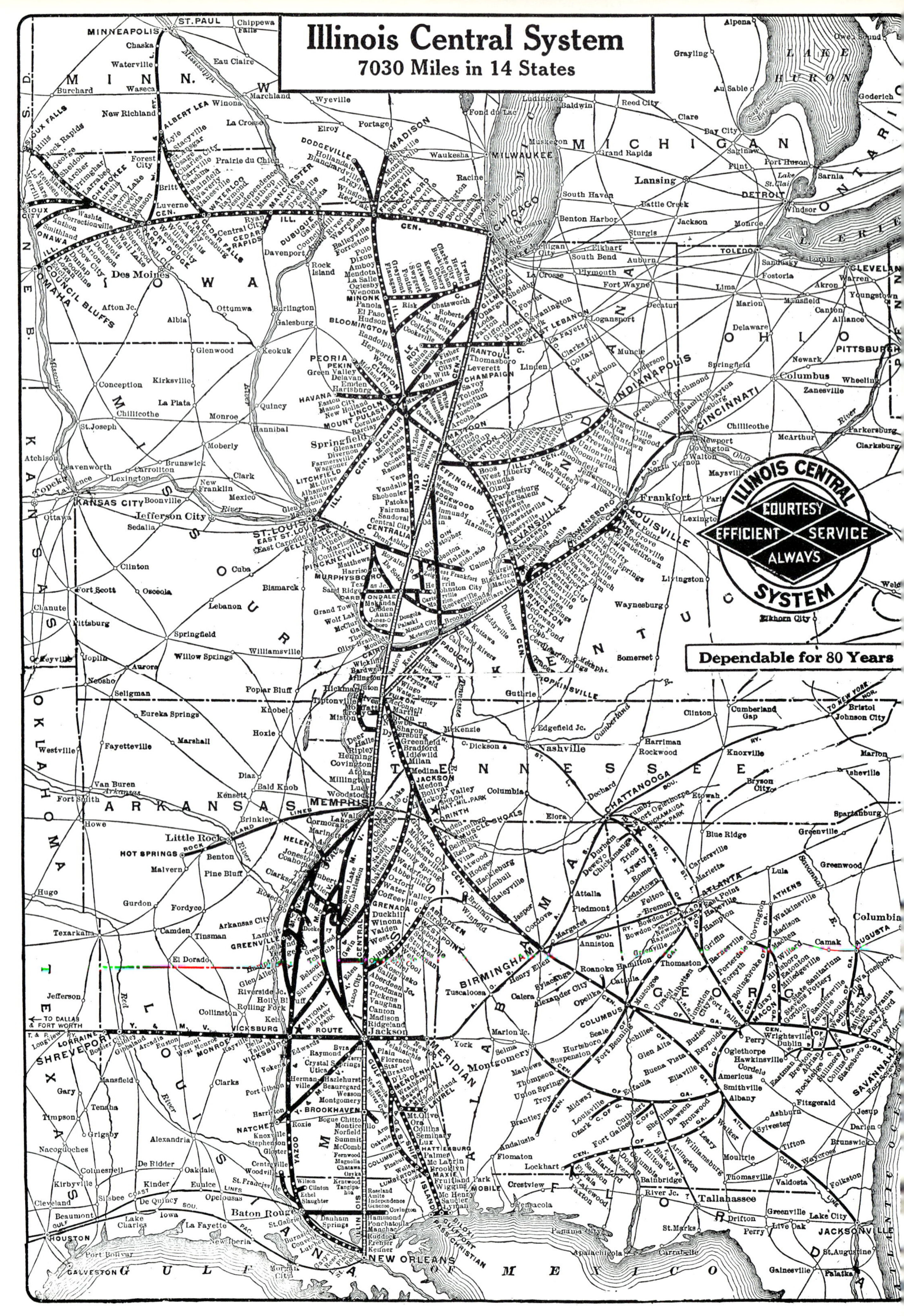
Illinois Central System
7030 Miles in 14 States
ILLINOIS CENTRAL
COURTESY
EFFICIENT
SERVICE
ALWAYS
SYSTEM
Dependable for 80 Years
MINN.
IOWA
MISSOURI
ARKANSAS
TENNESSEE
MICHIGAN
OHIO
INDIANA
KENTUCKY
GEORGIA
ALABAMA
MISSISSIPPI
LOUISIANA
TEXAS
OKLAHOMA
KANSAS
NEB.
S. D.
FLORIDA
LAKE HURON
LAKE ERIE
GULF OF MEXICO
CHICAGO
MEMPHIS
NEW ORLEANS
ST. LOUIS
MINNEAPOLIS
ST. PAUL
MADISON
OMAHA
SIOUX FALLS
BIRMINGHAM
ATLANTA
LOUISVILLE
EVANSVILLE
INDIANAPOLIS
CINCINNATI
JACKSON
VICKSBURG
SHREVEPORT
SAVANNAH
JACKSONVILLE

Despite snow on the ground, passengers on this Illinois Central train operating out of Chicago could enjoy the pleasure of having warm meals in the diner.

ILLINOIS CENTRAL

The Illinois Central Railroad, appropriately called the "Main Line of Mid-America," has been noted for developing recipes based on regional patronage over its substantial trackage between Chicago and New Orleans. The railroad's connections between the Gulf of Mexico and the Great Lakes as well as important farming and industrial areas has made it a strategic line. The system covers approximately 6,500 miles.

Dining car service for the Illinois Central began on December 7, 1897, with the use of two cafe cars on *The Daylight Special,* operating between Chicago and St. Louis. In addition to dining seats for six patrons, the two original dining cars--numbered 747 and 748--included smoking, parlor, and baggage accommodations.

Additional dining cars were quickly added to provide diner service between Chicago and other points. By the end of 1898, the capacity of individual cars had been increased so that 29 patrons could be seated at one time.

These improvements continued and by the 1960's two unit dining cars could seat 68 passengers. Greater elasticity than on standard dining cars was also developed with the diner-counter-lounge car, known as the "Palm Grove Cafe."

Until 1953 commissaries were operated at Chicago, Fulton, Kentucky, and Jackson, Mississippi. However, greater storage capacity and better refrigeration at that time eliminated need for all but the Chicago facility. Cars fully stocked at Chicago could make round trips with ease except for occasional emergency supplies at New Orleans or Miami.

The Illinois Central designed menus for attraction to travelers according to the train's origin or destination.

Trains carrying diners have included *The Panama Limited* and *The Creole* (Chicago to New Orleans), *The Floridan, The City of Miami,* and *The Seminole* (Chicago to Florida points), and *The Louisane* (Chicago to Houston via Southern Pacific, *The Panama Limited*).

A popular dinner feature on "The Panama Limited," the Illinois Central's crack streamliner, has been an elaborate menu containing both fish and meat courses--plus many extras--called the "King's Dinner." Included on the dinner are Manhattan or martini cocktail, appetizers, fresh gulf shrimp cocktail or crab finers, a 13-ounce bottle of imported wine, fish, charcoal-broiled boneless sirloin steak with buttered mushroom slices, potato and vegetable, a special salad created by the waiter, dinner bread, a heady cheese with fresh apple wedges, toasted saltines, coffee, and a choice of liqueur.

A price tag of $9.85 was set on the luxurious dinner in 1965.

The dinner was the brainchild of Charles Gibson, a native of Arkansas who was educated in Chicago and began dining car service in 1935, becoming associated with the Illinois Central as a waiter in 1940.

ALL PICTURES THIS CHAPTER: COURTESY ILLINOIS CENTRAL RAILROAD

The Illinois Central's "Daylight Special" between Chicago and St. Louis inaugurated the line's diner service. This picture was made in the teens.

SPAGHETTI CARUSO

This popular dish was developed for patrons of the Main Line of Mid-America. It serves eight portions.

2 lbs. chicken livers, cut in 1-inch squares
1 cup button mushrooms
1 small onion, chopped fine
1 clove garlic, chopped fine
2 tablespoons lemon juice
1 teaspoon salt
1 teaspoon pepper
1 teaspoon Ac'cent
1 cup canned tomatoes, crushed
1/4 cup shortening
1/4 cup flour
2 cups chicken stock

Sauce:

Place shortening in frying pan; add flour and brown. Then add onion and garlic and saute until soft. To this add chicken stock, mushrooms, crushed tomatoes, salt, pepper, Ac'cent, and lemon juice. Simmer for 10 minutes, stirring constantly to avoid sticking. Remove from fire, but keep hot.

Chicken livers:

Sprinkle livers with flour and saute lightly until done.

To serve, place 1 1/2 cups cooked spaghetti on dinner plate, and pour two tablespoons of chicken livers over spaghetti. Then pour four tablespoons of sauce over dish. Sprinkle chopped parsley and serve hot.

ORANGE PRALINE TOAST

This "different" dish was inspired by Illinois Central cooks from the Deep South and is certain to please guests.

1 cup brown sugar
1/4 cup orange juice
1 tablespoon grated orange rind
1/2 cup chopped pecans

Combine the above ingredients. Spread 1 tablespoon of mixture on each slice of buttered toast. Heat in medium-hot oven until sugar melts.

BAKED STUFFED LOBSTER TAIL

Lobster Tail became an Illinois Central favorite, especially on the "Panama Limited" where it developed into almost a "must". To vary this popular item, the line developed its own recipe.

Drop lobster tail in enough salted, boiling water to cover and boil for ten minutes. Remove lobster from water and allow to cool. Then split lengthwise and remove meat from shell, using a sharp, pointed knife. Cut meat into small chunks, about three pieces to each shell, and then replace cut pieces of lobster in shells. Sprinkle tops with crumb mixture. Pour tablespoon of melted butter over top and then place in moderate oven for 15 minutes, or until browned.

Crumb Mixture:

1/8 cup butter
1/2 clove garlic, chopped fine
3/4 cup bread crumbs, chopped fine
1/4 teaspoon salt
1/2 teaspoon paprika
1 tablespoon chopped parsley
2 tablespoons sherry wine
1 cash cayenne pepper

Cream the butter, garlic, and salt together; mix the bread-crumbs, paprika, parsley, sherry and Cayenne pepper--then add to the creamed mixture. The mixture should be crumbly.

A stainless steel kitchen helps make tasty meals on diners of the 1960's on the Chicago to New Orleans "Panama Limited" of the Illinois Central Railroad.

This is a dining car typical of the 1920's on the Illinois Central's "Panama Limited" crack train.

BAKED DEVILED CRAB MEAT

Crab Meat is a favorite all over the country, but it is probably appreciated a bit more in the Deep South. "Panama Limited" patrons hailed this recipe as soon as it was developed in the Illinois Central's dining car school.

1 lb. crab meat (fresh, frozen)
1 large onion, minced
1 large green pepper, minced
1 clove garlic
1/4 teaspoon cayenne pepper
1/4 teaspoon thyme
1/2 teaspoon salt
1 tablespoon Worcestershire sauce
3 eggs, hard-boiled and minced
4 slices bread, moistened and broken into small pieces
6 tablespoons melted butter
Juice of 1/2 lemon

Saute the onion, pepper and garlic in 2 tablespoons of butter for 10 minutes; add the thyme, pepper, salt, Worcester sauce and bread. Then add the crab meat, boiled eggs, and lemon juice. Mix the ingredients, being careful to avoid breaking up the crab meat. Place this mixture in four shirred egg dishes and pour one tablespoon of melted butter over each portion. Bake for 10 minutes. This recipe serves four persons.

CHICKEN ROYALE

Fowl helps make a good and well-balanced menu. Developed in the Illinois Central's diner training school, this dish was dubbed "Chicken Royale". It is a truly royal dish which is fit for a king.

Sauce: (one gallon)
2 onions, sliced
1 slice salt pork
1 tablespoon vinegar
1/8 teaspoon cayenne pepper
6 cups chicken stock
2 teaspoons salt
1/2 cup cornstarch paste
2 tablespoons raw carrots, grated
1 tablespoon raw green peas, chopped
1/4 cup melted butter
1 tablespoon lemon juice
1 teaspoon Ac'cent

Place sliced onion and salt pork in saucepan. Add vinegar and braise 10 minutes. Add chicken stock, salt and Cayenne pepper; boil 20 minutes. Remove salt pork, thicken sauce with cornstarch paste, strain, and return it to fire. Add chopped peas, grated carrots, and salt pork. Simmer 20 minutes until clear. Beat in butter, lemon juice, and Ac'cent. KEEP HOT.

CLAM CHOWDER - MID-AMERICA

Clam Chowder is a national favorite; yet, Illinois Central wanted something that could be identified with the midwest and, thus, with the Main Line of Mid-America. The line developed its own recipe and gave it an appropriate name. This recipe makes 3/4ths gallon of chowder.

2 cans chopped clams (Doxsee's brand, in 1-lb.-4-oz. cans)
1/2 cup salt pork, diced
1 cup onions, chopped fine
1 cup white potatoes, diced
2 cups water
2 tablespoons flour
Juice from the 2 cans of chopped clams
1 cup canned tomato meat, chopped
1 qt. fresh milk
2 teaspoons salt
1 teaspoon Ac'cent
1 teaspoon white pepper
3 tablespoons butter

Fry the salt pork until brown; remove from grease and place in saucepan; fry onions in remaining grease until soft, but do not brown. Add onions to pork; then add chopped clams, clam juice, water, tomatoes, and milk. Bring to a boil and skim off the grease; add potatoes and seasoning. Simmer until potatoes and pork are tender (approximately 25 minutes). Make reux with butter and flour and add to the chowder. Allow to thicken. Simmer an additional 10 minutes and stir frequently. Do not allow to boil. Garnish with chopped parsley. Serve hot.

POTATO CHEESE SOUP

1 qt. raw potatoes, peeled
8 cups cold water
1/2 cup finely chopped onions
1 teaspoon salt
1/4 teaspoon white or black pepper
1/2 cup American cheese, diced fine
1/2 cup Parmesan cheese, grated
2 cups hot cream
2 tablespoons flour
1/4 cup melted butter

Wash and peel white potatoes, cut in quarters, rinse and place in saucepan. Add cold water and cook until done. Remove from fire and force potatoes and liquid through sieve into another container.

Place melted butter in saucepan. Add finely chopped onion. Saute until soft - do not brown. Stir constantly to avoid burning. Stir in flour and add the strained potatoes and liquid. Season with salt and pepper. Cook slowly 15 or 20 minutes, being careful not to scorch. Remove from fire and strain. Add American and Parmesan cheese and hot cream. Garnish with chopped parsley. Serve hot; this recipe makes one-half gallon of soup.

SHRIMP GUMBO

4 tablespoons shortening
1 medium sized onion, chopped
2 blades celery, diced
1/2 clove garlic, chopped fine
1 cup canned tomatoes, crushed
1 cup tomato sauce
1 small bay leaf
1 teaspoon salt
1 pinch cayenne pepper
1/2 cup cooked rice
2 lbs. cooked shrimp (that have been shelled and deveined)
2 cups shrimp liquid
1 tablespoon cooking wine
1/4 cup cooked fresh or canned okra
1 medium sized green pepper, diced

Place shortening in saucepan. Add onions, green peppers, celery, and garlic. Saute until vegetables are soft (about 5 minutes). Stir in 2 tablespoons of flour, then add tomatoes, tomato sauce, and shrimp liquid. Season with salt and pepper, bay leaf, and wine. Simmer 20 minutes and stir frequently to prevent sticking. Last 10 minutes of simmering time: add cooked shrimp and okra. Remove bay leaf. Add one tablespoon of cooked rice to each cup or bowl; pour Gumbo over hot rice. Serve hot.

Here is a dining car typical of those being used during the 1960's on the Illinois Central Railroad.

ILLINOIS CENTRAL DRESSING

After much experimenting, IC developed a salad dressing that sent patrons soaring into the clouds with enthusiasm. What better name, then, than "Illinois Central Dressing"?

2 tablespoons chopped celery
2 tablespoons chopped dill pickle
2 tablespoons chopped green pepper
2 tablespoons chopped pimento
1 teaspoon chopped green onion
2 hard-boiled eggs, chopped (All the foregoing ingredients should be chopped very fine)
2 cups mayonnaise
1 cup chili sauce

Place celery, dill pickle, green pepper, pimento, green onion, and eggs in saucepan and mix thoroughly. Add mayonnaise and stir well. Add chili sauce and stir well. Store in cold place.

Note: All vegetables should be cleaned thoroughly and chopped very fine. This recipe makes one quart of dressing.

SHRIMP CREOLE

The word "Creole" in itself holds certain charm and evokes thoughts of the mysterious. Whence originated Creole cooking? In the first place, Creole cooking found its origin in New Orleans. From France came chefs to make their fortunes in the new world. From Spain came the best cooks. Later they borrowed ideas from one another. Still later, the people who learned from them adapted their techniques. The result? Creole cooking!

3 lbs. fresh shrimp
3 teaspoons salt
1 bay leaf
1 teaspoon cayenne pepper
1 small onion, cut in half
1 blade celery, diced
Juice of 1 lemon

Place shrimp in hot water. Season with the above, except lemon juice. Bring to boil and cook 20 minutes. Drain off liquor. Cool slightly. Remove shell and devein. Place shrimp in a container, cover with cold water. Add juice of one lemon and store in refrigerator until ready to use.

The Illinois Central's streamline all coach "City of New Orleans" crosses Big Muddy Creek near Carbondale, Illinois, on its way to southern cities.

OLD FASHIONED RAISIN PUDDING

1/4 cup milk
1/4 cup granulated sugar
1 cup brown sugar
3/4 cup flour
1 teaspoon baking powder
1/2 cup raisins
1 cup water
2 tablespoons butter

Mix the flour, baking powder, and raisins, and then add the milk and beat until smooth; spread in buttered pan, then prepare the sauce as follows: Mix brown sugar, water and butter in saucepan. Bring to boil and pour over the batter while hot. Bake in moderate oven (350 degrees) for 30 minutes.

Dinner

Table D'Hote

Price Opposite Entree Indicates Complete Meal Charge
Please Write "Dinner" on Meal Check, Listing Each Item Desired

FRIED DEEP SEA HALIBUT, Tomato Sauce 1.50
Longbranch Potatoes and Combination Salad, French Dressing

SAUTE CUTLET OF MILK FED VEAL 1.60
Spaghetti Milanaise and Buttered Lima Beans

ROAST YOUNG TOM TURKEY, Dressing, Jelly 1.75
Potatoes Whipped in Cream and Buttered Lima Beans

(Your Favorite Egg Dish Will be substituted for Entree if Desired)

Dinner Rolls
Chilled Melon
Pineapple Sundae
Peach Cobbler, Vanilla Sauce
Cheese with Saltines
Coffee
Milk
Tea

Cup of Soup or Plate Portion Lettuce and Tomato Salad Served with Table D'Hote Meals 20c Additional

A La Carte

Chef's Selection Soup, Cup 30
Chilled Tomato or Orange Juice 25
HOT CHICKEN SANDWICH WITH MASHED POTATOES 1.00
BOILED HAM SANDWICH 60
AMERICAN CHEESE SANDWICH 55
Longbranch Potatoes 25
Buttered Lima Beans 25
Sliced Tomatoes 45
Lettuce and Tomato Salad 40
Lettuce Salad, French Dressing 40
Assorted Bread 15
Rolls 20
Ry-Krisp 15
Chilled Melon 35
Cheese with Saltines 40
Peach Cobbler, Vanilla Sauce 30
Pineapple Sundae 35
Milk 20
Buttermilk 20
Coffee, Pot 25
Tea, Pot 30
Instant Sanka, Pot 30
Postum 30
Hot Chocolate, Pot 30

Saccharin Tablets are available upon request

A. C. Linton, Passenger Traffic Mgr., Illinois Central Railroad, Chicago (6)
N. L. Patterson, General Superintendent Dining Service, Illinois Central Railroad, Chicago (5)

City of Miami

ILLINOIS CENTRAL
CENTRAL OF GEORGIA
FLORIDA EAST COAST
ATLANTIC COAST LINE

CHICKEN AND HAM

2 oz. sliced chicken breast
1/2 thin slice ham
2 toast points
1 teaspoon sliced mushrooms

Service: Heat chicken in chicken stock and drain. Place toast points on plate and slice of broiled ham on toast points. Place mushrooms in center of ham and place hot chicken slices on each end of ham. Spoon liberal portion of hot Royale Sauce over all and serve hot.

TEA BISCUITS

3 1/2 cups sifted flour
3 1/2 teaspoons baking powder
1 teaspoon salt
3/4 cup shortening
1 whole egg
1 1/2 cups milk

Sift flour, baking powder and salt well, adding shortening and mix until flour crumbles; then add egg and milk. Stir well. Turn out on lightly floured board and roll dough to 3/4" thickness. Cut with biscuit cutter, place in greased pan, brush lightly with egg wash. Bake for approximately 15 minutes. This recipe makes 24 biscuits.

CREOLE SAUCE (One quart)

3 tablespoons shortening
1 medium-sized onion, diced
1 green pepper, diced
2 blades celery, diced
1 clove garlic, chopped fine
1 cup chicken stock or chicken cubes
1 cup canned tomatoes, chopped
1 tablespoon cooking wine
1 cup tomato sauce
1 bay leaf
1 teaspoon salt
1/4 teaspoon cayenne pepper
1/2 cup canned mushrooms, drained
1/4 cup cornstarch paste
1 lb. cooked rice

Place the shortening in saucepan. Add onions, green pepper, celery, and garlic. Saute 5 minutes. Add tomatoes, tomato sauce mushrooms, and chicken stock. Season with salt, Cayenne pepper, cooking wine, and bay leaf. Cook 30 minutes. Remove bay leaf. Add cornstarch paste. Simmer 10 minutes. Keep hot.

Place mold of cooked rice in center of plate or shirred-egg dish. Spread about 12 cooked shrimp (hot) around rice. Pour 1 cup of hot Creole Sauce over shrimp. Sprinkle with snipped parsley. Serve hot.

Rolling out of the Chicago yards, the Illinois Central Railroad's "City of New Orleans" heads southward. The train won acclaim for its fine food.

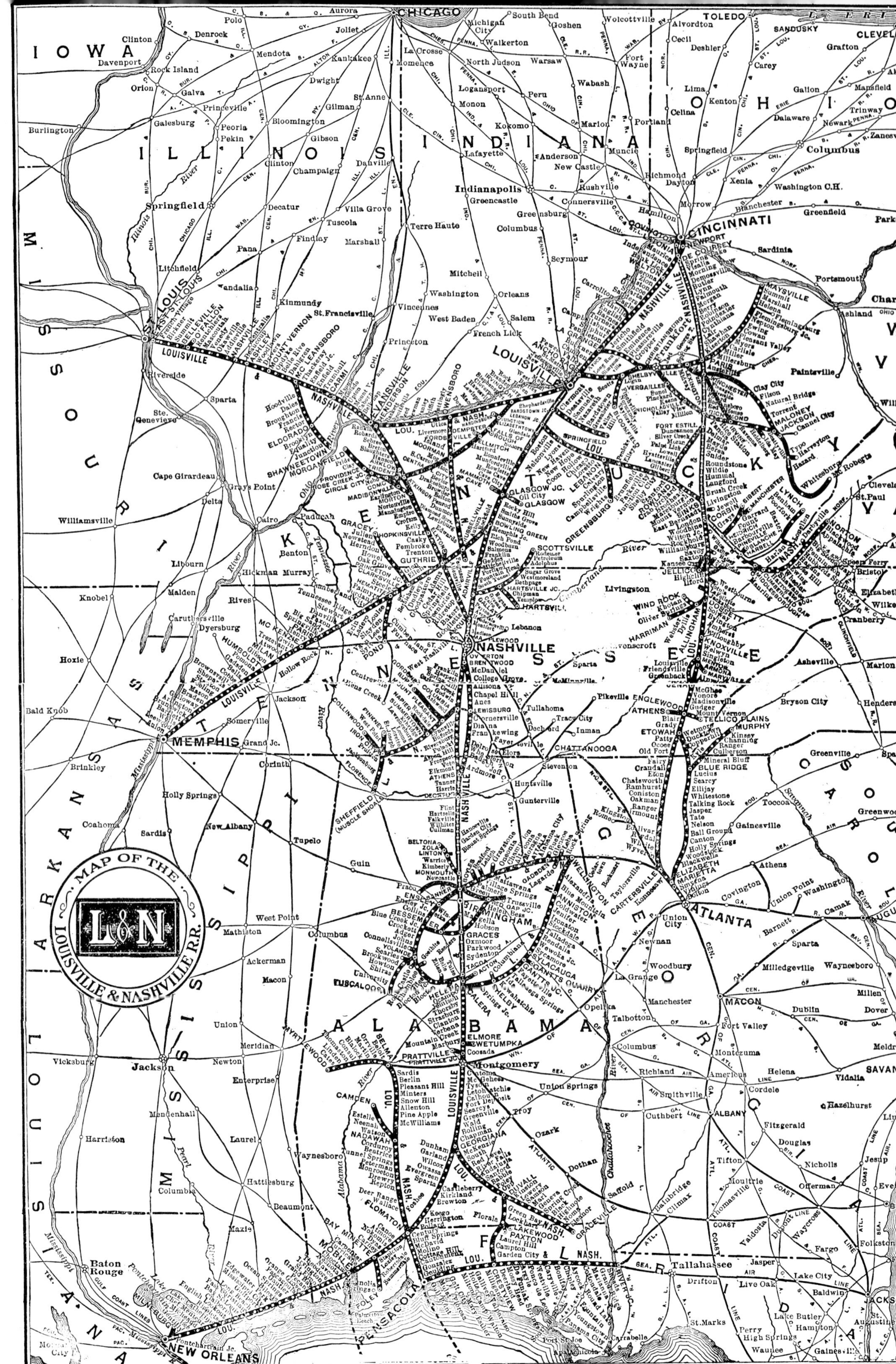
MAP OF THE
L&N
LOUISVILLE & NASHVILLE R.R.
IOWA
ILLINOIS
INDIANA
OHIO
MISSOURI
KENTUCKY
TENNESSEE
ARKANSAS
MISSISSIPPI
ALABAMA
GEORGIA
LOUISIANA
FLORIDA
CHICAGO
CINCINNATI
LOUISVILLE
ST. LOUIS
EVANSVILLE
NASHVILLE
MEMPHIS
KNOXVILLE
CHATTANOOGA
BIRMINGHAM
ATLANTA
MONTGOMERY
MOBILE
PENSACOLA
NEW ORLEANS
Indianapolis
Tallahassee
MACON

Here is the Louisville and Nashville "South Wind," steam-powered Chicago-Florida streamliner of the 1940's which won acclaim for speed and fine food.

LOUISVILLE & NASHVILLE

The Louisville and Nashville Railroad, completed between the two cities in 1857, grew during the years into a system with 4,700 miles of track serving 13 states. In addition to the cities that gave the railroad its name, the rails stretched to Cincinnati, St. Louis, Memphis, Birmingham, and New Orleans.

Prior to 1901, meals occasionally were served aboard Pullman dining cars on Louisville and Nashville trains. However, it usually was the practice to stop at designated stations so that travelers could appease their hunger at restaurants. Such arrangements, of course, stretched the lengths of trips considerably.

Even after the use of dining cars became widespread, stopping at restaurants continued--at least to a limited extent for certain trains--as late as the 1940's. Before World War II passengers also could arrange to have box lunches delivered aboard trains by having the conductor wire ahead.

The practice of avoiding the use of dining cars undoubtedly helped the railroad to save money--particularly in the instances where travel on trains was so light that there would be few patrons for a diner.

In October, 1901, the Louisville and Nashville placed its own diners--three cars to initiate the service--in operation. So popular did they become that many other dining cars soon were added to the system except in those cases where stops were scheduled for meals.

The Louisville and Nashville soon became noted for a fine tradition of Southern cooking. Food that built this reputation was prepared in the train's diner, and use of the railroad's commissary at Louisville was reserved primarily for storage.

Clifford J. Haury, who joined the railroad's dining car department in 1920 and advanced to become the division's superintendent, emphasized the need for careful selection of choice old hickory-smoked, country-cured ham. Its painstaking preparation made it highly popular as a breakfast item among travelers on such crack trains as *The Georgian, The Humming Bird, The Pan-American, The Crescent,* and *The Piedmont Limited.*

Above, distinctive chairs, white linen and fine flatwear were typical of the golden age of railroad diners on the all-Pullman L&N Pan-American *in 1925.*

Left, Christmas dinner on the Pan-American *en route from Louisville to Birmingham in 1955. A cook (left) makes a salad while the chef prepares to put the turkey in the oven.*

—Both: Donald Duke Collection

OLD KENTUCKY HAM

This recipe was issued to Louisville and Nashville chefs by Clifford J. Haury, superintendent of the railroad's dining cars, for cooking ham 18 months to two years old. The results are most delightful.

First carefully clean the ham by scrubbing with a stiff brush or coarse cloth, and then cut off the hock, which can be used as seasoning with beans or other dishes. Soak the ham 12 to 24 hours in cold water, but do not cook the ham in this soaking water. To boil or simmer your ham, place it in a large container, completely covering it with fresh, cold water; put it on the stove and bring to a boil, allowing it to simmer until the large bone in the butt end becomes loose and protrudes. The cooking time will average approximately 25 minutes to each pound. If necessary, add hot water to keep the ham completely covered. Remove the ham from water and when it has cooled, carefully remove the find and trim excess fat. Mix one cup of brown sugar with three tablespoons of Port wine or fruit juice, spreading this mixture over the ham. Decorate to your taste. Place the ham in the oven and bake at 375 to 400 degrees for 15 or 20 minutes. The ham should be served only after it has cooled to room temperature.

SERVING FRIED COUNTRY HAM WITH RED GRAVY

The ham should be cut in slices approximately one-fourth inch thick. Trim off the rind as well as the dark, hard edge from the meat side of the slice. Prepare a mixture of one pint of milk and one teaspoon of sweet syrup, an amount sufficient for soaking three slices of ham. Soak the ham in the milk mixture for approximately 20 minutes, and then drain and dry. Cut approximately one-half of the fat from the slice of ham; place the fat in a clean skillet and render. After all grease has been cooked from the fat, remove the fat from the skillet. Put the slice of ham in a hot skillet, brown quickly on one side and turn and brown on the other side. Repeat this the second time. The ham is now ready to be removed from the skillet (If cooked too long, it will become hard and dry.) Leave the grease and residue from the ham in the skillet to brown. When sufficiently browned, add a small amount of cold water to make red gravy. Pour the gravy over the ham and serve.

SHRIMP COCKTAIL SAUCE

1 cup mayonnaise
1 cup chili sauce
4 drops Tabasco sauce
1 tablespoon vinegar
Juice of 1/2 lemon
1 teaspoon anchovy paste
Salt to taste (The anchovy paste being salty, little additional salt is required)

In order to have the dressing smooth, dissolve the anchovy paste in vinegar and lemon juice, then mix in remaining ingredients.

In serving shrimp cocktail, Louisville and Nashville diner personnel were instructed to use a combination silver frame and glass over a tea plate; the inside cocktail glass was to be packed in crushed ice in a large outside glass. The shrimp and sauce were to be placed on a leaf of lettuce in the cocktail glass. An oyster fork with one-fourth of a lemon was to be placed on a tea plate used for an underline, while eight butter crackers or three double premium soda crackers being placed on a separate tea plate.

CORN MUFFINS

Instructions for preparing these muffins were explicit in ruling out use of sugar or wheat flour. The recipe makes 12 muffins of the size ordinarily served on Louisville and Nashville diners.

2 rounded cups corn meal
2 level teaspoons baking powder
1 level teaspoon salt
1 egg
2 cups milk
2 basting spoons bacon drippings or cooking oil (bacon drippings are preferable)

Bake until done.

FRESH SHRIMP GUMBO, NEW ORLEANS STYLE

1 qt. small chopped oysters
2 lbs. lake shrimp
1 1/2 gals. strained shrimp stock
1/2 gal. chicken stock (strained and not greasy)
3 onions
2 green peppers
3 sprigs chopped parsley
2 bay leaves
1/2 teaspoon thyme
1 lb. fresh or canned okra
1 No. 2 1/2-can tomatoes
1/4 lb. chopped raw ham
3 basting spoons cooking oil
3 basting spoons flour
1 level basting spoon paprika
1 round basting spoon file
Salt and Cayenne pepper to taste

Saute onions, green peppers, parsley, bay leaves, ham, thyme and paprika in large sauce pan in which soup is to be made. Add tomatoes and okra and let cook for a few minutes; do not let burn; add flour and make roux; brown but do not permit to burn. Add shrimp stock, chicken stock, salt, and cayenne pepper, letting mixture boil slowly for one hour and 30 minutes. Add the cooked shrimp and chopped oysters to gumbo 10 minutes before removing from range. After removing from range, add file (but do not permit to boil after adding this ingredient).

Put a teaspoon of boiled rice in cup and pour gumbo over the rice. A tablespoon of rice should be served with a tureen of gumbo. Never boil the gumbo with the rice and never add the file while the gumbo is on the fire, as boiling after the file is added tends to make the gumbo stringy and unfit for use. To reheat, place the gumbo in a jar and place in bain marie or on steam table. Do not reheat on a range.

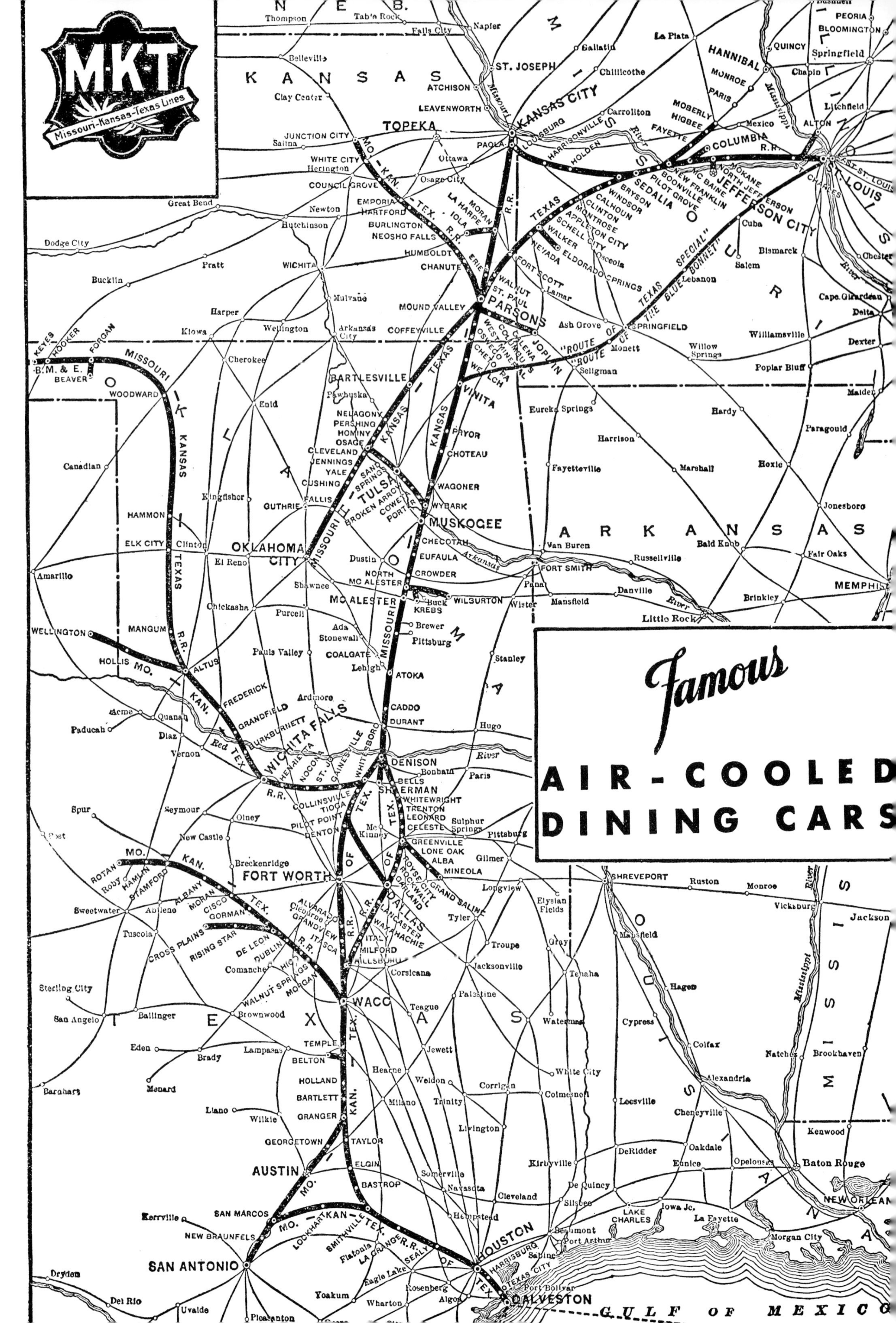
M-K-T
Missouri-Kansas-Texas Lines
Famous
AIR-COOLED DINING CARS
N E B.
K A N S A S
O K L A H O M A
T E X A S
A R K A N S A S
M I S S O U R I
L O U I S I A N A
GULF OF MEXICO
"ROUTE OF THE BLUE BONNET"
"ROUTE OF TEXAS SPECIAL"
MISSOURI-KANSAS-TEXAS R.R.
MO.-KAN.-TEX. R.R.
Thompson
Table Rock
Falls City
Napier
Belleville
Clay Center
ATCHISON
ST. JOSEPH
LEAVENWORTH
KANSAS CITY
TOPEKA
JUNCTION CITY
Salina
WHITE CITY
Herington
COUNCIL GROVE
Ottawa
Osage City
PAOLA
LOUISBURG
HARRISONVILLE
HOLDEN
Gallatin
Chillicothe
Carrollton
La Plata
HANNIBAL
MONROE
PARIS
MOBERLY
HIGBEE
FAYETTE
Mexico
COLUMBIA
QUINCY
PEORIA
BLOOMINGTON
Springfield
Chapin
Litchfield
ALTON
ST. LOUIS
ST. CHARLES
MOKANE
NORTH JEFFERSON
JEFFERSON CITY
BAINE
NEW FRANKLIN
BOONVILLE
PILOT GROVE
SEDALIA
BRYSON
WINDSOR
CALHOUN
CLINTON
MONTROSE
APPLETON CITY
SCHELL CITY
WALKER
NEVADA
ELDORADO SPRINGS
Osceola
Cuba
Bismarck
Salem
Chester
Cape Girardeau
Lebanon
SPRINGFIELD
Ash Grove
Monett
Seligman
Willow Springs
Williamsville
Poplar Bluff
Dexter
Delta
Great Bend
Newton
Hutchinson
EMPORIA
HARTFORD
BURLINGTON
NEOSHO FALLS
HUMBOLDT
CHANUTE
LA HARPE
IOLA
MORAN
ERIE
WALNUT
ST. PAUL
PARSONS
FORT SCOTT
Lamar
MOUND VALLEY
COFFEYVILLE
OSWEGO
CHETOPA
COLUMBUS
WEST MINERAL
GALENA
JOPLIN
WELCH
Dodge City
Pratt
Bucklin
WICHITA
Mulvane
Harper
Kiowa
Wellington
Arkansas City
KEYES
HOOKER
FORGAN
B.M. & E.
BEAVER
WOODWARD
Cherokee
Enid
BARTLESVILLE
Pawhuska
NELAGONY
PERSHING
HOMINY
OSAGE
CLEVELAND
JENNINGS
YALE
CUSHING
FALLS
GUTHRIE
TULSA
SAND SPRINGS
BROKEN ARROW
COWETA
PORTER
VINITA
PRYOR
CHOTEAU
WAGONER
WYBARK
MUSKOGEE
CHECOTAH
EUFAULA
CROWDER
NORTH MC ALESTER
MC ALESTER
KREBS
Buck
WILBURTON
Brewer
Pittsburg
Canadian
Kingfisher
HAMMON
ELK CITY
Clinton
El Reno
OKLAHOMA CITY
Dustin
Shawnee
Chickasha
Purcell
Ada
Stonewall
Pauls Valley
COALGATE
Lehigh
ATOKA
Ardmore
CADDO
DURANT
Hugo
Amarillo
WELLINGTON
MANGUM
HOLLIS
ALTUS
FREDERICK
GRANDFIELD
BURKBURNETT
WICHITA FALLS
HENRIETTA
NOCONA
ST. JO
GAINESVILLE
WHITESBORO
DENISON
Bonham
Paris
BELLS
SHERMAN
WHITEWRIGHT
TRENTON
LEONARD
CELESTE
GREENVILLE
LONE OAK
ALBA
MINEOLA
Sulphur Springs
Pittsburg
Gilmer
Acme
Paducah
Quanah
Diaz
Vernon
Red
Spur
Seymour
Olney
Post
New Castle
COLLINSVILLE
TIOGA
PILOT POINT
DENTON
Mc Kinney
Breckenridge
FORT WORTH
DALLAS
ROYSE CITY
ROCKWALL
GARLAND
GRAND SALINE
ROTAN
Roby
HAMLIN
STAMFORD
ALBANY
MORAN
CISCO
GORMAN
Sweetwater
Abilene
Tuscola
CROSS PLAINS
RISING STAR
DE LEON
DUBLIN
ALVARADO
Cleburne
GRANDVIEW
ITASCA
LANCASTER
WAXAHACHIE
ITALY
MILFORD
HILLSBORO
HICO
Comanche
WALNUT SPRINGS
MORGAN
Corsicana
WACO
Sterling City
San Angelo
Ballinger
Brownwood
Teague
Palestine
Eden
Brady
Lampasas
TEMPLE
BELTON
HOLLAND
BARTLETT
GRANGER
Menard
Barnhart
Llano
Wilkie
GEORGETOWN
TAYLOR
ELGIN
BASTROP
AUSTIN
Jewett
Hearne
Weldon
Milano
Trinity
Corrigan
Livingston
Somerville
Navasota
Hempstead
Cleveland
Kerrville
SAN MARCOS
NEW BRAUNFELS
LOCKHART
SMITHVILLE
LA GRANGE
Flatonia
SEALY
SAN ANTONIO
Dryden
Del Rio
Uvalde
Pleasanton
Yoakum
Eagle Lake
Rosenberg
Wharton
HOUSTON
HARRISBURG
TEXAS CITY
GALVESTON
Port Bolivar
Beaumont
Port Arthur
Sabine
Longview
Tyler
Troupe
Jacksonville
Elysian Fields
Gary
Tenaha
Waterman
White City
Colmesneil
Kirbyville
DeRidder
De Quincy
Silsbee
LAKE CHARLES
Iowa Jc.
La Fayette
Morgan City
Eunice
Opelousas
Baton Rouge
NEW ORLEANS
Oakdale
Cheneyville
Kenwood
Leesville
Alexandria
Colfax
Cypress
Hagen
Mansfield
SHREVEPORT
Ruston
Monroe
Vicksburg
Jackson
Natchez
Brookhaven
Eureka Springs
Hardy
Harrison
Fayetteville
Marshall
Hoxie
Paragould
Jonesboro
Malden
Van Buren
FORT SMITH
Russellville
Bald Knob
Fair Oaks
MEMPHIS
Brinkley
Pana
Wister
Mansfield
Danville
Little Rock
Stanley
Arkansas
River
Mississippi
Missouri

This Missouri-Kansas-Texas dining car includes the steward, waiters, and cooks. They are similar to crews assigned to diners on other railroads.

MISSOURI-KANSAS-TEXAS

The Missouri-Kansas-Texas Railroad, whose initials inspired the affectionate nickname of "The Katy" that eventually was emblazoned on its freight cars, began in 1865 by branching southward from the Union Pacific. Much of its growth came as the result of the end of the open range and the consequent end of the cattle drives from Texas and Oklahoma.

When farmers planted wheat and erected barbed wire fences to protect their crops, the cattlemen turned to the railroads to reach their markets.

Eventually operating approximately 3,200 miles of track, The Katy stretched from St. Louis to Kansas City and southward through Fort Worth and Dallas to Galveston. Branches carried Missouri-Kansas-Texas traffic to the cattle areas of Keyes, Okla. and Rotan, Texas.

Among the Missouri-Kansas-Texas Railroad's crack trains were *The Texas Special* (operated jointly with the St. Louis-San Francisco Railroad) from St. Louis to Dallas, Fort Worth, and San Antonio, and *The Blue Bonnet,* carrying passengers from St. Louis and Kansas City to Austin, Houston, and Galveston.

Other passenger trains operating over the line included *The Sooner, The Alamo Special,* and *The Katy Special.*

The competition of automotive and air travel gradually resulted in a reduction of The Katy's passenger service and consequently service ended for its dining cars, the meals on which once brought so much pleasure to travelers.

Representative recipes of dishes once enjoyed on the Missouri-Kansas-Texas diners are recorded here.

ALL PICTURES THIS CHAPTER: MISSOURI-KANSAS-TEXAS RAILROAD

ILLUSTRATION: THE BETTMANN ARCHIVE INC.

KATY KORNETTES

1 lb. white corn meal
1/2 cup butter
1 tablespoon sugar
1 teaspoon salt
1 qt. boiling sweet milk

Mix well all ingredients. Let stand about five minutes. Drop through pastry bag about the size of a silver dollar on baking pan which has been greased very lightly. Cool about 15 minutes at room temperature before baking. Bake in hot oven for about 20 minutes. Serves six persons.

KATY SPECIAL ONION SOUP

6 large onions
1/4 lb. butter
1/2 cup flour
1 gal. of rich stock
1/4 cup Worcestershire sauce

Cut onions into quarters, and then slice thin cross sections. Saute in butter to a golden brown. Add the flour to the onion and butter and blend well. Then add the hot stock and let simmer 20 minutes. Season with a bunch of parsley, bay leaves and a touch of garlic. Boil for a few minutes and then remove the bouquet. Season to taste with salt and pepper, and add the Worcestershire sauce. For each portion of soup prepare crouton fried in oil or butter. After soup is poured, place crouton in cup topped with a generous portion of grated Parmesan cheese. Place in hot oven a few minutes just before serving. Makes one gallon.

KATY CHICKEN PIE

1 cup diced chicken
1/3 cup finely diced salt pork
2/3 cup parisienne potatoes (boiled)
1/3 cup sliced mushrooms
1/8 cup green olives
1/4 cup small peas
1 qt. rich chicken roux
1/4 cup dry sherry cooking wine
1 teaspoon lemon juice
Parsley

Make the roux of stock from chicken seasoned with salt, pepper, nutmeg and minced parsley. Mix chicken, salt pork and mushrooms. Let simmer in roux. Add peas, olives, lemon juice and wine before serving. Serve in casserole topped with well browned crust with mixed parsley sprinkled on top. Chicken must be in good sized pieces with plenty of white meat. Never use turkey.

PEACH COBBLER

1/2 cup flour
Sugar
2 cups sliced peaches
1 tablespoon thick cooked tapioca
1/2 cup milk
Almond extract
1 1/4 teaspoon baking powder
1/2 cube butter

Prepare batter using flour, one-half cup sugar, one-half cup milk, and baking powder. Melt butter in baking pan and pour the batter over the top of the butter. Add one-third cup sugar to thinly sliced peaches and mix in 1/8th teaspoon almond extract and one tablespoon of thin cooked tapioca. Pour the peach mixture over the batter and bake at 400 degrees for approximately 35 minutes. During baking, the batter will rise to the top. Serves four.

Missouri Pacific Chef Henry Bausbach demonstrates the fine art of slicing turkey for a dish that will be appetizing to diners — on trains or at home.

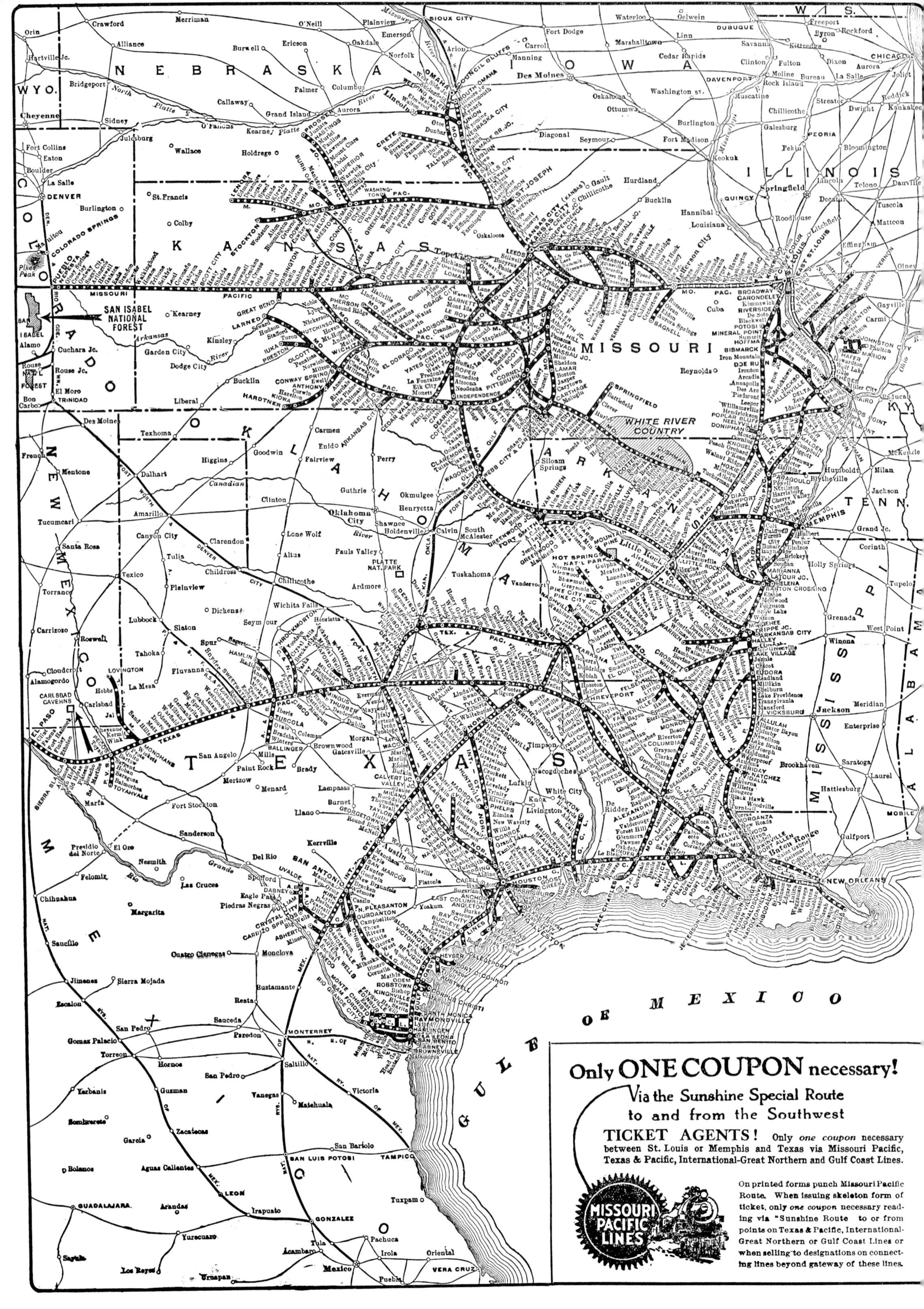
Only ONE COUPON necessary!
Via the Sunshine Special Route
to and from the Southwest
TICKET AGENTS! Only one coupon necessary between St. Louis or Memphis and Texas via Missouri Pacific, Texas & Pacific, International-Great Northern and Gulf Coast Lines.
On printed forms punch Missouri Pacific Route. When issuing skeleton form of ticket, only one coupon necessary reading via "Sunshine Route" to or from points on Texas & Pacific, International-Great Northern or Gulf Coast Lines or when selling to designations on connecting lines beyond gateway of these lines.
MISSOURI PACIFIC LINES
NEBRASKA
IOWA
ILLINOIS
KANSAS
MISSOURI
COLORADO
OKLAHOMA
ARKANSAS
NEW MEXICO
TEXAS
MISSISSIPPI
ALABAMA
TENN.
KY
WYO.
WIS.
MEXICO
GULF OF MEXICO
SAN ISABEL NATIONAL FOREST
WHITE RIVER COUNTRY
DENVER
KANSAS CITY
ST. LOUIS
MEMPHIS
Little Rock
NEW ORLEANS
HOUSTON
SAN ANTONIO
Dallas
FORT WORTH
OMAHA
CHICAGO

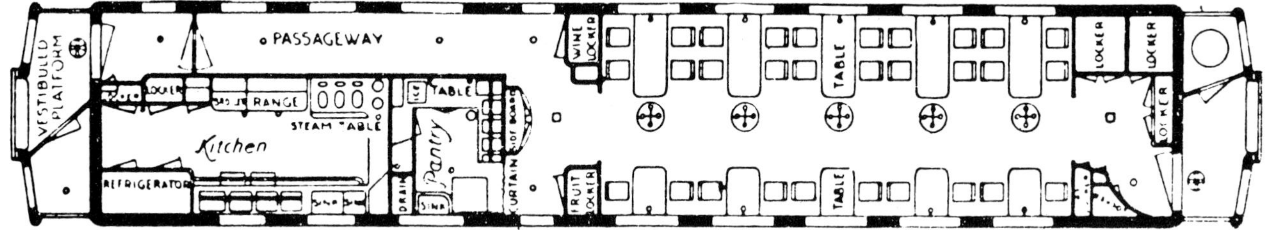

MISSOURI PACIFIC

Opening of the five mile rail line between St. Louis and Jefferson City in 1851 inaugurated what became The Missouri Pacific Railroad--eventually stretching over approximately 7,000 miles of track from Nebraska and Colorado to Texas and Louisiana.

The Missouri Pacific (its original name as a short line was The Pacific Railroad--a name highly popular for pioneering railways during the mid-19th century) helped develop a diversified area of farms, ranches, and industries.

The MoPac in the late 19th century became part of the 17,000 mile rail empire assembled by tycoon Jay Gould and subsequently operated by his son, George, until it crumbled amidst financial chaos in the early 20th century.

While the exact date that the Missouri Pacific began operating its own dining cars is unrecorded, it is known that diners were in use prior to the St. Louis World's Fair in 1904. Many travelers to this famous international exposition traveled on the MoPac and found their journeys all the more delightful because of the delicious cuisine served.

Since the Missouri Pacific served several colorful and diversified areas--ranging from the Rocky Mountains of Colorado on the west, Omaha and St. Louis in the north, to New Orleans and the Mexican border on the south--many tasty dishes were developed to pamper the tastes of the passengers. Recipes featuring Southern fried chicken and fresh mountain trout logically became favored items on the menus.

Among the MoPac's most famous passenger trains for travelers to enjoy dinner on the diner became *The Texas Eagle,* which was initiated to provide fast service between St. Louis and Memphis and Dallas, Fort Worth, Austin, and San Antonio. Companion trains providing good meals included *The Colorado Eagle,* linking St. Louis with points in the Rocky Mountains; *The Missouri River Eagle,* operating between St. Louis, Kansas City, and Omaha, and *The Valley Eagle,* speeding between Houston, Corpus Christi, and points in the Rio Grande Valley.

Fine food also became associated with crack MoPac trains of past years, including *The Texan* and *The Sunshine Special,* operated between St. Louis and points in Texas to Los Angeles in cooperation with the Texas and Pacific and Southern Pacific railroads. Other noted Missouri Pacific trains have included *The Southerner, The Missourian, The Rainbow Special,* and *The Tennessean.*

Under plans approved by the Interstate Commerce Commission during the 1960's, the MoPac and Texas Pacific eventually would be consolidated, in the interests of economy, as the Missouri Texas Pacific Railway. The merger was expected to produce mergers of routes as well as in dining car services.

The Missouri Pacific's outstanding dishes were developed by various chefs during the years for service on the famous trains.

The recipes offered here for Turkey Isabelle and Curry of Lamb Indian style were originated by Henry Bausbach, formerly supervising chef for the Missouri Pacific. He began MoPac service in 1930 and during the ensuing quarter of a century taught the line's chefs many fine points of European cuisine which helped to make journeys more memorable for numerous travelers.

ALL PICTURES THIS CHAPTER: MISSOURI PACIFIC RAILROAD

Dining was a pleasure on the "Scenic Limited," inaugurated by the Missouri Pacific in 1915 for travel to the Panama-Pacific Exposition in San Francisco.

COLD SLICED BREAST OF TURKEY, ISABELLE

This is a delightful summer dish which can be a year around favorite. It is colorful and has eye appeal in addition to being tasty and nutritious. The recipe can be scaled to serve various numbers of persons, depending on the size of the turkey.

1 Small boiled or roasted turkey
18 asparagus tips (fresh or canned)
6 dill pickles or 12 gherkins
1 small onion
1/2 bunch parsley
Green and ripe olives
Mayonnaise
Tabasco sauce
2 Green peppers
3 cups of cold boiled rice
1 head lettuce
1 pint Thousand Island dressing
1 bunch watercress
3 ounces sherry wine
12 slices of tomato
Sliced pimento
2 Hard boiled eggs

To serve, shred the lettuce finely and place on a large cold platter. In the middle of the platter place the cold rice, shaped in oblong form. Slice the turkey breast and place on top of the rice and cover the turkey with Isabelle sauce. On each end of the platter place nine asparagus tips, a thin strip of pimento and green peppers over the end part of the asparagus, and a dash of mayonnaise over the tips. On each side of the platter place the slices of tomato, flanked by the pickles cut in fan shape and the olives.

Preparation of Isabelle sauce:

Chop parsley, watercress, and onions together finely. To this add the Thousand Island dressing, a teaspoon of Worcestershire sauce, six drops of Tabasco sauce, and the sherry wine. When ready to serve, sprinkle finely chopped hard boiled egg over the entire dish.

RAINBOW MOUNTAIN TROUT, SAUTE BELLE MEUNIERE

1 Rainbow mountain trout
1 Egg
Parsley
Lemons
Flour
Butter
Mushrooms

Trout caught for the Missouri Pacific in the cold, clear waters of the Rocky Mountains of Colorado inspired this delightful dish. To prepare, clean and wash the trout and then dip in flour and beaten egg. Saute in just enough butter so that the fish will not stick to the frying pan. When browned, add a small lump of fresh butter, cover the pan, and place in the oven for six to eight minutes. In a small pan, heat a piece of butter and when lightly brown add two medium sized mushrooms, chopped fine, and saute until done. Then add a few drops of lemon juice to the butter and pour quickly over the fish. To serve, place fish on a silver platter and garnish with springs of parsley and lemon. Sprinkle with freshly chopped parsley. This recipe makes one portion.

PUMPKIN PIE WITH WHIPPED CREAM

1 No. 2 1/2 can pumpkin
1 teaspoon pumpkin spice
3 cubes of butter
1 cup milk
Pinch of salt
1 1/2 cups sugar
4 eggs
1/4 cup molasses
1/2 cup cream

Beat together cream, milk, sugar, butter, whole eggs, molasses, and pumpkin spice and then add pumpkin. Beat until smooth. Fill lined pie tins and bake in a moderate oven until done, or approximately 45 minutes. Serve with a dash of whipped cream on top of each portion.

SOUTHERN STYLE FRIED SPRING CHICKEN

1 Chicken	Lard
Flour	Toasted bread
Cream sauce	Pineapple
Sweet potato	Maraschino cherry

Clean and wash the chicken; cut off the wing at the second joint and split in half from the back, separating the breast into two parts. Cut off the drumstick at the joint. The chicken is now disjointed into six pieces. Heat a tablespoon of lard in a frying pan; dip the individual pieces of chicken in flour and beaten egg and place in the hot lard. Cover the pan and brown chickenon both sides. When browned nicely, remove all fat and place a large slice of butter in the pan; cover pan and place in the oven for 10 minutes. Arrange the chicken on a fresh piece of toast, putting a tablespoon ofcream sauce on the bottom of the platter. Garnish with a slice of glazed pineapple topped by a sweet potato cake.

To prepare the glazed pineapple, dry a slice of pineapple, sprinkle lightly with sugar and brown under the broiler or, if preferred, dip the pineapple in flour and brown in butter.

For the sweet potato cake, mash a boiled and peeled sweet potato, season lightly, form in the shape and size of a biscuit, dip in flour, and brown on both sides in butter. When done, place half of a maraschino cherry atop the cake.

OLD FASHIONED NAVY BEAN SOUP

3 slices bacon	1 carrot
1 medium sized onion	1 outside stalk celery
1 small green pepper	Butter
3/4 cup Navy beans	1 quart meat stock
1 medium sized potato	2 tomatoes

Fry bacon for one minute in sauce pan; add one ounce butter and the carrot, onion, celery, and pepper after cutting them in small dices. Cover pan and cook slowly for approximately 10 minutes or until vegetables are soft. Now add Navy beans (after soaking them in cold water for four to six hours). Add meat stock, cook for one hour, and then add raw potato cut in quarter inch dices; add peeled and cut tomatoes. Season to taste until all ingredients are well done. If the soup is too thick, add more stock. Four bouillon cubes to one quart of water may be substituted for the meat stock. If a ham bone is available, it may be cooked with the soup but in this case little salt should be used.

CREAM OF FRESH SPINACH SOUP, FLORENTINE

1 onion	3 tablespoons butter or chicken fat
3 tablespoons flour	12 ounces spinach
2 quarts meat or chicken stock	

Cut onion in small pieces and place in sauce pan with butter or chicken fat; cover tightly and cook slowly until onion is soft. Then add flour, blend well and cook for another three minutes. Gradually add two quarts of hot meat or chicken stock, blending well with the flour, and bring to a boil. Then add spinach (thoroughly washed) and boil slowly for 30 minutes. Season to taste and press through a sieve. Serve with bread croutons.

THE BETTMANN ARCHIVE, INC.

THE KITCHEN OF A PULLMAN CAR.

CASSEROLE OF PRIME BEEF, JARDINIERE

2 lbs. beef butt or chuck	Paprika
1 bunch carrots	1 bunch celery
2 onions	Allspice
Dash of flour	Small can tomato puree
4 ounces red wine	1/2 can turnips
1 can peas	1/2 can lima beans
6 small onions	Bay leaves

Remove excess fat and cut the meat in 1 1/2" squares. Roll meat in flour, season with salt and paprika, and brown in frying pan in clean fat. Meanwhile, saute carrots, celery, and onions, all cut in pieces, in a covered sauce pan. When the vegetables are soft, add the browned beef, a few bay leaves. a little allspice, and a small amount of flour. Cook for a few minutes until flour is lightly brown, then fill with enough meat stock to cover barely the meat. Add tomato puree for better taste and red wine. Cook slowly until meat is done. Then remove meat with a fork and strain the gravy over the meat. Have small diced carrots, turnips, and whole small onions cooked; add peas and lima beans. Drain well and saute with butter for a few minutes. Serve meat in casserole with the mixture of vegetables on top of the meat.

CURRY OF LAMB, INDIAN STYLE

2 lbs. lamb stew	2 onions
2 teaspoons curry powder	4 cubes of butter
3 tablespoons flour	

Cut onions finely and saute with two heaping teaspoons of curry powder in butter until onions are soft. Then add lamb stew, stirring well and steaming for several minutes; add water or meat stock to cover barely the lamb. Then add peeled and sliced apples. Now cook until meat is done. Melt four cubes of butter in sauce pan, adding three tablespoons of flour and cook for several minutes. After meat is done, place on a colander and add the liquid to the flour and butter (roux), making a sauce. Season to taste and pour over the meat. If coconut milk is available, add approximately four ounces to the sauce.

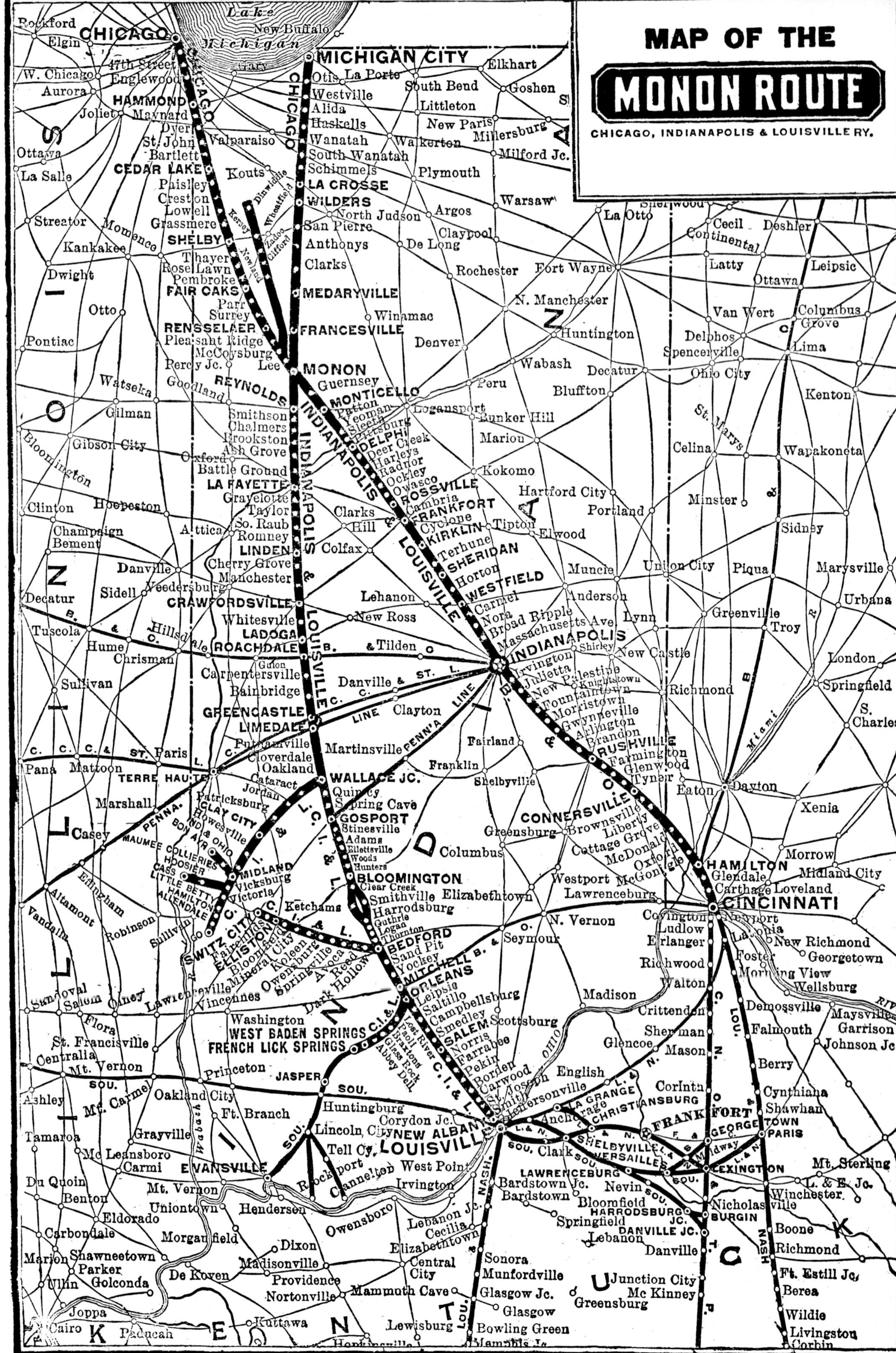
MAP OF THE
MONON ROUTE
CHICAGO, INDIANAPOLIS & LOUISVILLE RY.
Lake Michigan
CHICAGO
Rockford
Elgin
W. Chicago
Aurora
Joliet
Ottawa
La Salle
Streator
Kankakee
Dwight
Pontiac
Watseka
Gilman
Gibson City
Bloomington
Clinton
Hoopeston
Champaign
Bement
Danville
Decatur
Tuscola
Hume
Chrisman
Sullivan
Pana
Mattoon
Marshall
Casey
Effingham
Altamont
Vandalia
Robinson
Sandoval
Salem
Olney
Flora
St. Francisville
Centralia
Mt. Vernon
Ashley
Mt. Carmel
Tamaroa
Mc Leansboro
Carmi
Grayville
Du Quoin
Benton
Eldorado
Carbondale
Marion
Shawneetown
Ullin
Golconda
Joppa
Cairo
Paducah
New Buffalo
Gary
47th Street
Englewood
HAMMOND
Maynard
Dyer
St. John
Bartlett
CEDAR LAKE
Paisley
Creston
Lowell
Grassmere
SHELBY
Thayer
Rose Lawn
Pembroke
FAIR OAKS
Parr
Surrey
RENSSELAER
Pleasant Ridge
McCoysburg
Percy Jc.
Lee
Goodland
REYNOLDS
Valparaiso
Kouts
Dinwiddie
Wheatfield
Kersey
Nowland
Zadoc
Gifford
MICHIGAN CITY
Otis
La Porte
Westville
Alida
Haskells
Wanatah
South Wanatah
Schimmels
LA CROSSE
WILDERS
North Judson
San Pierre
Anthonys
Clarks
MEDARYVILLE
FRANCESVILLE
MONON
Guernsey
MONTICELLO
Patton
Yeoman
Sleeth
Pittsburg
DELPHI
Deer Creek
Harleys
Radnor
Ockley
Owasco
ROSSVILLE
Cambria
FRANKFORT
Cyclone
KIRKLIN
Terhune
SHERIDAN
Horton
WESTFIELD
Carmel
Nora
Broad Ripple
Massachusetts Ave
INDIANAPOLIS
Smithson
Chalmers
Brookston
Ash Grove
Oxford
Battle Ground
LA FAYETTE
Gravelotte
Taylor
So. Raub
Romney
LINDEN
Attica
Cherry Grove
Manchester
Veedersburg
CRAWFORDSVILLE
Whitesville
LADOGA
ROACHDALE
Hillsdale
Guion
Carpentersville
Bainbridge
GREENCASTLE
LIMEDALE
Putnamville
Cloverdale
Oakland
Cataract
Jordan
WALLACE JC.
Quincy
Spring Cave
GOSPORT
Stinesville
Adams
Ellettsville
Woods
Hunters
BLOOMINGTON
Clear Creek
Smithville
Harrodsburg
Guthrie
Logan
Thornton
BEDFORD
Sand Pit
Yockey
MITCHELL
ORLEANS
Leipsic
Saltillo
Campbellsburg
Smedley
SALEM
Norris
Farrabee
Pekin
Borden
Carwood
St. Joseph
Jeffersonville
NEW ALBANY
LOUISVILLE
Lost River
Paoli
Braxtons
Glass Rock
Abbey Dell
WEST BADEN SPRINGS
FRENCH LICK SPRINGS
Dark Hollow
Reed
Avoca
Springville
Owensburg
Koleen
Mineral City
Bloomfield
Fairfield
ELLISTON
SWITZ CITY
Ketchams
TERRE HAUTE
Patricksburg
CLAY CITY
Howesville
BON AYR
INDIANA & OHIO
MAUMEE COLLIERIES
HOOSIER
CASS
LITTLE BETTY
HAMILTON
ALLENDALE
MIDLAND
Vicksburg
Victoria
Sullivan
Lawrenceville
Vincennes
Washington
Princeton
Oakland City
Ft. Branch
JASPER
Huntingburg
Lincoln City
Tell Cy.
Rockport
Cannelton
Corydon Jc.
West Point
EVANSVILLE
Mt. Vernon
Uniontown
Henderson
Owensboro
Irvington
Morganfield
Dixon
Madisonville
De Koven
Providence
Nortonville
Kuttawa
Mammoth Cave
Lewisburg
Elizabethtown
Cecilia
Lebanon Jc.
Central City
Sonora
Munfordville
Glasgow Jc.
Glasgow
Bowling Green
Greensburg
Junction City
Mc Kinney
Bardstown Jc.
Bardstown
Bloomfield
Springfield
Lebanon
Danville
DANVILLE JC.
HARRODSBURG JC.
BURGIN
Nicholasville
LAWRENCEBURG
Nevin
VERSAILLES
SHELBYVILLE
Clark
Anchorage
LA GRANGE
CHRISTIANSBURG
FRANKFORT
GEORGETOWN
Midway
LEXINGTON
PARIS
Mt. Sterling
L. & E. Jc.
Winchester
Boone
Richmond
Ft. Estill Jc.
Berea
Wildie
Livingston
Corbin
Elkhart
South Bend
Goshen
Littleton
New Paris
Millersburg
Walkerton
Milford Jc.
Plymouth
Warsaw
Argos
Claypool
De Long
Rochester
Winamac
Denver
Peru
Logansport
Wabash
Bunker Hill
Marion
Kokomo
Tipton
Elwood
Clarks Hill
Colfax
Lebanon
New Ross
Tilden
Danville
Clayton
Martinsville
Franklin
Fairland
Shelbyville
Greensburg
Columbus
Elizabethtown
Westport
N. Vernon
Seymour
Madison
Lawrenceburg
Irvington
Julietta
New Palestine
Fountaintown
Morristown
Gwynneville
Arlington
Brandon
RUSHVILLE
Farmington
Glenwood
Tyner
CONNERSVILLE
Brownsville
Liberty
Cottage Grove
McDonald
Oxford
McGonigle
HAMILTON
Glendale
Carthage
CINCINNATI
Shirley
Knightstown
New Castle
Richmond
Muncie
Anderson
Lynn
Hartford City
Portland
N. Manchester
Huntington
Fort Wayne
Decatur
Bluffton
La Otto
Sherwood
Cecil
Continental
Deshler
Latty
Ottawa
Leipsic
Van Wert
Columbus Grove
Delphos
Spencerville
Lima
Ohio City
Kenton
St. Marys
Celina
Wapakoneta
Minster
Sidney
Union City
Piqua
Marysville
Greenville
Urbana
Troy
London
Springfield
S. Charles
Eaton
Dayton
Xenia
Miami
Morrow
Midland City
Loveland
Covington
Newport
Ludlow
Erlanger
Richwood
Walton
Crittenden
Sherman
Mason
Glencoe
English
Corinth
New Richmond
Georgetown
Foster
Morning View
Wellsburg
Demossville
Falmouth
Maysville
Garrison
Johnson Jc.
Berry
Cynthiana
Shawhan
OHIO
Wabash
C. C. C. & ST. L.
B. & O.
PENN'A LINE
SOU.
L. & N.
C. N. O. & T. P.
C. I. & L.
I. & L.
NASH.
LOU.
ILLINOIS
INDIANA
KENTUCKY

Here is an interior view of a dining-bar-lounge car used during the 1950's on the Monon Railroad for service between Chicago and Louisville.

MONON RAILROAD

The tracks of The Monon Railroad form a giant "X" across Indiana, crossing at the city of Monon--the community that inspired the system's nickname which subsequently was adopted as the line's corporate title.

The Monon Railroad stretches from Chicago (via leased tracks to Hammond) to Indianapolis and from Michigan City, Indiana, to Louisville, Kentucky. While the line's approximately 540 miles of tracks may be regarded as small in comparison to other major railroads, it has been regarded as an important rail system because of the heavily populated area served.

The system developed during the late 19th century as the Louisville, New Albany and Chicago Railway but was reorganized in 1897 as The Chicago, Indianapolis and Louisville Railway. The system grew considerably in 1916 when the Indiana Stone Railroad, Chicago and Wabash Valley Railway, and the Indianapolis and Louisville Railway were merged into it.

Box cars emblazoned with the motto, "The Hoosier Line," symbolized its service both to Indiana shippers and passengers.

The system's name officially was changed to The Monon Railroad early in 1956.

During the early 1950's the line became noted for its 75-mile an hour passenger trains--a speed made possible by reconditioning of the road bed.

Among the noted passenger trains on which the line's travelers enjoyed dinner in the diner were *The Hoosier, The Midnight Special,* and *The Tippecanoe. The Thoroughbred,* appropriately named because of its route between Chicago and Louisville that attracted spectators to the Kentucky Derby, also became famous for the cuisine in its diners.

Serving an area where there was considerable competition among railroads for passengers, The Monon provided exceptionally attractive dining and lounge cars.

The economic pressures resulting from losses of passenger traffic to automobiles resulted in the end of conventional diner service and the substitution of "snack" foods.

These recipes were salvaged from the era of gracious dining in luxurious cars on the Monon route.

ALL PICTURES THIS CHAPTER: MONON RAILROAD

CHICAGO HISTORICAL SOCIETY

This Pullman dining car with elaborate interior was displayed proudly at the 1904 St. Louis International Exposition to show the luxuries of travel by rail.

SPLIT PEA SOUP

Ham hock
1 onion
1 carrot
2/3 cup butter
1 lb. green split peas
1 pod garlic
1 stalk celery
1/3 cup flour

Boil ham hock in water until almost done; add peas, garlic, carrot, onion, and celery, cooking until done. Then remove vegetables and ham hock. Run the split peas through a strainer. Put the butter and flour in a sauce pan and stir to a smooth paste. Add one gallon of split pea stock and stir until well blended. Serve with one-half inch croutons fried in bacon fat or butter.

BARBECUED SPARERIBS

Combine and simmer 10 minutes the following ingredients:

1/4 cup minced onions
1/4 cup celery
1 tablespoon sugar
1/4 cup catsup
1 teaspoon dry mustard
1/4 teaspoon Tabasco sauce
2 tablespoons Worcestershire sauce
Salt

Have rib cut into small pieces. Brown thoroughly. Add about 1/4 cup water, cover pan and steam about 30 to 40 minutes. When meat is tender, pour barbecue sauce over ribs and bake for 20 minutes. Use about eight lbs. of spare ribs for six portions.

ROQUEFORT DRESSING A LA EARL

8 garlic cloves
2 lbs. bleu cheese
1 1/2 qts. mayonnaise
Juice of 3 lemons
1 pt. French dressing
Worcestershire sauce
1 tablespoon sugar

Work the soft cheese into the mayonnaise--this must be done slowly. Cut the garlic very fine. Add French dressing and other ingredients. It is best to allow to stand overnight before serving. If the dressing, when done, retains a mayonnaise taste, it can be cured by slightly increasing the proportion of sugar. In the recipe this is indicated by one tablespoon, but it can run as high as one soup ladle full to a gallon of dressing. It must be watched carefully, however, in the preparation, so that only enough sugar is used to kill the mayonnaise taste, and not enough to sweeten the dressing. In addition to the soft cheese worked into the mayonnaise, some lumps of roquefort are added for appearance. Sufficient Worcestershire sauce must be used to properly color the dressing and give the proper "bite." This is a matter of taste and the dressing must be tried frequently to be sure that it has a full roquefort flavor, and the "bite" desired.

ITALIAN SPAGHETTI

Sauce:

1 cup chopped onions
1/2 cup chopped celery
3 small cloves garlic chopped
2 lbs. hamburger
2 tablespoons oil or butter
2 cans tomato paste (small)
2 (No. 2 1/2) cans tomatoes
1/2 teaspoon oregano
1/8 teaspoon pepper
1/4 cup chopped parsley
1 teaspoon granulated sugar
1/4 cup Parmesan cheese

Fry onions, garlic, celery, and hamburger in oil or butter for about five minutes. Add tomato paste, tomatoes, and other ingredients and simmer in covered saucepan for about 1 1/2 hours. If sauce becomes too thick, add tomato juice. This will serve approximately eight portions.

Spaghetti:

Cook one pound of spaghetti in four quarts of boiling water for 15 to 20 minutes.

TWO-CRUST PIE RECIPE

1 1/2 cups flour
1/2 cup lard
Dash salt
5 tablespoons ice water

Use pie blender and blend together flour, lard and salt. Add five tablespoons of ice water. Roll out two thin crusts.

For filling:

3 lbs. apples
1 cup granulated sugar
2 tablespoons lemon juice
2 tablespoons butter
Cinnamon
Nutmeg

Brush with beaten eggs. Bake about 50 minutes in oven of 425 degrees F.

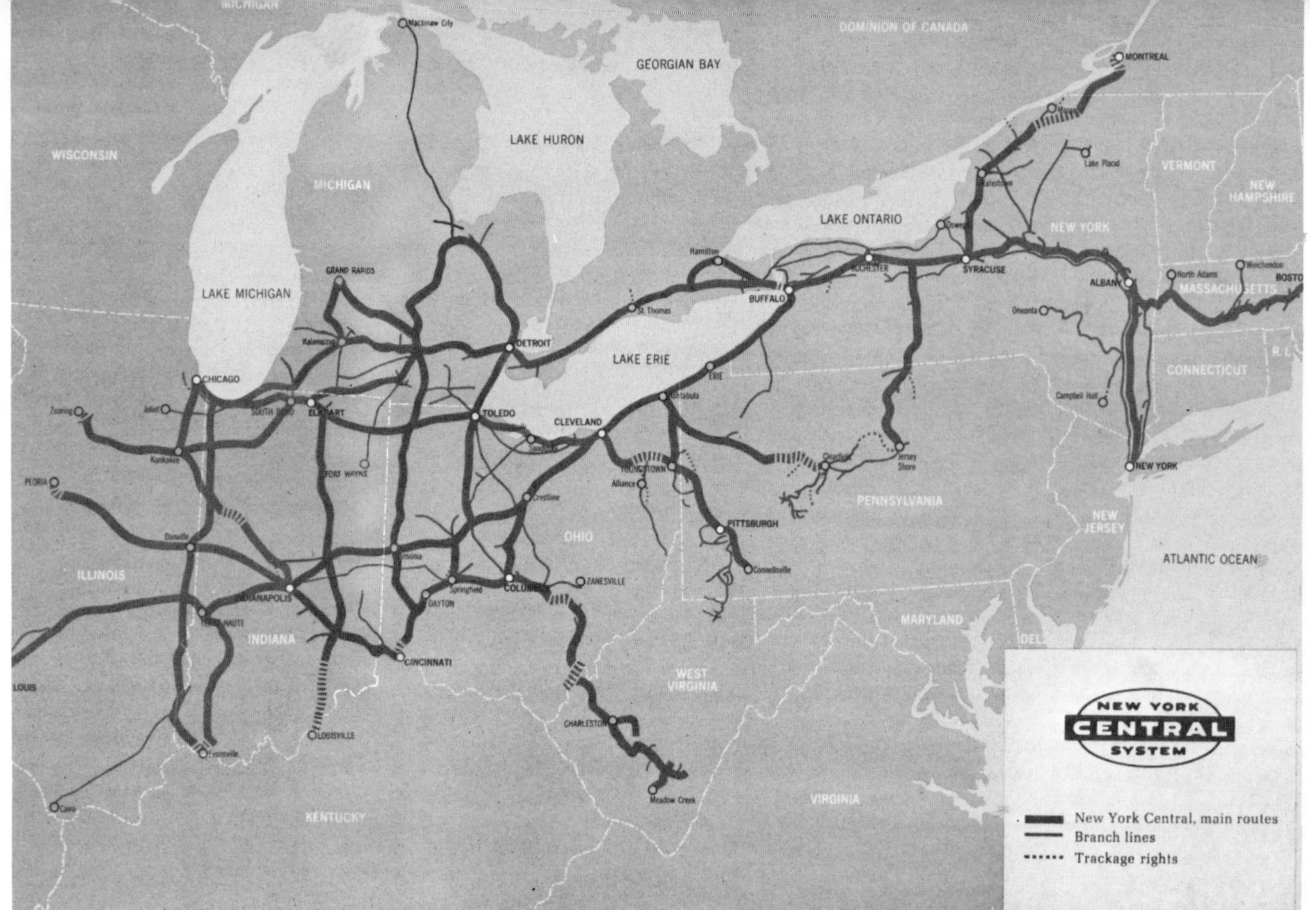

NEW YORK CENTRAL

Railway dining car service in the modern sense was pioneered in 1875 on the Michigan Central Railroad, a company later consolidated into The New York Central System. Through the years the New York Central, serving a heavily populated area that helped build an immense passenger service for the company, built a reputation of serving delicious dishes on its diners.

The system's most notable train--and one famed for its fine food--became *The 20th Century Limited,* speeding over the heavily traveled route between New York City and Chicago.

The New York Central was organized in 1853 through the consolidation of ten comparatively small railroads paralleling the Erie Canal --the area's main artery for freight prior to the rail era--and in the rich Mohawk Valley. The consolidated railway prospered, of course, as it funneled traffic to the port of New York and with other lines helped to secure New York City as the major American financial center.

Commodore Cornelius Vanderbilt, who had amassed a fortune from operating steamboats, turned his talents to railroading in 1862 when 68 years of age and five years later acquired control of the New York Central. The previous management had been content to transfer passengers and freight at Albany to ships (operated, incidentally, by Commodore Vanderbilt) for the remainder of the trip to New York City. When he became president of the New York Central, Vanderbilt consolidated the New York and Harlem and New York and Hudson railroads--which he had acquired on becoming interested in rail lines--into the railway and provided rail service directly to New York City.

The commodore's son, William H. Vanderbilt, became active in the railroad's management and directed a program of expansion by acquiring other railways. The New York Central's entry to Chicago in the 1870's was made possible by acquisition of several lines, including the

THE 20-HOUR FLEET

The New York Central Lines, the route overwhelmingly preferred by the public for their trips between New York and Chicago, now has in service a fleet of ten 20-Hour Limited Trains between these two great cities of America.

5 *Chicago to New York*

FAST MAIL
Lve. CHICAGO 9:50 a.m. Arr. NEW YORK 6:50 a.m.

THE WOLVERINE
(Via Michigan Central)
Lve. CHICAGO 11:00 a.m. Arr. NEW YORK 8:00 a.m.

ADVANCE 20TH CENTURY LIMITED
Lve. CHICAGO 11:40 a.m. Arr. NEW YORK 8:40 a.m.

20TH CENTURY LIMITED
Lve. CHICAGO 12:40 p.m. Arr. NEW YORK 9:40 a.m.

THE COMMODORE VANDERBILT
Lve. CHICAGO 3:00 p.m. Arr. NEW YORK 12:00 Noon

5 *New York to Chicago*

ADVANCE 20TH CENTURY LIMITED
Lve. NEW YORK 1:45 p.m. Arr. CHICAGO 8:45 a.m.

20TH CENTURY LIMITED
Lve. NEW YORK 2:45 p.m. Arr. CHICAGO 9:45 a.m.

THE COMMODORE VANDERBILT
Lve. NEW YORK 4:00 p.m. Arr. CHICAGO 11:00 a.m.

THE WOLVERINE
(Via Michigan Central)
Lve. NEW YORK 5:00 p.m. Arr. CHICAGO 12:00 Noon

THE IROQUOIS
(Via Michigan Central)
Lve. NEW YORK 10:40 p.m. Arr. CHICAGO 5:40 p.m.

Michigan Central on which American Diner car service was initiated.

By the mid-20th century the New York Central's tracks reached into 11 states and served such important cities as Buffalo, Boston, St. Louis, Chicago, Indianapolis, Columbus, and Cincinnati. In addition, the system extended into Canada to serve Ottawa and Montreal.

One of America's most famous steam locomotives, the 4-6-4 Hudson type, was placed in operation by the New York Central in 1927. Powerful and economical, these locomotives were used on most Central main line trains until the advent of diesel engines. The Hudsons remained a favorite with builders of model locomotives.

Dinner in the diner reached a high point among all railroads with the initiation in 1902 of *The Twentieth Century Limited,* New York City and Chicago in just 20 hours. Improvements in the road bed and the use of powerful diesel locomotives reduced the time so that the train was making the trip in 16 hours during the 1960's.

Travelers on such a crack train naturally came to expect foods as fine as the other services, which during the years have ranged from a barbershop to telephones for passengers wanting to maintain contact with their offices.

The railroad's commissaries in New York City and Chicago were stocked with choice foods to fill the menus, carefully developed by officials of the dining car service to cater to demands by travelers.

The task of supervising the operation of individual diners on *The Twentieth Century* as well as other New York Central passenger trains was assigned to a steward. Under his direction, the chef supervised kitchen workers preparing the food to be served.

While changes in dining car operations appeared inevitable when the New York Central and Pennsylvania Railroad eventually would be merged under rpinciples approved during the 1960's, the delightful dishes unquestionably would remain happy memories among NYC travelers for many years.

These dishes, which have appeared at various times on the menus of *The 20th Century Limited,* will bring pleasure to rail fans, people who have ridden the crack train, and anyone who enjoys superb food.

Above, dining car interiors looked like this when the "20th Century Limited" began operating in 1902.

Below, the crack train's diners had shed frills by the 1920's but offered the ultimate in service.

The New York Central's streamline "20th Century," powered by steam, rolls from New York in 1938.

NEW YORK CENTRAL SPECIAL WHEAT CAKES

2 egg yolks
2 cups milk
3 tablespoons maple syrup
2 teaspoons baking powder
5 tablespoons shortening
2 cups flour
1/2 teaspoon salt

Whip egg yolks, then add milk slowly, following with maple syrup. Sift salt, flour and baking powder together and add to mixture. Shortening to be added last. When entire mixture is smooth, let stand a few minutes before cooking. Do not turn cakes on griddle more than once and be sure griddle is not too hot. This makes 15 griddle cakes.

THE 20TH CENTURY SALAD BOWL

1/4 head of lettuce (medium size)
6 pieces finely sliced green onions
6 pieces finely sliced radishes
6 pieces finely sliced scored cucumber
6 pieces finely sliced celery
1/2 oz. bleu cheese

Separate the leaves of lettuce, place in well-chilled dry salad bowl, add the finely sliced onions, radishes, cucumbers and celery, which ingredients should fall in between the leaves of lettuce and should not be mixed; add the one-half ounce of crumbled bleu cheese and place four pieces of tomato around, cutting the tomatoes in quarters or sixths, depending on the size of the tomatoes. Shake dressing well in bottle and sprinkle over salad; this to be done at time of service to avoid ingredients becoming soggy. This makes one portion.

NEW YORK CENTRAL BAKED APPLE

Peel apple halfway, score and core thoroughly, peelings to be placed in bottom of pan. Fill apple center with sugar and squeeze a little lemon juice ovr sugar in each apple; this will form sufficient syrup for basting purposes. Baste continually until done. Under no circumstances is the apple core to be used. Do not turn apples upside down when cooked.

INDIVIDUAL DEEP DISH CHICKEN PIE

6 pieces boneless chicken, white and dark meat
3 whole Belgian carrots
4 Parisienne potatoes
3 button onions

Chicken should be boiled well done and cut in large chunks at least one inch square. Saute lightly and season with above vegetables. Do not brown. Assemble with chicken in deep pie dish with plenty of rich sauce. Cover with flaky pie crust; cut crust large enough to fit completely over pie, allowing enough so that the crushed may be pushed upward in the center. Crimp the edges with fork and glaze with egg wash.

FLAKY PIE CRUST

2 level cups shortening
1 level teaspoon salt
5 level cups flour
1 level teaspoon baking powder

Sift flour, salt, and baking powder together. Rub shortening into flour, but do not rub entirely smooth; leave some lumps the size of peas to make crust flaky. Moisten with ice water.

Many premier passenger trains featured distinctive table settings. Aboard the 20th Century Limited *custom chairs, menus and even matchbooks set off the silver service and linen.*
—Donald Duke Collection

CHICKEN TETRAZZINI

Spaghetti Bordelaise
Allemande Sauce
Fresh tomato (scalded, peeled and sliced)
Paprika
Sliced chicken
Boiled ham, slice
Corn Flakes
Parmesan cheese

Assemble as follows: Spread 4 tablespoons Spaghetti Bordelaise on bottom of large au gratin dish. Cover with nice portion sliced chicken, which has been incorporated in sauce (see above). Trim fat from slice of boiled ham, cut in half, and place on top of chicken. Place two thin slices of tomato on top of ham. Sprinkle liberal amount of crushed corn flakes and cheese mixture (two thirds corn flakes and one third grated Parmesan cheese) on top of this. Add paprika to get color. Place melted butter on top and brown in oven.

SPAGHETTI BORDELAISE

1/8 lb. butter
2 tablespoons flour
1 qt. beef consomme
Spaghetti
2 cups tomato juice
1/2 cup finely chopped green onions
1/2 cup finely chopped imported canned mushrooms

Melt butter in sauce pan. Add flour and cook thoroughly, stirring constantly. Add beef consomme and tomato juice (which have been mixed and heated) and continue to mix. Season with salt and pepper. Add green onions and mushrooms, which have been lightly sauted in butter. Incorporate well-cooked spaghetti into sauce and simmer to fairly thick consistency so that it sets firm when assembling order.

APRICOT AND ALMOND CUSTARD WITH SAUCE

3 cups of hot milk
4 eggs, whites separated from yolks, and well-beaten
1/4 teaspoon of salt
1/4 teaspoon of grated nutmeg
1/3 cup granulated sugar
1/2 teaspoon of lightly roasted and finely chopped plain almonds for each cup
1/2 apricot for each cup

Stir beaten whites and yolks of eggs in milk, add salt, nutmeg and sugar. Flavor with a little grated lemon and orange rind. Butter custard cups well, put finely chopped almonds on bottom, place apricot pit-side down on almonds. Fill cups with mixture and place in pan, surrounding cups with water. Cook until done in a medium oven. In the event custard browns too quickly, cover with buttered wax paper and finish cooking slowly. Allow to cool before removing from custard cups.

For Apricot sauce:

1 medium size can of apricots. Boil entire contents and strain.

SAUCE FOR CHICKEN PIE

3/4 cup sifted flour
3/4 cup butter
Salt and pepper to taste
4 qts. rich chicken stock
2 egg yolks

Make roux with flour and butter, cooking thoroughly. Add hot chicken stock gradually, stirring briskly with whip until smooth. Mix egg yolks with two teaspoons cold water, add to sauce, and whip in thoroughly. Season with salt and pepper. Sauce should be consistency of double cream. This recipe makes one gallon.

One of the delights of dining aboard a train was a freshly baked casserole. A New York Central chef rolls a pie crust onto a chicken pie before putting it into the oven.
—Donald Duke Collection

A modern New York Central dining car featured carpeting, wood panels and Venetian blinds.
—Donald Duke Collection

ALLEMANDE SAUCE

1/4 lb. butter
4 tablespoons flour
3 qts. rich chicken stock
1 qt. milk

Melt butter in sauce pan. Add flour and cook until mixture becomes creamy, stirring constantly. Add chicken stock and milk (which have been mixed and heated) and continue to mix. Season with salt, pepper, and juice of one-half lemon. Makes one gallon.

For this entree, to each quart of Allemande Sauce, add two ounces Sherry wine; four tablespoons sliced sauted mushrooms; four tablespoons small diced, boiled green peppers; four tablespoons small diced, washed pimientos. Mix in gently, and add good portion of sliced, cooked fowl (do not use drumsticks), incorporating into sauce.

BLUEBERRY PANCAKES

Place a portion of the batter for Special New York Central Wheat Cakes on the griddle iron. When the batter has set, sprinkle a few blueberries on the top. Then turn and complete frying.

CELERY FARCIE

Stuff celery stalks with following mixture: 2/3 lb. cream cheese, 1/3 lb. bleu cheese, 2 teaspoons mustard and 1 tablespoon Worcestershire sauce, blended to smooth consistency.

LOBSTER A LA NEWBURG

1 qt. cream
4 egg yolks
1 basting spoon flour
Butter
1 Lobster (boiled in advance)
1 lb. noodles (boiled in advance)
5 basting spoons sherry wine
1 cup sliced mushrooms
Salt
Pepper
1/2 lb. crushed corn flakes

Prepare sauce as follows, using double boiler. Make a roux of butter and flour. Heat cream and work in gradually. Place in steamer. Whip egg yolks and stir into sauce, let simmer, constantly stirring, and add sliced mushrooms. This should be of a thick consistency. Just before service, add heated sherry wine. Season with salt and pepper. Do not keep too hot, as it will have a tendency to break. Blend good portion of lobster chunks into sauce. Place portion on bed of fine buttered noodles in deep pie dish, sprinkle with finely crushed corn flakes, dot with butter and bake in oven.

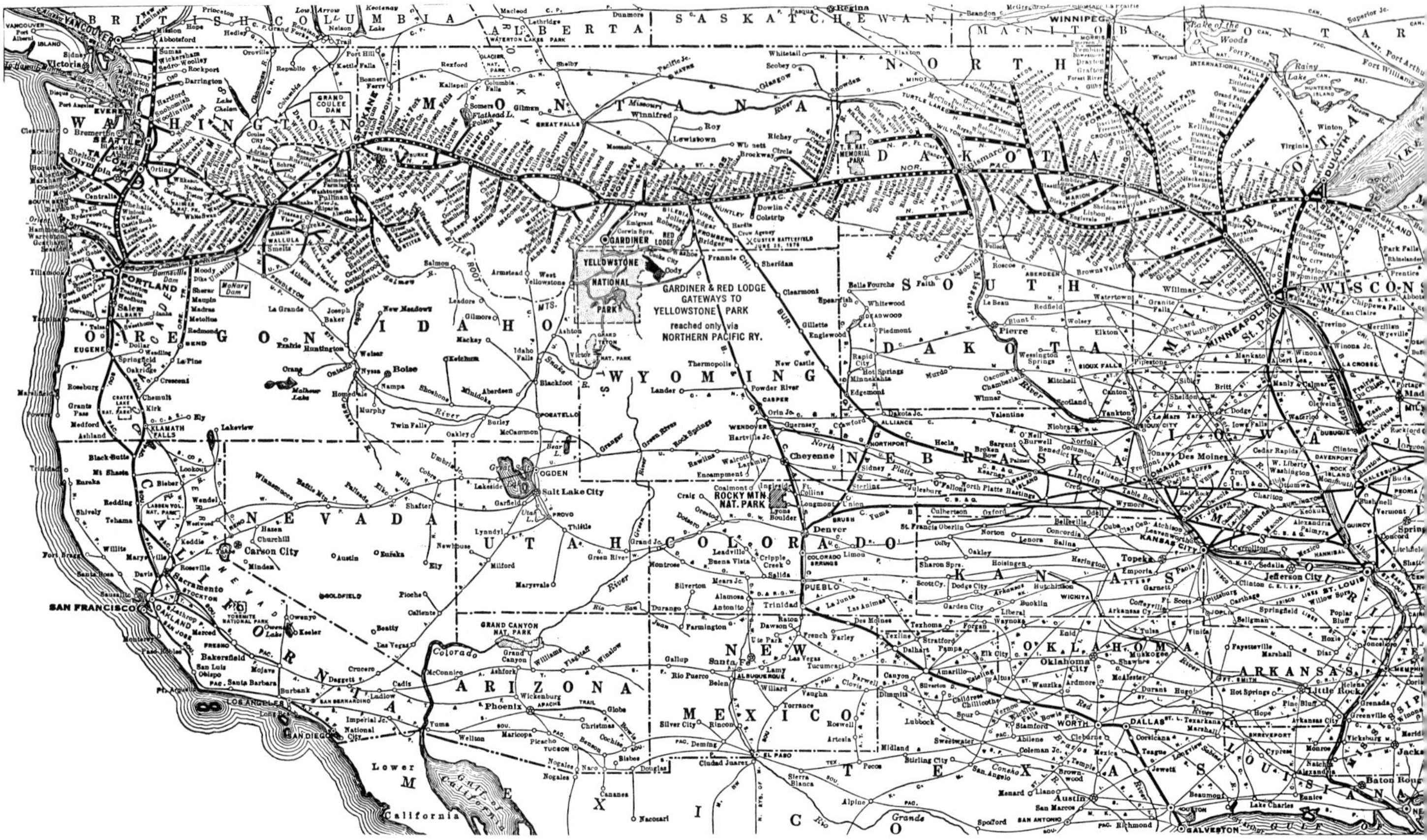

GARDINER & RED LODGE GATEWAYS TO YELLOWSTONE PARK reached only via NORTHERN PACIFIC RY.

Main Street of the Northwest

Spectacular scenery surrounds Northern Pacific's "North Coast Limited" of the 1960's as it rolls across the continental divide east of Butte, Montana.

NORTHERN PACIFIC

The Northern Pacific Railway pioneered service in the Pacific Northwest, opening its line between St. Paul, Minnesota, and Portland, Oregon, in 1883. However, even before achieving the distinction of being the first transcontinental line across the northwestern United States, the railroad offered meals to its passenders while traveling.

True to the early western spirit, this dining service was improvised in an attempt to give travelers the comforts they could expect on the Atlantic seaboard.

Northern Pacific crews erected a lunch room on a flat car so that passengers could satisfy their appetites.

Among those who enjoyed dinner in this primitive diner in 1876 were none other than General George A. Custer, who soon was to die tragically with his troops at the Little Big Horn, and his wife.

Mrs. Custer later described service on the improvised diner.

"Two men presided," she recalled, "one cooking and the other waiting on table. We were laboriously spearing our food with two tined forks and sipping muddy coffee with a pewter spoon when I heard, with surprise, the general asking for a napkin.

"It seemed as foreign to the place as a finger bowl," Mrs. Custer said. "The waiter knew him however, and liked him too well to refuse him anything, so he said, 'I have nothing but a towel, General.'"

The Northern Pacific grew considerably

ALL PICTURES THIS CHAPTER: COURTESY NORTHERN PACIFIC RAILROAD (Except as Noted)

This photo of Northern Pacific's "North Coast Limited" was made in 1930 with inauguration of new coaches.

during the ensuing years, and so did its dining car service.

The system became a network of approximately 6,900 miles of track stretching through Minnesota, North Dakota, Montana, Idaho, and Washington to Portland, with a line to Winnipeg. It developed extensive service in Washington, partially through using the tracks of the Spokane, Portland and Seattle Railroad (owned jointly with the Great Northern) and was able to offer fast service between Portland and Chicago through use of Burlington tracks between Chicago and St. Paul.

The Northern Pacific appropriately adopted the slogan, "Main Street of the Northwest."

The original lunchroom on a flat car became a memory after the Northern Pacific began operating its own diners early in 1899. Superb cuisine in dining cars that were more elaborate as the years passed became a tradition for passengers to enjoy as the trains rolled over the plains, through the spectacular Rocky Mountains, and then along the shores of the Pacific Coast where the tracks almost hugged the coast.

Commissaries in Seattle and St. Paul were built to prepare elaborate foods such as fruit cakes, plum puddings, and bread. Hot breads, biscuits, muffins, and ginger bread, baked en route in the galleys of the dining cars, became the delight of Northern Pacific passengers.

The line's most famous train, *The North Coast Limited,* early in the twentieth century took its place among America's finest trains as it sped travelers between Chicago and Portland.

The excellent cuisine did much to secure the train a highly popular place among travelers.

Other name trains that have operated over the Northern Pacific have included *The Manitoba Limited,* linking Winnipeg and Minneapolis-St. Paul; *The Alaskan,* running between Chicago and Portland; *The Puget Sound Limited,* connecting St. Louis (via the Chicago, Burlington and Quincy) to Portland and Seattle, and *The Main Streeter,* carrying passengers from Chicago and Kansas City (partially over Burlington tracks) to Portland and Seattle.

The nineteenth century travelers who ate in the improvised lunch room on a flat car would have many pleasant surprises if they were able to make the trip a century later.

Even the dining cars praised so much during the early twentieth century when *The North Coast Limited* began service gave way to even more deluxe equipment. Passengers on modern trains travel over territory retaining its beauty, but they can enjoy their dinner on the diner even more since meals are served on Vista-Dome cars commanding panoramic views of the countryside.

Among the Northern Pacific's best known dishes are "Big" baked potatoes. Their preparation is detailed here along with other offerings served on the railroad's diners.

Here is the observation-lounge car of Northern Pacific's "North Coast Limited," one of America's famous trains soon after inauguration in 1900.

Here is the way the famed and delicious "Big Baked Potato" looks when served on the Northern Pacific.

BIG BAKED POTATOES

This dish became famed on the Northern Pacific soon after its introduction in 1909, and these instructions from the railroad follow the method of preparation that makes the potatoes so tasty.

To qualify for serving in the fashion of Northern Pacific dining cars, potatoes must be free from all blemishes, including bruises, knobs, and cuts. Each potato must weigh 16 ounces or more; some potatoes used may even weight as much as three pounds. Potatoes used in this recipe come from the fields of Washington and Montana through which the Northern Pacific tracks were pushed. Premium prices, of course, must be paid for these prize potatoes, and they require a special method of baking.

Potatoes should be washed thoroughly and then pierced at both ends with an ice pick; place in a moderate oven. During fall and winter months, approximately two hours is required for baking. The potatoes should be turned several times during baking. In spring and summer, potatoes will bake in approximately an hour and a half. At that time of year, it is well to place a pan of water in the oven with the potatoes to compensate for some of the natural moisture which has evaporated during the storage period. (The fact the potatoes contain more natural moisture during the fall and winter months increases the baking time.)

When the potatoes are done, they should be taken from the oven and rolled gently to loosen the meaty part from the skin. Cut from end to end, spread open, and serve with a large piece of butter in the center.

BIG BAKED APPLES

8 large tart apples
1/4 teaspoon cinnamon
1/2 cup sugar

Core the apples and place them in a baking dish. Fill the centers with the sugar and cinnamon. Cover the bottom of the dish with boiling water and bake in a hot oven until soft, basting often with syrup in the dish. Serve hot or cold with cream.

HOT RICE AND CHOPPED HAM GRIDDLE CAKES

1 cup sifted flour
5 teaspoons baking powder
1/2 teaspoon salt
2 eggs
1 cup cooked rice
2 cups milk
1 cup diced, cooked ham
3 tablespoons melted butter

Sift together the flour, baking powder, and salt. Beat the eggs and add the rice, milk, ham, and butter. Mix well. Add this liquid mixture to the dry ingredients and beat until well-blended. Spoon onto a hot greased griddle to form cakes of desired size. Cook on one side until a number of bubbles appear. Turn over and cook to a golden brown. Serve hot with butter and syrup.

STUFFED JUMBO PRUNE SALAD

Thus recipe was provided by E. M. Shepherd, a dining car steward who began his association with the Northern Pacific in 1927. While the recipe is for a single serving, it may be increased to provide for guests.

4 large prunes
Lettuce
Cream
Chopped walnuts
4 sections of grapefruit
Cream cheese
Dash of salt

Cut open prunes and remove seed, replacing with cream cheese softened with cream and seasoned with salt. Sprinkle creamed cheese with chopped walnuts. Using a lettuce leaf as a base, arrange the prunes and sections of grapefruit in a wagon wheel effect. Top with a salad dressing of your choice.

SPECIAL NORTHERN PACIFIC SAUCE FOR BAKED HAM

1 pint orange juice
1/2 cup granulated sugar
1/2 cup white raisins
2 ounces quartered maraschino cherries
1/2 cup orange marmalade
Juice of 1/2 fresh lemon
Grated rind of one orange
1 teaspoon corn starch
Juice of pineapple or maraschino cherries

Place all ingredients (except corn starch and juice or pineapple or maraschino cherries) into a sauce pan or pot; bring to a boil on a slow fire and thicken with corn starch which has been dissolved in a cup containing approximately one tablespoon of cold water. Remove pot or pan containing sauce; mix corn starch liquid into sauce and set aside until ready for use. The juice of pineapple or maraschino cherries can be added to blend to desired thickness prior to using when reheated in a double boiler.

BANANA NUT BREAD

4 cups sugar
2 cups shortening
8 eggs
4 cups mashed bananas
6 tablespoons sour milk
4 teaspoons lemon juice
8 cups bread flour
4 teaspoons baking powder
1 teaspoon salt
1 teaspoon baking soda
4 cups chopped nuts
Banana flavoring

Mix ingredients and bake until done. This recipe makes four loaves.

The eastbound "North Coast Limited" enters Rocky Canyon, near Bozeman, Montana, in 1925.

The Minnetonka was the Northern Pacific's first engine. Built in 1870, it was used to construct the line.

STRAWBERRY PARFAIT PIE

This recipe, used in the Northern Pacific's St. Paul and Seattle bakeries for pies served on the Vista-Dome *North Coast Limited* and *The Mainstreeter,* was originated by J. W. Welligrant, employed by the railway beginning in 1912 and who in the 1960's was head baker in the St. Paul commissary. He is also responsible for the recipes for banana nut bread, the apple, lemon, and "Pearadise" lattice pies, and for Northern Pacific French dressing.

Graham cracker crust:

1/4 cup brown sugar
20 graham crackers, rolled fine
1/4 cup softened butter

Pie filling:

1 package frozen strawberries
1 pint vanilla ice cream
1 package lemon gelatin

Drain 1 1/4 cups of juice plus water from strawberries; put into a two quart sauce pan and bring to a boil. Remove from head and add gelatin, stirring until dissolved. Add the ice cream to the hot mixture, permitting it to melt. Chill in freezer until mixture is thickened but has not set. Fold drained strawberries and mixture into pie shell and chill until firm.

Mix above ingredients, stirring well, and place into pie tin.

OLD FASHIONED BEEF STEW

This recipe was provided by Fred Hagen, originally from Norway and a chef with 38 years service with the Northern Pacific.

2 lbs. beef
1 bunch rutabagas
1/2 bunch celery
Butter
1 bunch carrots
2 onions
1 clove garlic
Flour

Mix ingredients and bake until done. This recipe makes four loaves.

HONEY FRUIT MAYONNAISE DRESSING

This recipe was developed by E. T. Paulson, a chef with 47 years of service with the Northern Pacific.

1 pt. mayonnaise
1/3 cup honey
2 tablespoons orange juice
1 tablespoon orange rind

Mix well.

SEAFOOD SALAD

This recipe was issued by W. F. Paar, who became superintendent of the Northern Pacific's dining car department after 42 years of service with the railway during which he worked in virtually every position on diners. The following recipe was his choice for a popular salad for use on Fridays or during the Lenten season. The following directions will make a serving for one person.

Lettuce
Tomato
Cooked crab meat
Capers
Pimiento
1/2 boiled egg
Parsley
Celery
Cooked lobster meat
5 large shrimp
Green pepper
3 Sardines
Lemon
Mayonnaise

Using a green salad bowl, place crisp lettuce in the form of a cup, with the edges above the rim of the bowl. Place pieces of broken (but not cut) lettuce in the bottom of the lettuce cup; place small pieces of celery cut lengthwise on top of lettuce and slices of tomato should be placed upright around the cup of lettuce. On top of the broken pieces of lettuce, place six large pieces of lobster meat, a similar amount of crab meat, and the shrimp. Sprinkle with capers, chopped green pepper, and pimiento.

Salt and pepper to taste and top with the sardines. Garnish with the one-half hard-boiled egg, wedge of lemon, and sprig of parsley. Serve mayonnaise on the side. Be sure that the lettuce is fresh and crisp and that the salad ingredients, as well as the bowl, are chilled.

Northern Pacific's streamline Vista-Dome "North Coast Limited" of the 1960's rolls through spectacular Rocky Canyon just east of Bozeman, Montana.

The Lewis and Clark Traveller's Rest car on Northern Pacific's Vista-Dome North Coast Limited *featured a buffet and a lounge section. A uniformed stewardess (r.) was aboard to attend to the passengers' needs.*
—Donald Duke Collection

LEMON PIE

Filling:

4 ounces butter	10 ounces sugar
Pinch of salt	3 ounces flour
12 egg yolks	1 cup lemon juice

Place butter and one pint of water in double boiler and bring to a boil; then add (mixed together) the sugar, salt, flour, and egg yolks. Cook until thick and then add the lemon juice.

Meringue:

12 egg whites	1 cup granulated sugar

Beat egg whites stiffly, gradually adding the sugar. Fill pie crust (previously prepared) with filling and top with meringue. Place in oven long enough to brown the top of the meringue.

This recipe will make approximately 10 individual pies.

APPLE PIE

5 or 6 apples	1/2 cup water
1 cup sugar	1 teaspoon lemon juice
Cinnamon	Mace

After peeling and slicing apples, boil them in sugar with water until tender. Add cold lemon juice and fill pie plates lined with pastry. Wet edges and cover with pastry; wash with milk. Sprinkle a small amount of sugar on top of pie and bake in a steady, moderate oven for approximately one-half hour. Small amounts of cinnamon and mace should be sprinkled on apples before placing the top crust on the pie.

LEMON MERINGUE PIE

1 baked pastry 8" pie shell	1 1/3 cups (15 oz. can) Sweetened condensed milk
1/2 cup lemon juice	2 eggs, separated
1 teaspoon grated lemon rind or 1/4 teaspoon lemon extract	1/4 teaspoon cream of tartar
	4 tablespoons sugar

Combine lemon juice and grated lemon rind or lemon extract; gradually stir into sweetened condensed milk. Add egg yolks. Stir until well blended. Pour into cooled pastry shell. Add cream of tartar to egg whites; beat until almost stiff enough to hold a peak. Add sugar gradually, beating until stiff but not dry. Pile lightly on pie filling. Bake in slow oven (325 degrees F.) until done.

NORTHERN PACIFIC FRENCH DRESSING

Garlic	3 eggs
3/4 cup sugar	1/2 cup catsup
2 tablespoons dry mustard	1/3 cup paprika
2 quarts salad oil	1 pint tarragon vinegar
1/2 cup lemon juice	1/3 cup salt

Rub the mixing bowl with garlic before mixing ingredients. Then add three eggs, well beaten. Adding to the eggs slowly, add the sugar, catsup, mustard, paprika, and a dash of the salad oil. Then add the balance of the salad oil, the salt, vinegar, and lemon juice. Be sure to stir constantly while mixing ingredients.

Above, steam reigned when this 1941 photo was made of the "North Coast Limited" at the St. Paul depot.

Below, this late 19th century scene shows a wooden Northern Pacific trestle near St. Regis, Montana.

The steward of this beautifully appointed Northern Pacific diner invites you to your table. The car seats 48 persons, 32 in the main center section and eight each in two glass-partitioned areas, called "banquettes," one at each end of the car.

—Donald Duke Collection

NORTHERN PACIFIC FRUIT CAKE (LIGHT)

The recipe for this cake and the dark fruit cake which follows originated at the Paris International Exposition of 1900 and was modified during the years by Fred Kaul and J. W. Welligrant, head bakers for the Northern Pacific.

Fruit and nut ingredients:

2 1/2 lbs. white raisins
2 lbs. candied cherries
2 lbs. candied pineapple
1 lb. sliced or diced mixed fruit

Mix these ingredients with one ounce of brandy or wine and allow to stand over night in a cool place before proceeding.

2 cups shelled walnuts
2 cups shelled pecans
2 cupt shelled almonds

The nuts are to be added with the fruit ingredients and placed with the following cake mixture.

Cake mixture:

1 lb. granulated sugar
1 teaspoon salt
2 1/4 lbs. bread flour
12 whole eggs
1/2 cup milk
1/2 lb. butter
1/2 lb. shortening
1/2 teaspoon mace
1 teaspoon vanilla
1 1/4 lbs. bread flour

Cream the sugar, salt, 1 lb. bread flour, butter, shortening, mace, and vanilla for approximately five minutes with a rotary mixer at a slow speed. Gradually add the whole eggs, creaming for approximately eight minutes at medium speed. Add the milk and 1 1/4 lb. bread flour. Mix for approximately three minutes at slow speed; add fruits and nuts, mixing well. Bake for about three hours at 325 degrees F.

NORTHERN PACIFIC FRUIT CAKE (DARK)

2 lbs. washed seedless raisins
2 lbs. washed currants
1 lb. sliced or diced mixed fruit
1/2 lb. candied cherries
1/2 lb. candied pineapple
1 oz. port wine
1 oz. sherry wine

Prepare these ingredients the day before and let stand in a cool place.

1 cup shelled walnuts
1 cup shelled almonds
1 cup shelled pecans

These are to be added when fruit is mixed with cake mixture.

Cake mixture:

1 lb. granulated sugar
6 oz. shortening
6 oz. butter
1 teaspoon salt
12 whole eggs
1 teaspoon cinnamon
1 teaspoon mace
1 teaspoon nutmeg
1 teaspoon cardamon seed
1 1/4 lbs. bread flour

Cream the above ingredients (except the eggs and flour) at a slow speed in a rotary mixer. Then gradually add the whole eggs and bread flour. Add the fruits and nuts, mixing well. Bake for approximately three hours at 325 degrees F.

Northern Pacific's luxurious "North Coast Limited" of the 1960's rounds a curve on Butte Mountain near Spire Rock, Montana, while passengers enjoy the scenery from Vista Dome cars or in the diners.

Indians arrived to greet passengers on the open-end observation car of Northern Pacific's "North Coast Limited" for this 1923 picture at Arlee, Montana.

SIRLOIN OF BEEF WITH MUSHROOM SAUCE

This recipe was originated by Steven Porter, a chef credited with 42 years of service with the Northern Pacific.

Sirloin of beef (28 portions)
2 Sliced carrots
3 Outside stalks of celery
Salt and Pepper
2 onions

Remove flank and all bones from the sirloin, trimming part of the fat and sinew with a sharp knife. Season with salt and pepper. Place in roasting pan with a small amount of the fat and a few beef bones; cook in a hot oven for 30 minutes and then add carrots, onions, and celery. Put this back into a medium hot oven and roast for an additional 30 minutes, or until medium done. Be careful not to burn the vegetables. Then remove the meat from the pan and place on a large platter; keep warm, but not too hot, until time for serving.

Mushroom sauce:

1 lb. fresh mushrooms
Beef gravy
Butter

Cut stems from fresh mushrooms and wash them carefully to remove sand. If the mushrooms are small (button sized), leave whole; if large, cut stems and heads into one-half inch dices. Place in a sauce pan with a piece of butter; season with salt and cook slowly for approximately 10 minutes with cover on tight. Now add beef gravy (made your favorite way) and simmer for an additional 15 minutes.

"PEARADISE" LATTICE PIE

8 canned Bartlett pear halves (1 lb, 4 oz.)
3/4 cup sugar
1 tablespoon fresh orange juice
1 tablespoon fresh lemon juice
1/2 cup coffee cream
1 tablespoon butter
1/8 oz. nutmeg
1/8 oz. cinnamon

Drain and slice pears into pastry-lined pan. Add sugar to pears. Then add orange juice to mixture without stirring in, then the lemon juice. Pour coffee cream over mixture. Add butter in bits and sprinkle nutmeg and cinnamon over filling. Top with lattice crust. Bake 40 to 45 minutes at 375 to 400 degrees F. (No thickening is used in this pie which may be served warm or cold.)

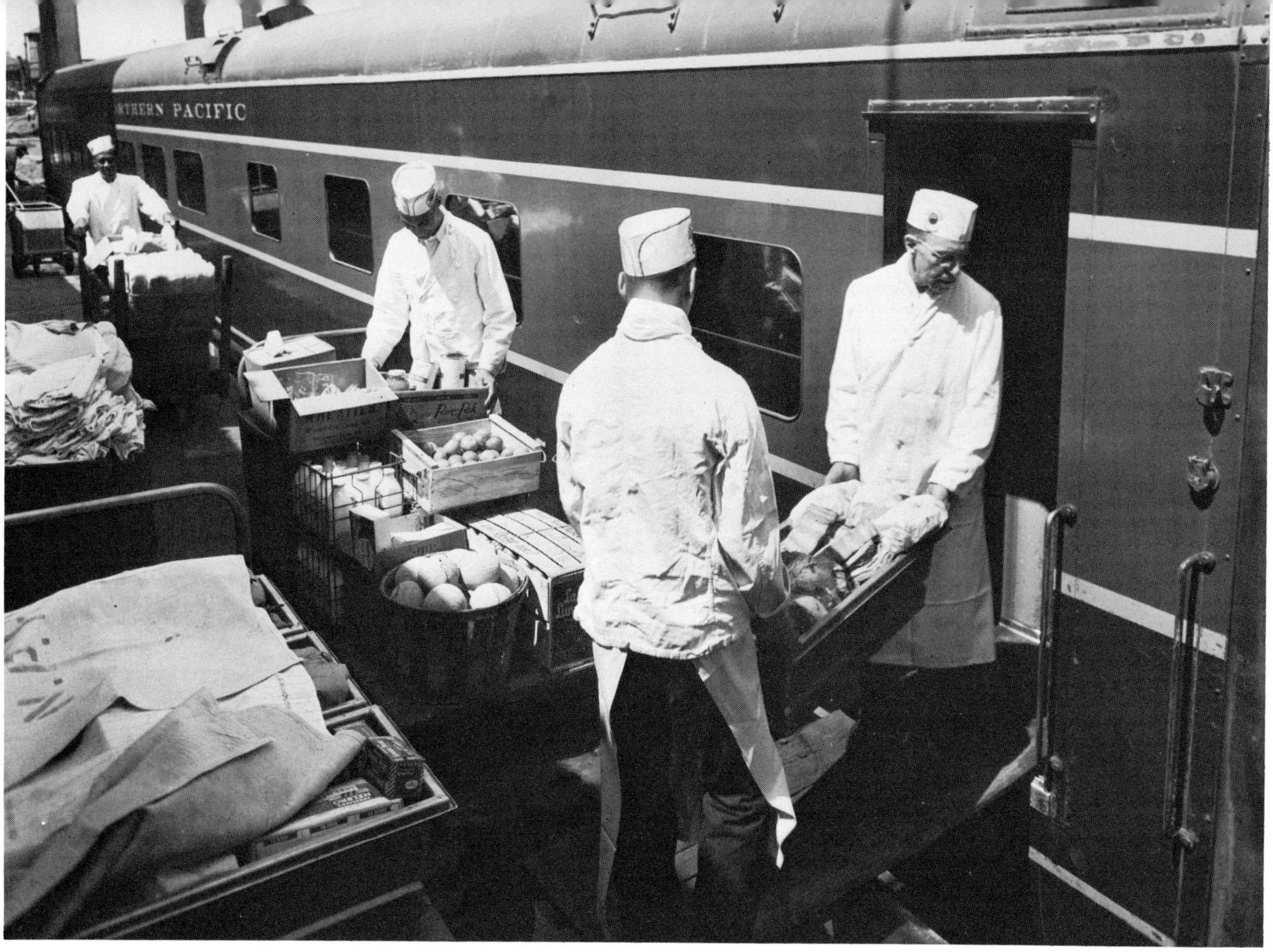

Above, supplies are loaded on N.P.'s "North Coast Limited" diner to serve transcontinental travelers.

Below, the streamline "North Coast Limited" arrives with passengers at Seattle's King Street station.

CHICAGO HISTORICAL SOCIETY

This 19th century photograph shows painters placing the finishing touches on coaches in the Pullman shops. Era rail cars were noted for being ornate.

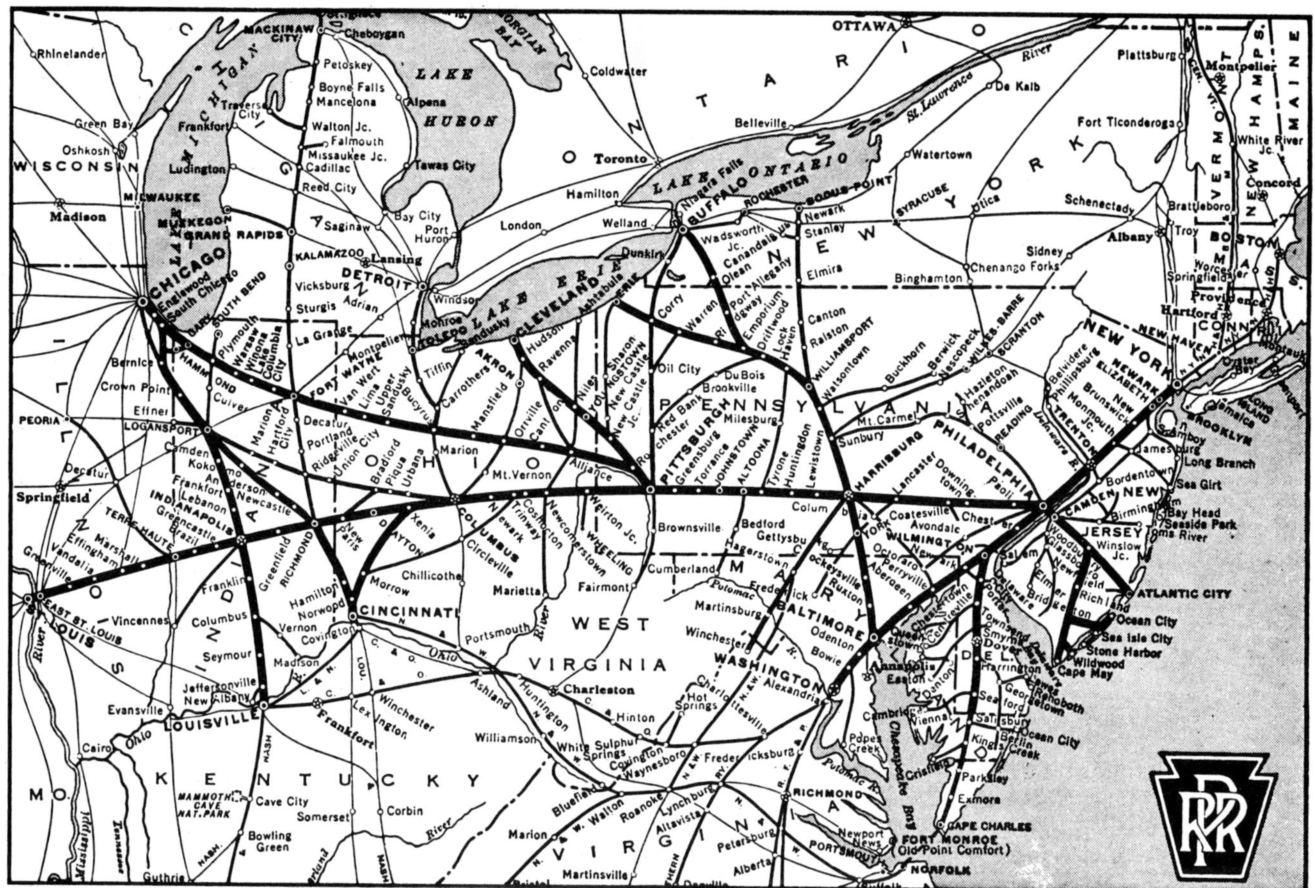

PENNSYLVANIA RAILROAD

Founded in 1846 to build a line between Philadelphia and Pittsburgh, The Pennsylvania Railroad developed into the giant of American railways. Its tracks, serving 13 states, linked many major cities, including New York, Chicago, Detroit, Buffalo, Washington, D. C., Cleveland, Columbus, Cincinnati, Louisville, Indianapolis, Peoria, and St. Louis as well as the two cities it originally connected.

The P.R.R. initially was promoted by Philadelphians who regarded a rail line as essential to tap the growing commerce with mid-America if their community were to prosper. The Pennsylvania not only helped Philadelphia grow into one of America's great cities but also provided the impetus for the development of other major metropolitan areas.

The Pennsylvania grew not only by building its lines but also through the acquisition of more than 600 other railroads. By the 1960's, the Pennsylvania system covered approximately 10,000 miles of track and while it was fourth among American railroads in total mileage, it rated first in revenues. Even so, there were economic pressures from automotive and air competition and plans were made for eventual consolidation of the P.R.R. with the New York Central.

The P.R.R., serving a densely populated area, early in its history began carrying relatively large numbers of passengers. Its famous trains have included *The Manhattan Limited,* connecting Chicago and New York; *The St. Louisan,* rolling between New York and St. Louis; *The*

ALL PICTURES THIS CHAPTER: PENNSYLVANIA RAILROAD (Except as Noted)

THE BETTMANN ARCHIVE, INC.

The rush for meals at a depot restaurant between train stops before the general use of dining cars was depicted in this early day railway drawing.

Red Arrow, serving New York, Philadelphia, Baltimore, and Washington, D. C., to Detroit; *The American,* also serving New York and St. Louis; *The Buckeye Limited,* speeding between New York and Cleveland; *The Washington,* providing fast service to the nation's capitol, and *The Sea Gull,* to Atlantic City.

But the train that brought the most fame to The Pennsylvania undoubtedly was *The Broadway Limited,* inaugurated in 1902 to match the 20-hour schedule offered between New York City and Chicago by The New York Central.

The Broadway Limited became the pride of the system, offering luxurious accommodations, powerful engines that gave speed to the trip, and diners serving the most delicious of foods appealing to gourmet appetites.

Handling most of the main line passenger traffic was the P.R.R.'s K-4 Pacific type locomotive, introduced in 1914. The railroad eventually built 424 of these powerful steam engines and they served efficiently for 30 years--being replaced by diesel locomotives following the end of World War II.

Passengers on *The Broadway Limited* traveled with the assurance that their trips would not only be speedy but also would be memorable for the quality and variety of food served on the diners.

While kitchens were established in New York City and Chicago to prepare such foods as roasts, stews, and pies, most of the work of cooking the meals remained the duty of the chefs in the dining car kitchens. Commissaries for supplying these foods were set up in Washington, D. C., Philadelphia, Harrisburg, and Pittsburgh as well as Chicago and New York City.

To indicate the emphasis placed on appetizing meals and service for passengers, The Pennsylvania prepared a 271-page book of recipes and instructions for dining car personnel.

The preface of this book gives hints which are of importance to a cook at home or aboard a railway dining car.

"A well prepared meal requires dedicated attention to the work to be performed," the book advises. "Food must not only taste good, but appeal to the eye as well if it is to be thoroughly enjoyed."

Here are recipes which became favorites on *The Broadway Limited* as well as on other Pennsylvania trains.

The Pennsylvania Railroad's "Broadway Limited" of the steam era races to New York from Chicago, making the trip in 20 hours. The service began in 1902.

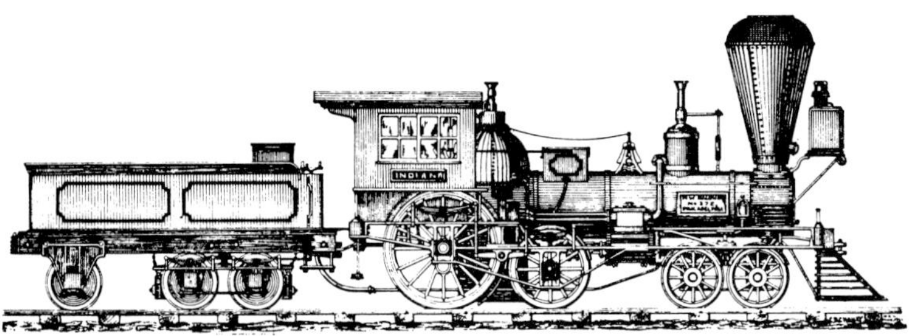

Built in 1850, "The Indiana" was among the Pennsylvania's first locomotives used for passenger service.

MARYLAND BUTTER

6 hard-cooked egg yolks
1/4 lb. butter

To be mixed thoroughly and passed through pastry tube.

ENGLISH BEEF BROTH WITH BARLEY

1 tablespoon shortening
1 cup celery: cut in 1/4" dice
1 cup turnips: in 1/4 " dice
2 cups carrots· in 1/4" dice
2 cups onions: in 1/4" dice
3 cups tomato juice
1 gal. brown beef stock
1/2 cup barley
1 cup cooked lean beef cut in small dice
2 tablespoon flour
2 tablespoon chopped washed parsley
Worcestershire sauce

Place shortening in saucepan, melt, add vegetables (after cutting them into one-fourth inch dices), and saute for five minutes. Add flour, tomato juice, stock, and barley; then cook slowly until barley and vegetables are done. Add meat and parsley. Season with salt and pepper and a teaspoon of Worcestershire sauce. This recipe makes one gallon and will serve 20 portions.

PENNSYLVANIA CLUB SANDWICH

3 slices fresh toast
3 slices broiled bacon
4 heart leaves of crisp lettuce
1 branch parsley
Mayonnaise
2 pickle chips
Sliced breast of chicken from 4 lb. chicken
2 slices of tomato

Spread a lettuce leaf with mayonnaise; lay three slices of broiled bacon on the lettuce, cover with another lettuce leaf and place on slice of toast. Put the second piece of toast on top and cover with another lettuce leaf spread with mayonnaise. Next put the slices of white meat of chicken on the lettuce and cover with the last leaf of lettuce and then the third slice of toast. Cut in four triangular sections, each section to be pierced with a wooden toothpick to hold it together. Garnish with a leaf of lettuce in the center of dinner plate; place the tomato slices and pickle chops on top of the lettuce. Arrange the four triangular shaped sections in stand-up position around the tomato slices.

TUNA FISH SALAD FRITTER

8 slices of white bread
4 whole eggs
2 cups of milk
1 cup of finely diced celery
1 tablespoon of mayonnaise
16 3/4 oz. cans of tuna fish

Beat eggs, milk and salt together until thoroughly mixed. Mix tuna fish and diced celery together with mayonnaise. Season with a little pepper. Spread one slice of bread with approximately two tablespoons of tuna fish salad. Place a second slice on top. Trim carefully, then soak the sandwish well on both sides in the beaten mixture of eggs and milk. Fry in butter in frying pan until well browned on both sides and heated through completely. This sandwich must be served immediately upon completion. Do not cut. Recipe makes four sandwiches.

BROILED TENDERLOIN STEAK ON TOAST

Place the steak on one slice of toast and the garniture consisting of two slices of tomato and a thin slice of raw Bermuda onion in lettuce leaf on a second slice of toast. Additional garniture of five pieces of freshly cooked French fried potatoes are to be placed alongside sandwich. Serve on a hot dinner plate with two pickle chips on one side of sandwich and a branch of parsley on the other.

SEA FOOD NEWBURG

12 oysters
24 cooked shrimps (each cut in half)
6 mushroom caps (washed and cut in halves)
12 scallops (each cut in 3 pieces)
8 tablespoons Sherry wine
3 egg yolks (well beaten)
1 teaspoon chopped shallets
2 oz. butter
1 tablespoon paprika
1 1/2 cups cream
1 1/2 cups cream sauce

Blanch the oysters and scallops, then strain through a colander. Place the juice in a pot and allow to reduce for 5 minutes. Saute the shallots until cooked, then add mushrooms; and simmer slowly until done; add the cream sauce and juice. Then put in the seafood, add the paprika and mix for a second, add the cream and cook slowly five minutes. Next add the yolk of the eggs, beaten well with the wine; shake well. This recipe makes six portions.

PUMPKIN CUSTARD PIE
(Two pies)

1 1/2 cups pumpkin (canned)
6 eggs
2 cups granulated sugar
1 teaspoon salt
1 teaspoon ground nutmeg
1 teaspoon ground cinnamon
1 teaspoon ground ginger
1 1/2 cups hot milk
1 1/2 cups hot cream
1 tablespoon melted butter

Beat eggs and sugar for at least five minutes. Then, in a separate dish, mix the spices in a small amount of the milk and cream until smooth. Add balance of the milk and cream and stir into the mixture of eggs and sugar. Now place pumpkin puree in bowl and gradually add the liquid mixture to it. Fill the pie to within one-fourth inch of top of pan; before placing in oven, sprinkle each pie with one-half tablespoon of melted butter. Bake until well done and of good color.

Above, here is the crew of a Pennsylvania Railroad dining car in the 1920's. Note jugs of water on each table for passengers. Right, this drawing depicts "deluxe" P.R.R. passenger coaches of the 1860's.

This is a Pennsylvania Railroad dining car typical of those used by the system during the 1960's.

CELERY ROOT SALAD

Cut off green stalks, wash celery roots well and put them in cold water with salt, bring to boil and cook until done. When soft, drain well and let cool. When properly cold, peel, cut into quarters and slice thin. Place in bowl, add some finely chopped onions and parsley. Then mix with dressing consisting of one cup of P.R.R. dressing to which two tablespoons of mayonnaise have been added. Salad should be ready at least one hour before dinner is called in order that celery root will have chance to absorb some of the dressing. Serve on lettuce leaf.

P.R.R. SALAD BOWL

1/4 head crisp lettuce (core removed, leaves pulled apart)
1 good-size ripe tomato (cut into eight (8) portions)
2 green onions or scallions, cleaned, well washed and thinly sliced
1/4 cucumber (peeled, seeds removed and cucumber thinly sliced)
3 radishes, well washed and thinly sliced
1 stalk celery, cleaned, well washed and thinly sliced
3/4 oz. Roquefort or similar cheese
1 small china creamer full of French Dressing (3 tablespoons)

Wash all vegetables, except tomatoes; place them in a clean towel to dry. This is a very important thing for if not dry, dressing will not mix. Then place all vegetables (including tomatoes) in a round pan, crumble the cheese and sprinkle over, add dressing and mix well. Place in salad bowl and serve with rye or wheat wafers on a tea plate. This recipe produces one portion.

PENNSYLVANIA DRESSING

Yolks of 4 hard-boiled eggs made into a smooth paste with tarragon vinegar
2 level teaspoons paprika
2 level teaspoons celery salt
2 teaspoons powdered sugar
2 green peppers chopped medium fine
12 chives, cut very fine
2 springs parsley, chopped fine
Whites of 4 hard-boiled eggs (chopped)
Juice of 1 lemon (strained)
1/2 cup olive oil
1 1/2 cups mayonnaise

Mix ingredients well together in a bowl in the order given; beat with an egg whip. Transfer into a quart jar, cover tightly, and keep in an ice box. This recipe makes one quart of dressing.

POACHED EGGS, CRAB MEAT AND CHEESE ON TOAST

1 6-oz. can crabmeat (drain and clean thoroughly--remove all small tendons and fibers
1 1/2 tablespoons melted butter
1 1/2 tablespoons flour
6 poached eggs
Parsley
1/4 cup milk
Salt - paprika
1 tablespoon sherry wine
3 rounds of buttered toast cut to fit shirred-egg dish
Grated cheese

Melt butter, add and blend the flour. When hot stir the milk in slowly. Add the crabmeat. Season with salt and paprika. Remove from fire and add the sherry wine. Place round of buttered toast in shirred-egg dish and cover with crabmeat. Place two poached eggs over and sprinkle each with grated cheese; place in oven to brown. Top with a sprig of parsley. Serve hot. Recipe makes three portions.

SCRAMBLED EGGS, COUNTRY STYLE, ON DEVILED VIRGINIA HAM CROUTON

7 oz. of deviled ham
16 eggs--two to be used for each serving
8 slices of white bread
Parsley

For each serving, prepare a slice of toasted white bread; trim off the crust carefully; spread the surface of the toast with deviled ham. Place on pie tin and then in oven. Prepare the scrambled eggs and then place neatly on the toast. Cut the toast diagonally, place on hot dinner plate, and arrange with toast to the outside. Garnish with a branch of well washed, crisp parsley. This recipe makes eight portions.

AVOCADO AND ORANGE COCKTAIL

1 Avocado
2 consomme spoons of mayonnaise
2 consomme spoons of strained cocktail sauce
1 Orange
Juice from orange pulp
Lettuce

Remove skin and pit from avocado; cut avocado and place in a bowl with peeled orange. Add orange juice, mayonnaise, and sauce. Mix well, and then place into lettuce lined cocktail glasses to be served. This recipe serves four persons.

Coffee shops were the order of the day for most short-distance travelers aboard the Pennsylvania Railroad's Congressional and Senator trains in the high-speed corridor between New York and Washington, D.C.
—Donald Duke Collection

Right, this Pennsylvania Railroad food cart brought sandwiches, drinks and snacks to passengers throughout the train.
—Donald Duke Collection

The locomotive "Lancaster" pioneered rail service from Philadelphia to the inland trading areas.

ROAST BEEF HASH, SOUTHERN STYLE

1 qt. 1/4-inch diced cold roast beef
1 pt. 1/4-inch diced, peeled raw Irish potatoes
1 cup 1/4-inch diced, peeled raw white onions
6 cups cold water
1 cup 1/4-inch diced, raw green pepper (flower & seeds removed)
4 tablespoons well-washed, finely chopped parsley
Salt and very little pepper
2 oz. of table butter

Saute the pepper and onion in the butter over slow fire and let smother with lid on saucepan for about 10 minutes. Add the meat, potatoes, salt and pepper seasoning, and water; let cook slowly for about forty minutes. If the hash becomes too dry during the cooking process, add a little more water as needed. Half of the chopped parsley is to be added to the hash when cooked, and the remainder to be kept for sprinkling over each portion when served.

For service, place two large spoons of Southern Hash in a hot casserole, placing each casserole as it is filled on top of the range for a few minutes until it becomes boiling hot. Wipe the bottom of the casserole with a kitchen towel, place a tea plate under the dish, and sprinkle approximately one-half teaspoon of chopped parsley over the hash; add other dishes such as corn fritters or potato pancakes, cover with lid, and serve with hot dinner plate.

This recipe makes 12 portions.

SWEDISH MEAT BALLS

1 lb. ground beef
1 lb. ground veal
1 lb. ground pork
1 cup cut onion
1 egg
Juice of 3 lemons
1 cup bread crumbs
1/2 pint sour cream
2 quarts cream sauce
Salt
Pepper

Saute onions, and mix with meat, egg, crumbs, salt, and pepper. Shape in balls of one ounce each and saute. Add meat balls to hot cream sauce mixed with sour cream and lemon juice. Serve five meat balls with sauce for each portion. This recipe will make 15 portions.

BAKED APPLES FILLED WITH SAUSAGE MEAT

Wash six large apples. Cut a slice from the tops. Scoop out the cores and pulp, leaving shells 3/4-inch thick. Cut the pulp from the cores. Chop the pulp and combine with one cup of well-seasoned sausage meat. Sprinkle the shells with teaspoonful of salt and two tablespoons of brown sugar. Fill shells heaping full with sausage mixture. Bake in a moderate oven until apples are tender. Caution: Do not overcook as apples will fall apart.

PENNEPICURE PIE

1 bottom crust
1 heaping tablespoon granulated sugar
1/4 teaspoon ground cinnamon
1/4 teaspoon ground nutmeg
1/4 teaspoon ground cloves
3 egg yolks
1 whole egg
1 1/2 cups of boiling cream
1/2 cup seedless raisins, well washed and finely chopped

For meringue:
3 egg whites (beaten dry and stiff)
1 tablespoon powdered sugar

Mix sugar and spices (cloves, cinnamon, nutmeg) and salt well together and add to egg yolks and beat until perfectly smooth. Add cream slowly and last of all the chopped raisins, beating mixture well during this process. Pour mixture into unbaked bottom crust in pie tin and bake in moderate oven until well done and colored. Allow to cool. For meringue, add sugar to the beaten egg whites and cover pie. Bake on top shelf of moderately hot oven until meringue is delicately colored. Cut pie as usual, but it will be helpful if the blade of the knife is first dipped in boiling hot water before each portion is sliced. Recipe makes one pie.

P.R.R. BAKED GRAPEFRUIT

3 Large grapefruit
6 tablespoons granulated sugar
6 tablespoons Sherry wine
6 tablespoons melted butter

Cut grapefruit in halves, loosen segments of fruit, and remove seeds. Sprinkle each half grapefruit with sugar, sherry wine, and melted butter. Keep well chilled in refrigerator until needed. To serve, place prepared grapefruit in pan in hot oven, baking until of a nice color. Serve while hot in grapefruit dish. Recipe makes six servings.

SWEET POTATO AND SAUSAGE STUFFING
(Sufficient for a 14 lb. turkey)

Saute until light brown: one-half pound (one cup) sausage meat. Break it up with a fork. Remove it from the pan. Add to the pan and saute for three minutes, three tablespoons chopped onion and one cup chopped celery. Add the sausage meat, four cups mashed sweet potatoes, two cups dry bread crumbs, 1 1/2 teaspoonfuls salt, one-fourth teaspoonful paprika and three tablespoonfuls chopped parsley. Mix these ingredients well.

BREAST OF CHICKEN WITH VIRGINIA HAM

Remove the breasts fron a 3 1/2-pound roasting chicken. Remove the skin and season the breasts with salt and pepper, roll in flour. Put two ounces of butter in a shallow saute pan, and fry the breasts for about fifteen minutes, or until golden brown. Take a slice of cooked Virginia ham and just heat through on the broiler, or in pan with a little butter. Do not allow to become hard or crisp. Place Virginia ham and chicken breast on slice of toast and serve with a little Supreme Sauce poured over.

HARD COOKED EGGS A LA KING

12 hard boiled eggs	3 Green peppers cut in 1/2" pieces
3 cups medium thick cream sauce	1 tablespoon melted butter
12 fresh mushrooms (sliced)	Salt for taste
Toast	Chopped parsley

Saute the mushrooms and green peppers in butter for approximately five minutes, but do not let them brown. Add the cream sauce and simmer until well heated, salting to taste. Keep warm on steam table or hot plate until ready for use.

To serve, remove crusts from toast; cut diagonally and arrange in diamond shape on hot dinner plate. Place four halves of eggs on toast (cut side down) and cover with sauce. Sprinkle with chopped parsley. Serve very hot. Recipe makes six portions.

BAKED EGGS AND CHEESE IN BREAD CASES

1 Loaf unsliced bread	Butter
1/2 Cup grated cheese	4 Eggs
Parsley	Salt and pepper

Prepare four bread shells in this manner: cut four 1 1/4" slices from a whole loaf of bread with a large biscuit cutter. Press a small biscuit cutter into these rounds, but not through them. Hollow the centers, leaving a shell and a bottom at least one-fourth inch thick. Butter the sides lightly and place the shells in a slow oven until they are toasted.

Then spread the bread shells with melted butter and sprinkle with one-fourth cup grated cheese. Drop a whole egg into each bread case. Sprinkle tops with the remainder of the grated cheese. Bake until eggs are firm and the cheese is brown. Season with salt and pepper; garnish with chopped parsley. A hot mushroom sauce may be served if desired; however, let guests pour the sauce over the dish if desired. This recipe makes four servings.

OMELET, PLAIN

Add a tablespoon of milk to two eggs and beat with fork thoroughly. Season with salt only. Pour mixture into greased omelet pan, which must be very hot. Shake pan quickly back and forth until mixture is set. Then fold omelet away from you and turn onto a hot plate or platter. Do not under any circumstances turn omelet over as this tends to make it tough and leathery.

OMELET ARGENTINE (WITH EGG PLANT)

Cut egg plant in one-half-inch squares. Put in omelet pan with small amount of butter and fry until cooked. Use about six squares per omelet, add egg mixture and cook in usual manner. Serve omelet with tomato sauce around it.

TOMATO SAUCE ONION OMELET

4 medium sized onions	Tomato sauce
1 1/2 tablespoon shortening	Eggs

Peel onions and cut in thin slices and fry until brown. Turn occasionally with a fork or shake the pan so that the onions do not burn. Season with salt before taking from fire. Make omelet as usual and when approximately half done, place one tablespoon of fried onions on top of the egg mixture. Continue cooking until of creamy consistency. Fold and turn on large, hot plate. Serve tomato sauce alongside omelet.

WESTERN OMELET

2 onions (sliced and diced)	1 green pepper (diced)
2 tablespoons of diced, cooked ham	Eggs

Saute the ingredients in a pan until the onions and peppers are soft but not burned. Add this mixture to eggs and cook as ordinary omelet. This amount is enough for four omelets.

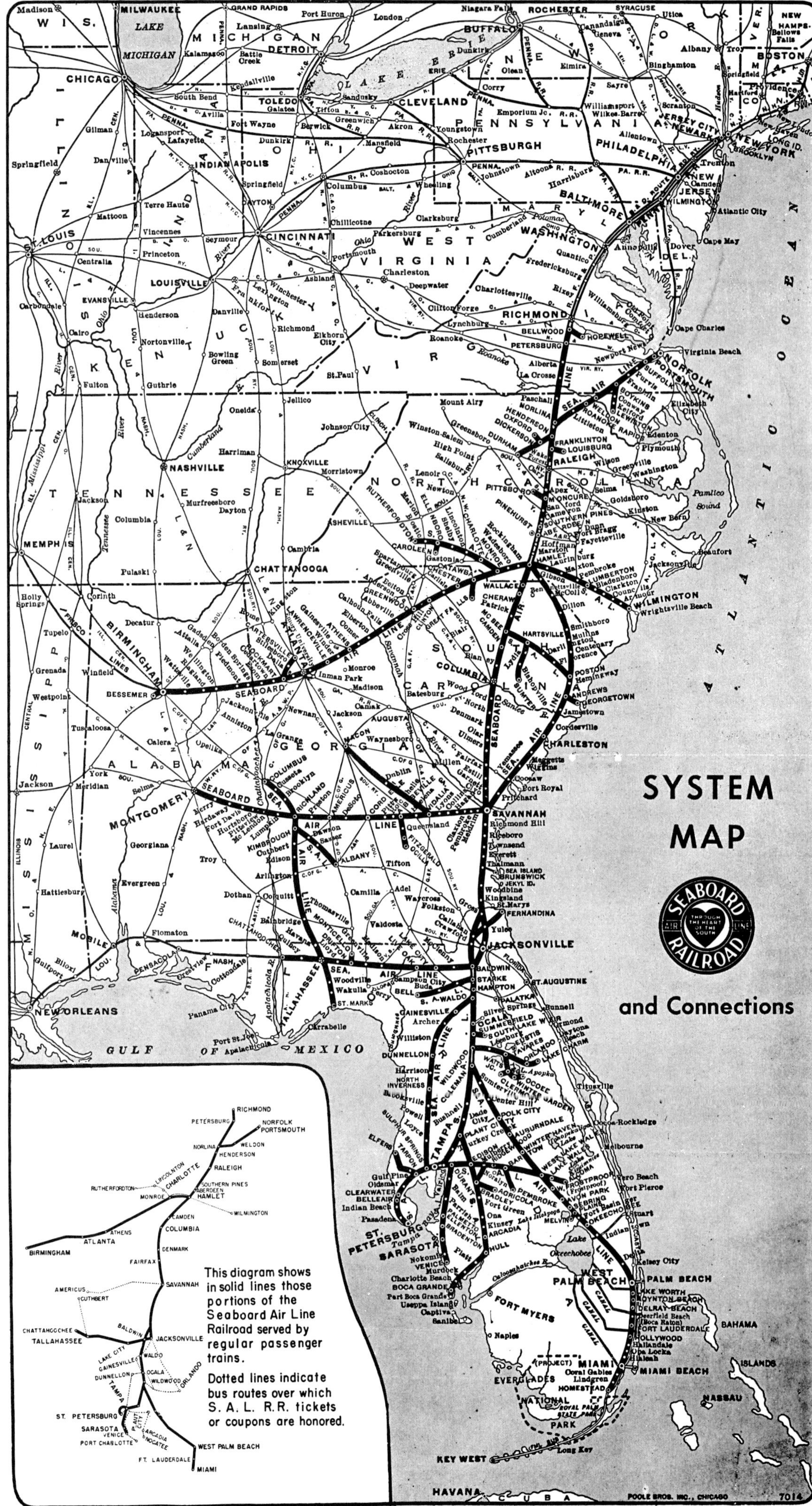
SYSTEM
MAP
and Connections
SEABOARD RAILROAD
THROUGH THE HEART OF THE SOUTH
This diagram shows in solid lines those portions of the Seaboard Air Line Railroad served by regular passenger trains.
Dotted lines indicate bus routes over which S. A. L. R.R. tickets or coupons are honored.
ATLANTIC OCEAN
GULF OF MEXICO
POOLE BROS. INC., CHICAGO
7014

The Seaboard Air Line Railroad's "Silver Meteor," crack New York-Florida streamliner, rolls across the Trout River near Jacksonville, Florida.

SEABOARD RAILWAY

The Seaboard Air Line Railway, serving six Southern states, was organized in 1900 under the leadership of John S. Williams, a young Richmond, Virginia, banker. The system originally had approximately 2,600 miles of track but expanded to cover about 4,100 miles through the acquisition of smaller railroads. Stretching from Richmond and Norfolk, Virginia, to Tallahassee and Miami, Florida, the Seaboard's service area also includes Atlanta and Albany, Georgia, and Birmingham and Montgomery, Alabama.

The Seaboard became a popular line for Easterners to travel (via Pennsylvania Railroad connections) to spend winters in the Florida sun.

Among the railroad's noted trains have been *The Southern States Special* and *The New York-Florida Limited.* The success of the streamline *Silver Meteor,* connecting New York City with St. Petersburg and Miami in 1939, prompted the introduction of *The Silver Comet,* speeding between New York City and Birmingham, and *The Silver Star,* rolling between New York City and Miami, following World War II. The name of the crack streamliner *Palmland* reflected the road's Florida traffic.

Dining on The Seaboard Air Line followed the tradition of Deep South hospitality. The railroad's dining car service began in approximately 1902 when two day coaches were converted into diners for service between Atlanta, Georgia, and Hamlet, North Carolina.

Keeping with the geographical area served by the railroad, Southern-style dishes became features that delighted the appetites of passengers headed for relaxation in the sun.

The Southern recipes detailed here are representative of the dishes that became identified with the Seaboard's dining car service.

ALL PICTURES THIS CHAPTER: SEABOARD AIR LINE RAILROAD

Dining car personnel load supplies to prepare delicious foods to be served Seaboard Air Line passengers.

SOUTHERN SPOON BREAD

3/4 cup corn meal
1 teaspoon salt
2 tablespoons shortening
2 eggs
1 cup sweet milk
2 teaspoons baking powder
1 cup boiling water

Mix meal, salt, shortening. Scald with the boiling water. Add well-beaten eggs, sweet milk and baking powder. Bake in moderate oven.

BAKED SMITHFIELD HAM

Wash ham thoroughly and cover with cold water. Allow ham to soak in water overnight. Change water and cook slowly for three hours (10- to 12-pound ham). Let ham cool in water in which it cooked. Remove skin from ham, sprinkle with brown sugar and brown in oven.

CREAM OF PEANUT SOUP

1 qt. veal or chicken stock
1 lb. peanut butter (pure)

Work the peanut butter into a light roux, add to the veal stock and let simmer gently for an hour. Just before serving add a little hot cream to be thoroughly infused with the soup.

FLORIDA SHRIMP CREOLE

1 1/2 cups uncooked rice
6 outside branches celery, diced
3 medium onions, chopped
1 large green pepper, chopped
1/2 lb. fresh mushrooms, sliced
4 cups canned tomatoes
1/4 cup pimientos, chopped
1 clove garlic, very finely chopped
1/2 teaspoon black pepper
2 teaspoons salt
2 teaspoons chili powder
4 tablespoons butter or bacon fat
2 cups water
2 teaspoons sugar
1 tablespoon vinegar
2 lbs. fresh shrimp
2 tablespoons flour

Saute celery, onions, green pepper and mushrooms slowly in butter or bacon fat for 10 minutes. Add flour and seasonings and mix well. Add tomatoes, pimientos and garlic. Add water slowly and simmer for about an hour or until thick, stirring constantly. Add fresh shrimp which have been previously cooked. Simmer about five minutes or until shrimp are thoroughly heated. Serve on a hot platter around a mound of fluffy rice. Serves six to eight portions.

To prepare fluffy boiled rice:

1 1/2 cups rice
4 teaspoons salt
10 cups boiling water

Wash rice thoroughly, add salt to boiling water in deep saucepan. Add rice slowly so boiling does not stop. If water is very hard, add one teaspoon lemon juice or one tablespoon vinegar to keep rice white. Boil gently without stirring for 12 to 25 minutes, depending upon variety, or until rice is entirely soft when pressed between fingers. Drain into sieve, wash with hot water, cover with cloth and set over hot water to separate grains.

To prepare green shrimp:

1 qt. boiling water
1/2 chopped onion
1 branch celery
2 teaspoons salt
1 bay leaf
1 teaspoon black pepper
1/2 lemon

Cook these ingredients for 15 minutes in boiling water. Add shrimp and cook for 10 to 15 minutes. Let cool in broth. Remove shell and black sand vein.

SOUTHERN CORN MUFFINS

1 cup sifted flour
1 cup water-ground corn meal
3 teaspoons baking powder
1/2 teaspoon salt
3 tablespoons sugar
1 egg, well-beaten
1 cup milk
3 tablespoons shortening, melted

Mix and sift dry ingredients. Combine egg, milk and shortening and add to flour mixture, stirring only until mixed. Use tablespoon to dip batter into greased muffin pans and fill them two-thirds full. Bake in hot oven for 20 to 30 minutes. Approximate yield: one dozen medium-sized muffins.

SOUTHERN FRIED CHICKEN

Disjoint chicken. Salt and pepper heavily. Dredge in flour. Fry very slowly in one-half inch fat in uncovered pan.

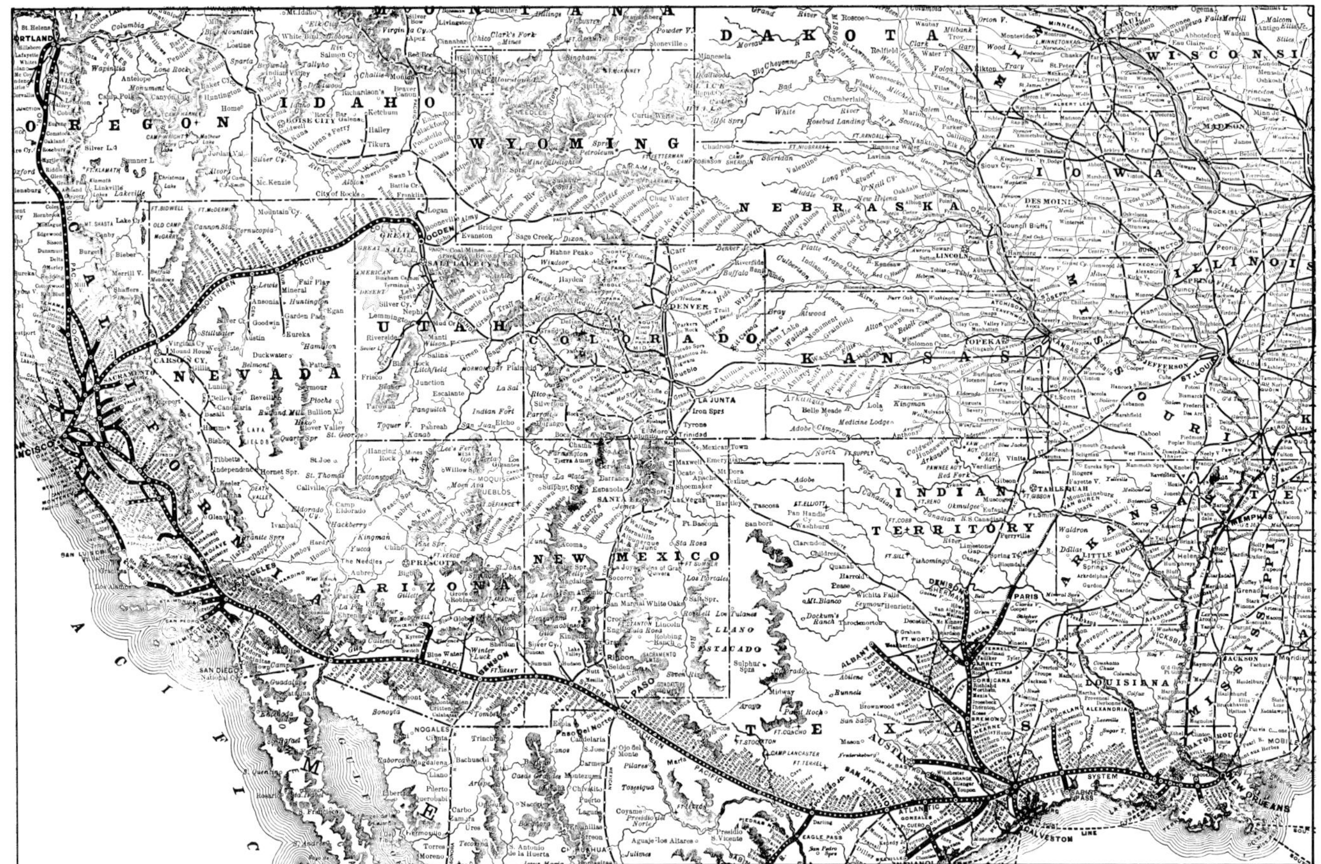

SOUTHERN PACIFIC

Operating over 12,000 miles of track, the Southern Pacific rolls through contrasting geographical and climatic areas. The immense system (exceeded in mileage only by the Santa Fe) uses plows to clear snow high up in the Sierra Nevada while on the same day its trains may be speeding through sizzling desert temperatures near the Salton Sea, which is 245 feet below sea level.

The Southern Pacific's diversity of operating areas can be noted by its route from New Orleans through Houston, San Antonio, El Paso, and Phoenix to Los Angeles, its line from Oakland through California's coastal mountains and past the Oregon pines to Portland, its service from California through the Sierra to Utah, and its lines between Los Angeles and Oakland and San Francisco.

The Southern Pacific system was formed in 1885, taking over the Central Pacific Railroad famed for its "gold spike" ceremony celebrating completion of the first transcontinental train route. Subsequently it built new lines and consolidated smaller railroads into its system.

The company began operating its own dining cars in 1892, setting a high standard of meals for passengers headed west to settle or enjoy the scenery.

Noted Southern Pacific passenger trains have included *The Sunset Limited,* traveling from

ALL PICTURES THIS CHAPTER: SOUTHERN PACIFIC RAILROAD

Here is a tavern car that was included in Southern Pacific "Daylight" trains during the 1950'*s.*

San Francisco and Los Angeles to New Orleans; *The Argonaut,* speeding from Los Angeles to New Orleans; *The Golden State Limited,* linking Chicago (via the Chicago, Rock Island and Pacific) and Los Angeles; *The Overland Limited* and *The Pacific Limited,* both rolling between Chicago (over the Chicago and Northwestern) and San Francisco, and *The Shasta, The Cascade,* and *The Klamath,* all speeding between San Francisco and Portland.

In addition, service between San Francisco and Los Angeles came with *The Owl, The Daylight, The Lark, The Padre,* and *The San Joaquin.*

Dinner in the diner became a delight affair on whatever Southern Pacific train the passenger rode.

Menus featuring fresh foods from the areas served were developed for dining cars operating on various routes.

Trains bound to or from New Orleans featured such southern favorites as gumbo, specially roasted coffees, and fish from the Gulf of Mexico. In California, recipes were found to present fresh fruits and vegetables and mountain trout in the tastiest dishes. Salmon found its way into special recipes for menus on trains operating in the Pacific Northwest.

Of notable interest was the Southern Pacific's introduction in 1961 of the first automatic buffet car in the United States. The initial car went into service on *The San Joaquin Daylight* and railroad officials promptly pronounced it a success. More cars were constructed and placed into operation.

The automatic buffet cars, providing hot and cold foods from vending machines, eliminated conventional dining cars from many trains. While the food provided was considerably less distinguished than that offered on traditional diners, the automation helped to reduce the Southern Pacific's cost of serving meals--a service which rarely provided profits and most frequently brought substantial losses.

Many other railroads subsequently began introducing automated buffet cars to replace the more costly diners presided over by chefs and waiters.

The first collection of recipes used on the Southern Pacific's famous trains was organized in 1921 by Allen Pollok, at the time manager of the system's dining car service.

Otto Paul Riess, who became the Southern Pacific's head chef prior to his retirement from the company, advised that any housewife following the recipes carefully, could produce dishes as delicious as those served aboard the railroad's fine dining cars.

The recipes described here were served frequently on Southern Pacific main line trains, adding considerable pleasure to journeys.

FRENCH TOAST

4 slices white bread, each 1/2 inch thick or better
3 eggs
1 heaping teaspoon sugar
1/2 cup cream
4 drops vanilla
Shortening for frying
Powdered sugar

Cut each slice of bread crosswise and trim. Beat eggs, add cream, vanilla, and soak bread thoroughly therein. Fry in hot shallow shortening on both sides until nicely browned and done. Sprinkle with powdered sugar when serving.

SOUTHERN PACIFIC DATE BRAN MUFFINS

3 cups flour
1/3 cup shortening
1/3 cup sugar
1 teaspoon baking powder
1/4 teaspoon salt
2 cups all-bran (prepared)
1 cup dehydrated dates
2 eggs
2 cups milk

Blend flour and shortening thoroughly. Add sugar, baking powder and salt. Sift. Crush bran with rolling pin and add to blend; fold in dates. Beat eggs in milk and combine with dry mix. Fill into muffin tin and bake for about 12 minutes in hot oven. Makes 24 medium-sized muffins.

HOT CAKES

1 cup flour
1/2 cup milk
1 tablespoon sugar
1 tablespoon melted butter
1 teaspoon baking powder
1 egg
Pinch of salt

Blend flour with dry ingredients and pass through sieve. Beat egg and melted butter in milk, add blend making a soft batter. Makes six cakes.

SOUTHERN PACIFIC SALAD BOWL

2 heads of lettuce, broken small
4 tomatoes, plunged for one minute into boiling water, skinned, cooled, then quartered
1 cucumber, peeled, scored, and sliced thin
1/2 bunch radishes, sliced thin
1/2 bell pepper, cut into strips, fingerwide, then shredded fine
1 teaspoon sugar
Pinch salt

Mix in the bowl, and moisten with French dressing to suit taste. Makes enough for six servings.

SOUTHERN PACIFIC FRENCH DRESSING

1 qt. olive oil
1 teaspoon paprika
1 tablespoon English mustard
1/2 tablespoon salt
Pinch of garlic powder
1/2 tablespoon white pepper
1/2 cup tarragon red wine vinegar
1/4 cup cold water
White of one egg

Blend spices; moisten with a few drops of vinegar and stir with whip until forming a paste. Add white of egg; beat thoroughly and combine with oil, which is to be added in small portions gradually. Add balance of vinegar, then water. Work until smooth. This recipe makes one quart of dressing.

The Southern Pacific's "Shasta Daylight" rounds a curve with its mountain namesake in the background.

TENDERLOIN TIPS, SOUTHERN PACIFIC

1 lb. thinly sliced beef tenderloin tips
1 green pepper, shredded
1 medium-sized onion, sliced
4 fresh mushrooms, sliced
1 large tomato, skinned, seeds removed, and cut small
1 cup beef broth or water
6 tablespoons butter
1 tablespoon flour
Salt
White pepper

Saute onions, peppers and mushrooms in butter. Add tomato and let simmer gently. Season tips with salt and pepper, saute in butter and sprinkle with flour. When nicely browned cover with broth or water and add vegetables. Let cook slowly until done, or about 15 minutes. Makes three servings.

HOT SLAW

1 large head of cabbage, shredded
1 onion, shredded
2 apples, sliced
1/2 cup sugar
1/2 cup cider vinegar
1/2 teaspoon English mustard
1 bay leaf
1 small onion with 4 cloves inserted
Rind of a 2-lb. piece of bacon
2 oz. butter
Salt

Smother cabbage, onion and applies in butter. Add other ingredients, and water to fairly cover cabbage. Salt to taste, cover saucepan and cook until soft. Remove onion with cloves and bay leaf before serving. Makes six to eight servings.

The Southern Pacific's "San Francisco Overland Limited" rolls over the 13-mile Salt Lake Trestle during the 1920's enroute to Chicago.

PEPPER POT

1 lb. tripe, cut into half-inch squares
2 bell peppers, core and seeds removed and diced
1 medium-sized onion, minced
1 leek, white part only, quartered and diced
3 branches celery, shredded
2 tablespoons butter
1 tablespoon flour
1 cupful raw potatoes, diced
2 tablespoons Worcestershire sauce
1 tablespoon crushed black pepper
1 qt. beef broth

Boil tripe partly done and braise in butter. Add bell peppers, onion, leek and celery. Braise lightly, stir in flour and cover with broth. Let boil slowly. Add potatoes when vegetables are about two-thirds done. Skim and salt. Finish with Worcestershire and crushed pepper. Recipe makes four servings.

CHIOPINO SAUCE

1/2 cup olive oil
1 cup minced onions
1/2 cup minced celery
4 medium-sized fresh mushrooms, minced
Clove of garlic, crushed
Few leaves of spinach, finely chopped
Few sprigs of parsley, finely chopped
Small bay leaf
1 qt. tomatoes, passed through sieve
Salt, pepper, paprika
1 tablespoon vinegar

Heat olive oil and fry onions. Add celery, mushrooms and garlic, then pureed tomatoes. Bring to a boil. Add balance of ingredients and season to taste. Let cook until thick. This recipe makes one quart of sauce.

SOUTHERN PACIFIC CHICKEN GUMBO

2 lbs. chicken, including bones chopped into small pieces
3 oz. veal, cut small
2 oz. raw, lean ham, cut small
1/2 cupful onions, cut small
1/2 cupful celery
1/2 cup cut bell peppers
Salt
Thyme
1/2 cupful okra, sliced
2 medium-sized tomatoes, skinned and quartered
1/2 cupful shrimps, sauted in butter
1 qt. water
White pepper
Gumbo file
Butter
1 cup rice

Prepare rice separately. Braise meats in butter, adding onions celery and peppers; when these ingredients are soft, add the tomatoes and okra. Cover with water and boil slowly for 30 minutes. Add shrimps. Let simmer an additional 10 minutes. Salt and season. To serve, mold rice in center of coup plate and cover with gumbo. This recipe makes four servings.

BEEFSTEAK AND KIDNEY PIE

16-oz. sirloin steak
1 sliced lamb kidney
1/4 cupful diced raw potatoes
1/2 oz. butter
1 tablespoon chopped onions
Pinch flour
2 oz. pie dough
Pinches of salt and white pepper

Season meats, sprinkle with flour and arrange in an oval earthenware dish with slices of kidney on top. Add potatoes, onions and butter. Fill dish to rim with cold water and cover with dough. Brush with milk and bake for about 25 minutes in a medium-hot oven. Makes one serving.

Tasty meals became associated with the Southern Pacific-Rock Island jointly operated "Golden State Limited," operated between Los Angeles and Chicago.

OMELET ECLAIR

3 eggs
1 tablespoon cream
1 sugar cookie or macaroon
1 tablespoon thick chocolate
2 tablespoons whipped cream
1 teaspoon melted butter

Beat eggs and cream, break in cookie or macaroon and pour into buttered pan. Shuffle about, and when fairly set, shape. Hold over hot fire until fluffy. Turn out on platter. Glace with syrup and garnish with whipped cream. This is one serving.

FRENCH APPLE PIE

2 lbs. apples, peeled, cored and quartered
6 oz. sugar
Pinch cinnamon
Pinch nutmeg
1 chip butter
Pie dough, 8 oz.
Apricot preserves

Drop prepared apples into salted water to preserve color. Line pie tin with dough the usual way, crimp edge and firm in refrigerator. Drain apples, add sugar and spices; fill shell and top with butter. Bake at 400 degrees for about 40 minutes, or until apples are done. Let pie stand for about 30 minutes until free of steam and heat; cover with hot apricot glacing, made from apricot preserves heated and strained.

Dinner time was a pleasure aboard Southern Pacific's "Lark," former Los Angeles-Oakland night train.

SOUTHERN PACIFIC CASSEROLE

2 1/2 lbs. lamb shoulder, skinned and boned
1 medium-sized onion, minced
1/4 lb. butter
2 branches celery
1 bunch young carrots, shaped small
4 young turnips, quartered and shaped
12 boiling onions
1 heaping tablespoon flour
1 cup tomatoes, pureed
1 pt. broth, made of the lamb bones
12 small rounded potatoes, boiled in salted water, then browned
1 cup peas, boiled in plain water
Salt
White pepper
Parsley

Cut lamb into 1 3/4-inch squares, dredge mildly with salt and white pepper and saute in pan without browning. Sprinkle with the chopped onion and celery, move meat about and continue cooking until ingredients added become soft. With the moisture disappearing add flour, and when the latter has nicely browned, tomato puree and broth. Bring to a boil and put into casserole. Braise carrots and turnips in butter. Brown onions and add to meat. Cover casserole, place in oven and bake until contents are done, or about 40 minutes. Remove lid, take off surplus fat and garnish with potatoes, peas, and a sprinkle of chopped parsley. Makes six servings.

DUMPLINGS

1 cup flour
1 tablespoon shortening
1 teaspoon baking powder
1/4 cup milk
1 teaspoon chopped parsley
Pinch of nutmeg
Salt

Blend shortening and flour, fold in dry ingredients, and mix with milk, making a firm dough. Scoop with spoon, and use as directed.

CHIOPINO

1 dozen clams in the shell
1 only, large crab
1 rock cod, medium size
1 cup olive oil
1 cup onions, minced
1 clove of garlic, crushed
1 qt. tomatoes passed through strainer
Salt and pepper to taste

Fry onions in oil. Add garlic and tomatoes, and bring to boil. Put clams well-washed into saucepan. Place over it the crab, cleaned, broken apart and cracked. Cut cod across bone into meat, covering with tomato sauce. Cover and cook slowly for approximately 25 minutes. Recipe serves four persons.

Above, "The City of San Francisco" on the route to Chicago became noted for its delicious meals.

Below, here is the type of club car used in Southern Pacific trains during the 1920's and early 1930's.

Many railways devised special menus for children. Here a young traveler looks over the offerings for small fry as she rides on the Southern Pacific.

PLANTATION SHORTCAKE

Corn Bread:

- 2 cups cornmeal
- 1 cup flour
- 3 teaspoons baking powder
- 1 teaspoon salt
- 2 tablespoons sugar
- 2 cups milk
- 2 eggs
- 2 tablespoons melted butter

Filling:

- 6 slices ham, raw
- 1 chicken (4 lbs.) boiled
- 12 fresh mushrooms
- 1 tablespoon flour
- 1 oz. butter
- 1 cup chicken broth
- 1 cup cream
- Chopped parsley

Blend dry ingredients and sift. Beat eggs, add milk, and stir in dry blend. Add butter last. Pour into buttered baking pan and bake in a hot oven. Cut into squares while hot. Fry ham, slice chicken and place in between squares of corn bread, figuring three to one portion. Pour off some ham drippings and add butter. Slice mushrooms and saute in same. Add flour, and when absorbed, chicken broth and cream. Let simmer until thick. Pour over filled layers, sprinkle with chopped parsley and serve. Makes six servings.

TROUT A LA PRESIDENT

- 2 large trout
- 1 tablespoon finely chopped onions
- 1 tablespoon finely chopped celery
- 1 tablespoon finely chopped fresh mushrooms
- 3 tablespoons butter
- 3/4 cupful fresh bread crumbs
- 1 egg
- Pinch of chopped parsley
- Pinch of thyme
- Salt and pepper to season
- Lemon juice

Saute onions, celery and mushrooms in butter. Add bread crumbs, seasonings, and bind with egg. Clean trout and remove backbone by sliding point of knife along each side of bone, breaking it off at the neck and lower part, leaving head and tail fins intact. Rub trout with salt, pepper and lemon juice, stuff and fold into oiled paper, closing all ends tightly. Bake for about twenty minutes in moderately heated oven, or until trout are done. Remove paper when serving, and sprinkle with parsley butter. This recipe serves two persons.

OLD FASHIONED CHICKEN POT PIE

- 1 chicken (4–5 lbs.)
- 1/2 cup butter
- 1/2 cup flour
- 1/2 cup white mushrooms
- 1 cup French carrots, diced
- 1 cup small potatoes, shaped round
- 1/2 cup green peas
- Seasonings and salt

Put chicken, covered with cold water, on fire, bring to boil, and skim. Salt and season; add two medium-sized carrots, one small onion, branch of celery, and boil until done.

Skin chicken, remove all meat from bones, and cut into large pieces. Dice boiled carrots. Cook peas rapidly in boiling water, without salt, for about twenty minutes. Boil potatoes in chicken broth. Saute mushrooms in butter. Arrange meat and vegetables alternately in casserole.

Melt butter in saucepan, add flour and let cook a few minutes. Add the chicken broth, strained through a cloth, making a thin sauce. Cook thoroughly and pour sauce over ingredients. Place dumplings, made to your own liking, or follow recipe on page 124, over same. Cover and bake in oven for about twenty minutes or until dumplings are done. Makes six servings.

ROULADE OF BEEF

- 4 slices (5 to 6 oz. each) top round
- 4 slices bacon
- 1 small carrot, quartered
- 1 sour pickle, quartered
- 4 olives
- 1 tablespoon minced onion
- 2 tablespoons flour
- 2 medium-sized tomatoes
- 1 oz. butter
- White pepper
- Salt

Pound meat flat, season and sprinkle with onions. Roll in bacon, carrot, pickle, and olives. Tie securely. Dredge with flour and fry in butter until brown. Remove meat to a saucepan. Sprinkle balance of flour into frying pan, let brown nicely, then add enough water or stock to stir up a sauce. Break in tomatoes, and boil for about ten minutes. Strain over roulades and braise until soft. Remove strings before serving. Makes four servings.

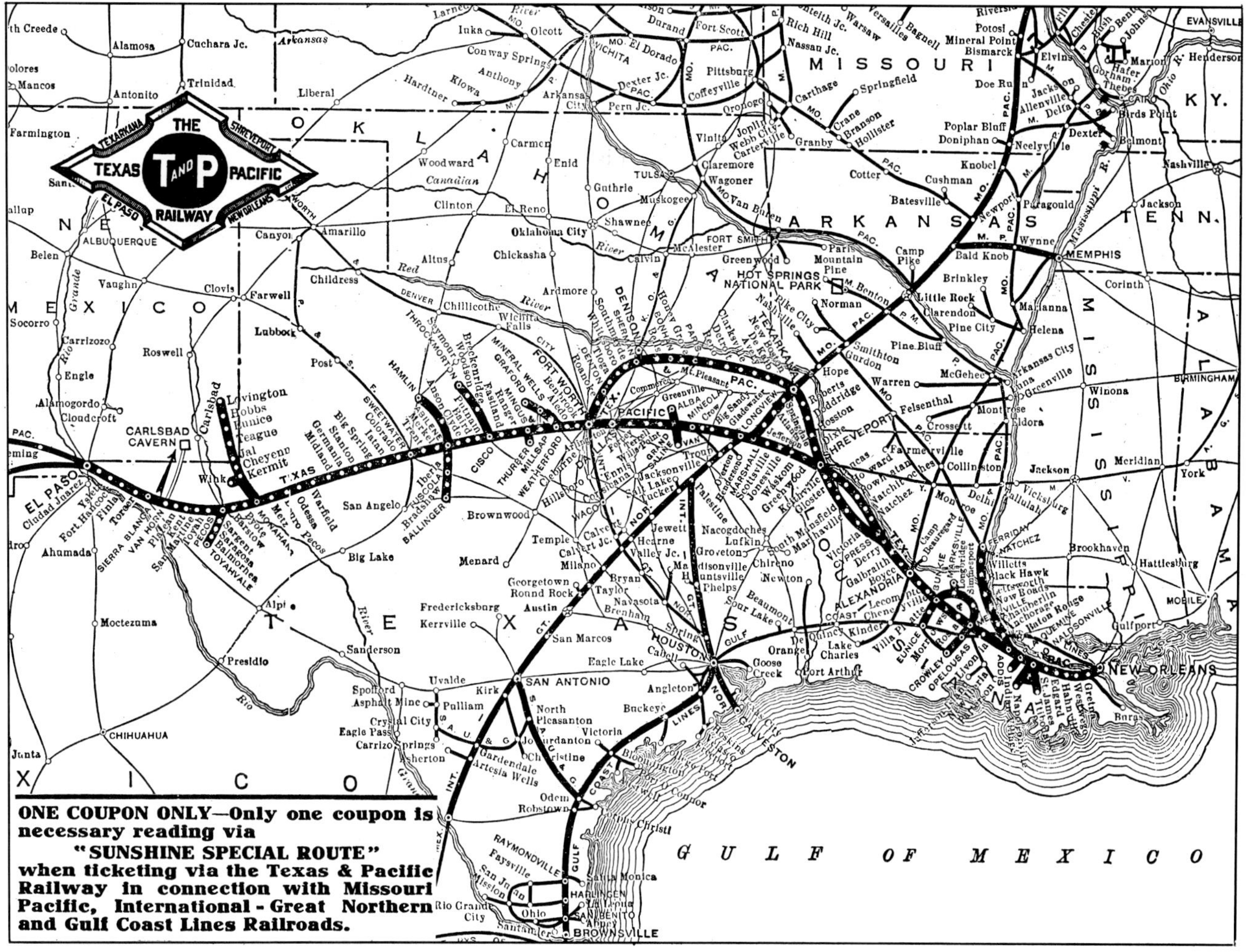

TEXAS and PACIFIC

The Texas and Pacific Railway, organized in 1871, grew into a 1,820-mile system--of which approximately 1,160 miles were the main line between El Paso and New Orleans--through the acquisition of several smaller railroads.

Among the railway companies consolidated into the T and P included the Southern Trans-Continental, the Memphis, El Paso and Pacific, the New Orleans Pacific, the Mississippi and LaFourche, and the Texarkana, Shreveport and Natchez.

In the mid-1960's preliminary plans were approved for merger of the Texas and Pacific with the Missouri Pacific Railroad, owner of most of the company's stock.

The T and P's most famous trains have been *The Texas Eagle,* operating (in cooperation with the Missouri Pacific) from St. Louis to Dallas, Fort Worth, and El Paso, and to Houston and San Antonio. Among the delicious dishes favored on Texas and Pacific dining cars has been cantaloupe pie, the recipe for which is given here.

ILLUSTRATION: THE BETTMANN ARCHIVE INC.

CANTALOUPE PIE A LA TEXAS AND PACIFIC

1 well ripened cantaloupe	1 1/2 cups sugar
2 tablespoons flour	3 tablespoons butter
1/8 teaspoon nutmeg	1 cup cold water

Strain juice from seeds of the cantaloupe and put meat of cantaloupe through a ricer. Preserve both the meat and juice. Pour this mixture into a sauce pan and add the cup of cold water. Place on stove and boil for five minutes. Mix flour and sugar together and slowly add to the hot mixture, stirring constantly. Add the butter and nutmeg. When the mixture is cool, pour into ready-baked pie shell and cover with meringue. Brown in oven.

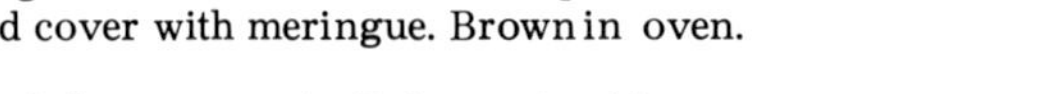

For Meringue: Whites of three eggs (well beaten) with one teaspoon of sugar.

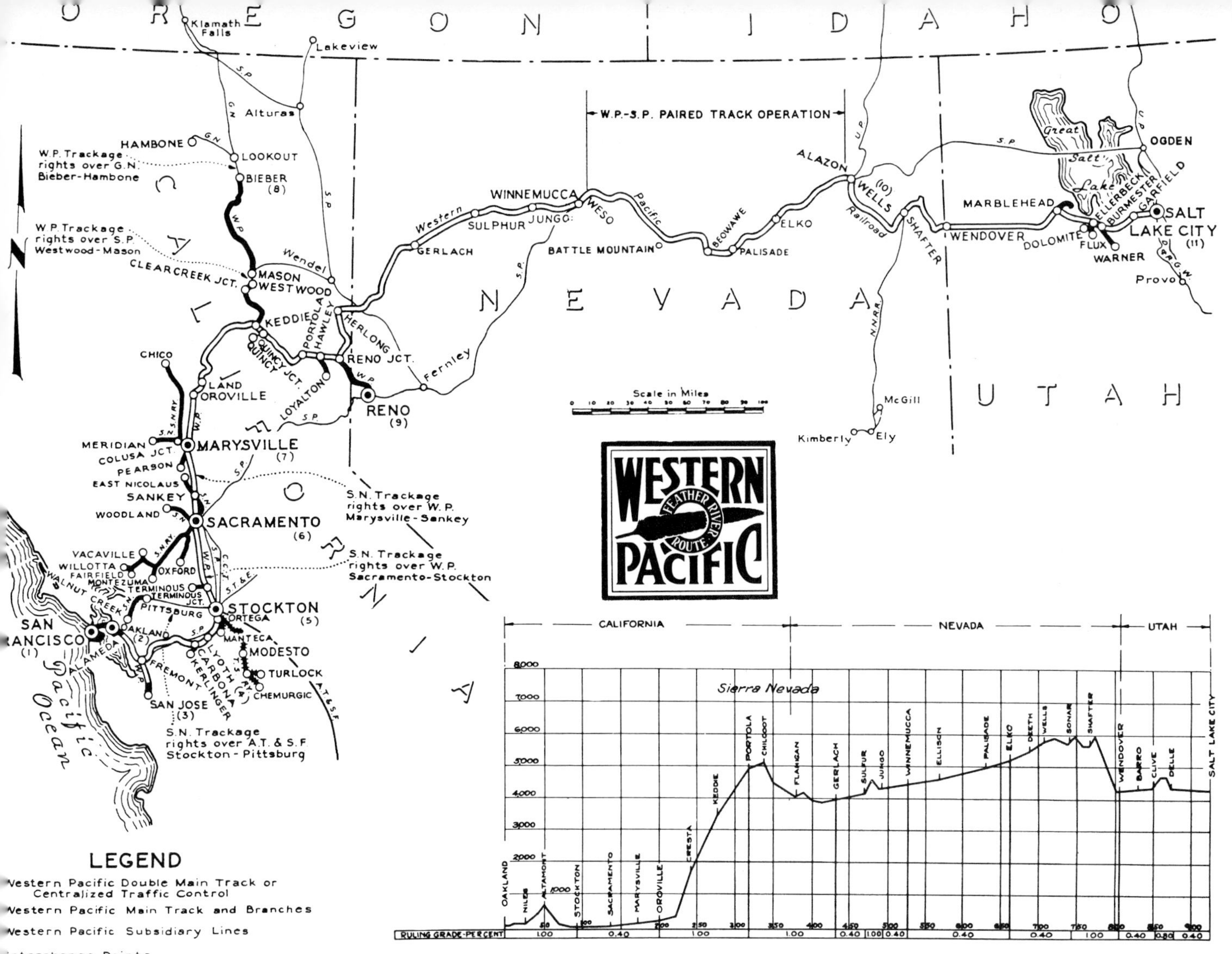

WESTERN PACIFIC

Stretching 927 miles from San Francisco Bay (at Oakland) to Salt Lake City, the Western Pacific Railroad was completed in 1909 as part of a transcontinental route designed to compete with the Southern Pacific. The line was the pride of George Gould, son of tycoon Jay Gould who developed a rail empire that included the Wabash, Missouri Pacific, St. Louis and Southwestern, and Denver and Rio Grande Western railroads.

The line's construction cost much more than was anticipated and was completed on the verge of a business recession, resulting in substantially less freight and passenger revenues than were anticipated.

The big debt created by building the Western Pacific helped to topple the Gould rail empire.

The Western Pacific survived, although under new ownership, and eventually took its place as a progressive and profitable railroad. Its approximately 1,500 miles of track reached important industrial and agriculture areas of California and connected with the Great Northern for service to the Pacific Northwest.

So strategic and well managed had the Western Pacific become over the years that during the

ALL PICTURES THIS CHAPTER: WESTERN PACIFIC RAILROAD

This Western Pacific dining car crew posed for a picture in about 1914 while awaiting arrival of patrons.

1960's substantial blocks of its stock were acquired by the Atchison, Topeka and Santa Fe and the Southern Pacific. Both railroads sought to control the line.

Two of the Western Pacific's famous trains took their names from international expositions. *The Panama Pacific Express* carried many visitors to San Francisco's Panama-Pacific Exposition, held to celebrate the opening of the Panama Canal in 1915, and *The Exposition Flyer* was launched for the San Francisco International Exposition of 1940.

The menus of both trains featured delicious dishes designed to delight the cosmopolitan appetites of the travelers attending these fairs.

The Western Pacific's best known passenger train has been *The California Zephyr,* a crack streamliner that began service in 1949 between Oakland and Chicago (as a joint operation with the Denver and Rio Grande Western and the Chicago, Burlington and Quincy railroads).

The streamliner made the overland trip in approximately 49 hours and almost as soon as it began service was pronounced a success. The train's luxurious cars, including Vista-Dome coaches for enjoyment of the scenery, lured many travelers from airplanes.

The food served on the crack train's diners also made the trip attractive.

These recipes represent concerted culinary efforts during the years of Western Pacific passenger service. Several dishes have an Italian flavor because an emphasis on this type of cooking once was featured on *The California Zephyr.*

"As you travel over this bountiful land of ours, may you be ever reminded of the grace Almighty God has bestowed upon us. Let us acknowledge our debt to Him with prayers of thanksgiving."

Select Dinners

To insure prompt service, please write each item on meal check.
It will be a pleasure to serve any dish not listed that you may wish if it is available.

"Table Flowers are Colorado Carnations"

Following Items Will Be Served with Meals at Additional Prices Shown:

Assorted Relish .45 — Shrimp Cocktail .60

(Price opposite each entree includes Soup or Fruit Cup, Vegetable, Potato, Rolls, Dessert and Beverage)

Choice of One:

Green Turtle Soup, Anglaise — Hot or Jellied Consomme — Chilled Fruit Cup

Broiled Filet of Barracuda, Lemon Butter.......... 3.65
Baked Tunafish Tetrazzinni, au Gratin.......... 3.20
Baked Individual Chicken Pie en Casserole.......... 3.10
Cottage Fried Pork Chops, Country Gravy.......... 3.50
Roast Top Sirloin of Beef, au jus.......... 3.95

Baked Potato with Butter — Whipped Potatoes

Spinach, German Style — Peas in Butter

Hot Rolls — French Rolls

Waldorf Salad
(Served with these meals 35c additional)

Butterscotch Sundae — Chilled Grapefruit — Cherry Cream Pie

Peach Melba — Orange Sherbet

Individual Cheese - Wafers

Coffee — Tea — Milk — Hot Chocolate — Decaffeinated Coffee

Broiler Special

$5.25

Broiled Sirloin Steak (12 oz.)
Button Mushrooms — Long Branch Potatoes
Waldorf Salad
Hot Rolls
Choice of Beverage

En Casserole

$3.25

Tomato Juice or Fruit Cup
Ragout of Beef a la Creole
Whipped Potatoes — Demi-Tossed Salad
Hot Rolls
Choice of Dessert
Choice of Beverage

A la Carte

APPETIZERS — Shrimp Cocktail .85
Assorted Relish .60

SOUP — Cup .40

ENTREE (Served with Bread and Butter)

Broiled Filet of Barracuda, Lemon Butter.......... 2.90
Chilled Red Salmon, Potato Salad, Garni.......... 2.30
Baked Tunafish Tetrazinni, au Gratin.......... 2.45
Baked Individual Chicken Pie, en Casserole.......... 2.35
Cottage Fried Pork Chops, Country Gravy.......... 2.75
Roast Top Sirloin of Beef, au jus.......... 3.20
Broiled French Lamb Chops, Rasher of Bacon.......... 2.75
Sugar Cured Ham with Two Eggs.......... 1.75
Golden Omelette with Preserves or Jelly.......... 1.60

SANDWICHES Combination - Double Deck

Sliced Chicken on Toast
Sliced Combination Salad
Choice of Beverage
2.10

Lettuce, Bacon and Tomato
Potato Salad
Choice of Beverage
1.95

Steward in Charge of this Car is ....

Managers of Dining Car Service
P. M. Scott, Burlington, Chicago
F. J. Corrigan, Rio Grande, Denver
W. J. Powell, Western Pacific, Oakland

No. 1/4
3-65

VEGETABLES — Baked Potato with Butter .55
Whipped Potatoes .35
Spinach, German Style .45
Peas in Butter .45

SALADS (Includes Saltines and Melba Toast)

Chilled Fruit Salad Plate, Cottage Cheese 1.75
Sliced Combination Salad Plate .75
Head Lettuce, Half Portion .50
California Zephyr Combination Salad Bowl 1.85
Choice of Dressings
French-Olive Oil and Vinegar, Italian, 1000 Island, Bleu Cheese or Mayonnaise

DESSERT

Cherry Cream Pie .45 — Butterscotch Sundae .55
Chilled Grapefruit .50 — Peach Melba .70
Individual Cheese - Wafers .50

BEVERAGES

Pot Service for One — Coffee, Tea, Chocolate,
Decaffeinated Coffee .35
Individual Milk or Buttermilk .25

Additional charge will be made for service outside the dining car.
This service is subject to delay when dining car is busy.

Diners aboard the Chicago–San Francisco California Zephyr *made selections from this menu in 1965.* —*Donald Duke Collection*

Western Pacific's "Panama-Pacific Express," crack passenger train inaugurated in 1914, became noted for fine food. Here it stops in the Feather River Canyon after leaving a tunnel in the Sierra.

TOSSED GREEN SALAD

Romaine
Leaf lettuce
Cucumbers
Green peppers
Garbanzo beans
Pimientos
Green onions
Tomatoes, skinned, cut in 1/8 wedges
Radishes
Olive oil and vinegar Italian dressing
Salt
White pepper

Marinate garbanzo beans in olive oil and vinegar Italian dressing for about four hours. Adjust amounts of ingredients to the number of persons being served.

Prepare equal portions of romaine and leaf lettuce in small pieces. To each two quarts add one cup of thin julienne sliced one and one half inch lengh green peppers, one cup of thin sliced radishes, one cup of diced cucumbers, one-half cup of chopped green onions, one-half cup of small square-cut pimentos, and one cup of marinated garbanzo beans. All ingredients should be kept chilled and crisp.

Just prior to service, place the mixed salad ingredients in a large wooden salad bowl and then add olive oil and vinegar Italian salad dressing; season lightly with salt and pepper. Toss salad lightly until all ingredients have a slight covering of dressing. Garnish salad with skinned tomatoes cut into one-eighth wedges in a circle around the salad bowl. Place six or eight pieces of tomato on top of the salad in a pin wheel pattern. For serving, two pieces of tomato should be placed on each individual portion. Above measurements will serve approximately eight persons.

ANTIPASTO (as served on the *California Zephyr)*

On silver compote:

Red beans (see recipe below)
Tiny sweet green peppers
Dried olives
Sardines

A leaf of lettuce is to be placed in compartments of the compote (in accordance with serving on the *California Zephyr* and filled with the above items. Bouillon spoons and cocktail forks are to accompany the compote to the table. Adjust amount of ingredients in accordance with number being served.

On silver platter:

Sliced salami
Thin sliced prosciutto
Celery hearts
Green onions

The food should be served on a chilled platter, and amounts should be adjusted to the number being served.

STEAMED FINNAN HADDIE

Finnan haddie
Butter
Lemon juice

Remove bone and skin from haddie and cut into portion sized filets. Steam in colander (tightly covered) over boiling water until tender. Serve piping hot with maitre d'hotel butter over fish. Garnish with slice of lemon and sprig of parsley.

FILET OF FISH BAKED MARGUERY

6 lbs. filet of fish
6 tablespoons melted butter, oil or margarine
Salt and pepper
3/4 cup minced onion
2/3 cup butter or margarine
3/4 cup flour
2 cups milk
3 cups light cream
6 teaspoons bottle thick meat sauce

6 teaspoons lemon juice
6 tablespoons sherry wine
3 teaspoons salt
1 egg
6 teaspoons Parmesan cheese
A little white pepper
Dash of cayenne pepper

Arrange the filets in a hot greased baking pan; brush over with melted butter and sprinkle lightly with salt and pepper. Then sprinkle top with finely chopped onion and bake in a hot oven of 450 degrees F. until easily flaked and moist.

Meanwhile melt two-thirds cup butter in a double boiler, add flour, and stir until smooth. Stir in milk and cream; cook until smooth and thickened. Stir in the remaining ingredients, except egg yolk. Heat and pour slowly over beaten egg yolk. Continue to stir; blend well and reheat quickly in double boiler; then pour at once over the baked fish. Just before service brown the top lightly.

SALMON-MACARONI, AU GRATIN

1 1/2 lbs. elbow macaroni
1/4 lb. butter or margarine
1 cup finely chopped green peppers
6 cans 10 1/2 oz. cream of celery soup
4 lbs. canned red salmon
1 pt. milk
2 lbs. grated American cheese
3 teaspoons salt
Cracker crumbs

Cook elbow macaroni in salt water until tender. Drain and blanch with cold water. Melt butter, add finely chopped green peppers. Cook until tender. (Do not brown.) Gradually stir in soup. Add three teaspoons salt. Drain and flake salmon. Combine one cup of salmon liquid with milk and stir into soup mixture. Heat and add cooked macaroni, flaked salmon and 1 1/2 lbs. of grated American cheese. Turn into buttered au gratin dish of sufficient portion to be rounded; sprinkle with cracker crumbs and remaining grated American cheese. Dot with butter. Bake in moderate oven (350 degrees F.) until golden brown. Be sure to serve piping hot. This is enough for 20 portions.

CHICKEN CACCIATORA

4 lbs. spring chicken cut into pieces
1/2 cup flour
1 teaspoon salt
1/2 cup fat
1/4 cup chopped onion
1 clove garlic, chopped fine
1/4 cup chopped carrots
1 basil or bay leaf
3 sprigs parsley
4 cups tomatoes
1 teaspoon salt
Dash of pepper
1/4 cup sherry or white wine

Dredge chicken in flour, sprinkle with salt and brown in fat until golden on all sides. Place in covered dish in warm place. Brown onion, garlic, carrots, parsley, basil or bay leaf in fat left in frying pan. Strain tomatoes (when strained, you will have two cups tomato pulp), add tomato pulp to brown vegetables in frying pan. Add one teaspoon salt and dash of pepper and bring to boil; add chicken and wine and simmer until chicken is tender. Serve with sprig of celery. This makes four portions.

VEAL SCALOPPINI A LA PARMESAN

1 lb. veal steak or cutlets
1 cup mushrooms, drained
1/2 cup Parmesan cheese
Flour
Garlic
3 medium tomatoes
1/2 cup dry white wine
Olive oil
Salt
Pepper

Cut the veal in about two-inch squares, season veal with salt and pepper, roll in flour, saute veal with one clove of garlic in oil until golden brown (remove garlic). Add tomatoes and mushrooms to veal and place in baking pans. Mix white wine and Parmesan cheese and pour over veal and sauce. Bake in 400-degree oven for 20 to 30 minutes, or until cheese is brown. This is enough for four portions.

RAVIOLI AND SPAGHETTI

Spaghetti sauce (any good prepared canned sauce)
Ravioli
Spaghetti

Spaghetti is to be cooked in salted boiling water until tender, (however, be sure not to overcook); blanch in cold water to whiten, then place in hot water. Ravioli to be cooked in salted boiling water until tender; then remove from water and place in colander on steam table and cover with clean wet towel. Heat spaghetti sauce in double boiler and keep hot.

Pasta service and portion (Italian dinner): Place four ounces of hot spaghetti on hot six-inch service plate; place two ravioli on top of spaghetti; two cookspoons of spaghetti sauce over ravioli and spaghetti. Sprinkle with cheese and serve piping hot.

ITALIAN RED BEANS

Red kidney beans
Chopped chives
Chopped parsley
Red wine vinegar
Olive oil
Juice of 1 clove of garlic
Salt

A good grade of red kidney beans is to be crained of juice and blanched in cold water; drain beans thoroughly. Mix olive oil and wine vinegar, using 1/3 cup of wine vinegar to each half cup of olive oil. Chop chives fine, add to beans; add juice of one clove of garlic. Marinate beans in the olive oil and wine vinegar for approximately four hours; season slightly with salt. Sprinkle lightly with freshly chopped parsley just before serving. Keep well-chilled at all times. Vary amounts of various ingredients according to the number of persons to be served.

MARSALA WINE NUT SUNDAE WITH WAFERS

Ice cream
Marsala wine
Pignoli nuts (pine nuts)
Wafers

Pignoli nuts are to be toasted in oven slightly or until very light brown.

Place dipper of ice cream in chilled sherbet glass and pour 3/4 ounce of chilled Marsala wine over ice cream. Sprinkle with toasted Pignoli nuts. Underline sherbet glass with doily on six-inch plate with two wafers on same plate, and spoon for service.

FRESH SHRIMP A LA NEWBURG EN CASSEROLE

Shrimp (fresh or frozen)
Egg yolks
Butter
Sherry wine
Cayenne pepper
Cream
Milk
Cornstarch
Salt

Remove shell from raw shrimp. Split down back and clean. Wash thoroughly and drain. Saute the shrimp in a little butter over fast fire for about 20 minutes. During the cooking, add a little sherry wine. Shuffle or flip the shrimp several times during cooking to insure they are cooked evenly. Add salt and a little cayenne pepper during the cooking. Then pour over sufficient hot cream and milk to cover, using two-thirds cream and one-third milk. Simmer slowly for approximately 15 minutes. Beat six egg yolks to each quart of liquid. Add a small amount of corn starch mixed in cold water to the egg yolks; mix well. Slowly stir the egg yolk and corn starch into the shrimp mixture to thicken. Add sufficient sherry wine to give good flavor. The sauce should be medium thick when properly prepared. If it is too thick when finished, it may be thinned by using equal amounts of hot cream and milk.

TOASTED GARLIC ROLLS

Vienna rolls
Olive oil
Garlic

Marinate garlic in olive oil not less than four hours. Split Vienna roll lengthwise, brush very lightly with garlic flavored olive oil; toast in oven until very light brown, serve very hot.

STUFFED PORK TENDERLOIN WITH CREAM GRAVY

3 large or 6 small pork tenderloins
1 tablespoon flour
2 oz. butter
1 cup cream

Split pork tenderloins lengthwise and fill with dressing (Raisin, see recipe), tie and dredge with flour, arrange in roasting pan, brush with butter and roast about 20 minutes in hot oven. Remove the tenderloins, sprinkle a little flour in pan, add cream, let simmer for a few minutes and strain. When serving, remove string, place open side down on platter and cover with pan gravy. Makes six servings.

RAISIN DRESSING
(For Stuffed Pork Tenderloin)

1 cup fresh bread crumbs
1/4 cup seedless raisins
1 oz. butter
1 egg
Pinch of salt
Pinch of cinnamon
Milk to moisten

Mix ingredients well.

SPRING VEGETABLE SOUP

1 No. 3-can meat tomatoes
1 cup diced raw carrots
1 cup diced raw celery
1 cup diced raw turnips
1 1/2 gal. (approx.) stock (chicken, beef, or veal)
2/3 cup fresh or frozen lima beans
2/3 cup fresh or frozen peas
1 cup diced onions
2/3 cup fresh green beans
1 oz. butter
1 potato
Seasoning
Parsley

Wash all vegetables well in colander, drain and place in stock pot with one ounce butter. Season with salt and pepper. Cover pot and saute slowly for about 15 minutes, stirring a few times during cooking to be sure vegetables do not brown or burn. Add tomatoes and approximately 1 1/2 gallon meat stock. Drop one large raw, peeled potato into soup to absorb the acid from tomatoes. Simmer until vegetables are tender; skim grease from top of soup. Season to taste, remove potato from pot, and serve. Sprinkle each serving with freshly chopped parsley. This recipe makes approximately 24 servings.

Above, the Western Pacific's California Zephyr *crosses a trestle near Portola, California.*

The steward aboard the California Zephyr *gives menus to this traveling family.* —*Donald Duke Collection*

INDEX

APPETIZERS

SALADS

DRESSINGS, SAUCES, AND GRAVIES

SOUPS AND CHOWDERS

Left, Interior of Pullman car of the 1870's.

ILLUSTRATION: THE BETTMANN ARCHIVE, INC.

EGG DISHES

FISH

Above, note ornate furnishings of a diner during the teens on the Panama Limited on the Illinois Central.

A dining car tradition, Louisville & Nashville's famous Country Ham Breakfast. —Donald Duke Collection

A delicious salad bowl was offered to these happy diners aboard the Burlington–Rio Grande–Western Pacific California Zephyr.
—Donald Duke Collection

FOWL

MEAT

VEGETABLES

BREADS

FRENCH TOAST, HOT CAKES, AND FRITTERS

Left, "The Chief," Santa Fe's Chicago-Los Angeles streamliner, enters a tunnel in rugged Cajon Pass.

Above, the Civil War locomotive "The General" is shown in 1962 by the Tennessee Capitol at Nashville.

PIES AND CAKES

OTHER DESSERTS

SPENCER CRUMP COLLECTION

The compact kitchen of a Central Pacific diner was shown in this illustration of the 1870's.

MISCELLANEOUS

Above, Great Northern's first Empire Builder is seen here at St. Paul in inaugural year of 1929.

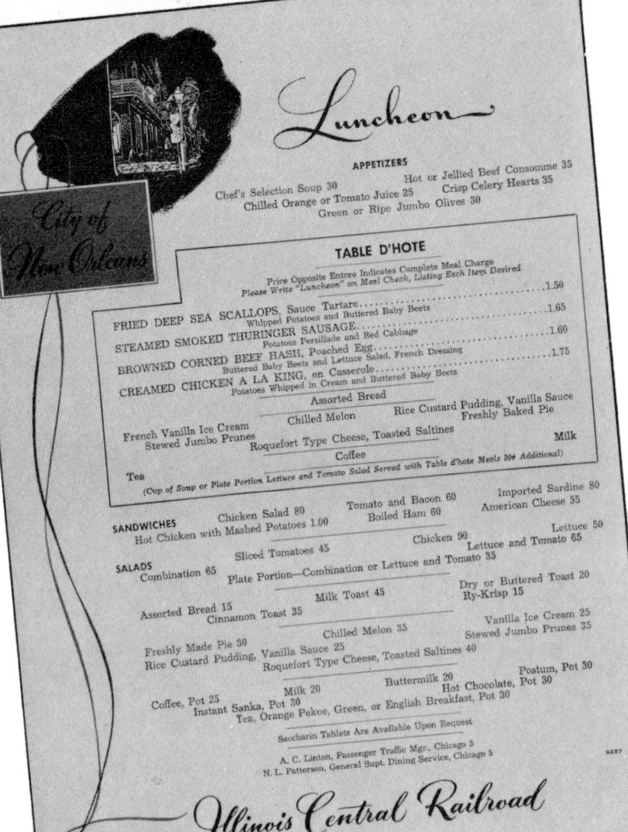

City of New Orleans

Luncheon

APPETIZERS

Chef's Selection Soup 30 — Hot or Jellied Beef Consomme 35
Chilled Orange or Tomato Juice 25 — Crisp Celery Hearts 35
Green or Ripe Jumbo Olives 30

TABLE D'HOTE

Price Opposite Entree Indicates Complete Meal Charge
Please Write "Luncheon" on Meal Check, Listing Each Item Desired

FRIED DEEP SEA SCALLOPS, Sauce Tartare....1.50
Whipped Potatoes and Buttered Baby Beets
STEAMED SMOKED THURINGER SAUSAGE....1.65
Potatoes Persillade and Red Cabbage
BROWNED CORNED BEEF HASH, Poached Egg....1.60
Buttered Baby Beets and Lettuce Salad, French Dressing
CREAMED CHICKEN A LA KING, en Casserole....1.75
Potatoes Whipped in Cream and Buttered Baby Beets

Assorted Bread

French Vanilla Ice Cream — Chilled Melon — Rice Custard Pudding, Vanilla Sauce
Stewed Jumbo Prunes — Freshly Baked Pie
Roquefort Type Cheese, Toasted Saltines

Tea — Coffee — Milk

(Cup of Soup or Plate Portion Lettuce and Tomato Salad Served with Table d'hote Meals 30¢ Additional)

SANDWICHES — Chicken Salad 80 — Tomato and Bacon 60 — Imported Sardine 80
Hot Chicken with Mashed Potatoes 1.00 — Boiled Ham 60 — American Cheese 55

SALADS — Sliced Tomatoes 45 — Chicken 90 — Lettuce 50
Combination 65 — Lettuce and Tomato 65
Plate Portion—Combination or Lettuce and Tomato 35

Assorted Bread 15 — Milk Toast 45 — Dry or Buttered Toast 20
Cinnamon Toast 35 — Ry-Krisp 15

Freshly Made Pie 30 — Chilled Melon 35 — Vanilla Ice Cream 25
Rice Custard Pudding, Vanilla Sauce 25 — Stewed Jumbo Prunes 35
Roquefort Type Cheese, Toasted Saltines 40

Coffee, Pot 25 — Milk 20 — Buttermilk 20 — Postum, Pot 30
Instant Sanka, Pot 30 — Hot Chocolate, Pot 30
Tea, Orange Pekoe, Green, or English Breakfast, Pot 30

Saccharin Tablets Are Available Upon Request

A. C. Linton, Passenger Traffic Mgr., Chicago 5
N. L. Patterson, General Supt. Dining Service, Chicago 5

Illinois Central Railroad

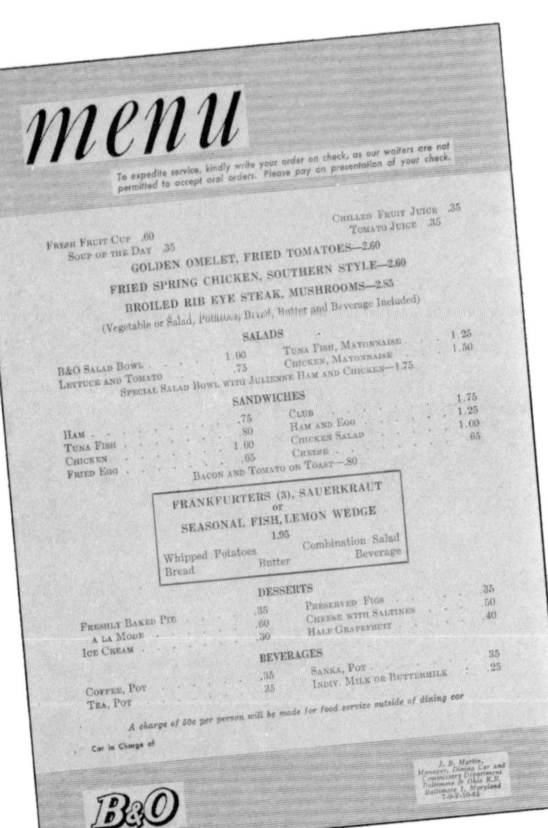

menu

To expedite service, kindly write your order on check, as our waiters are not permitted to accept oral orders. Please pay on presentation of your check.

Fresh Fruit Cup .60 — Chilled Fruit Juice .35
Soup of the Day .35 — Tomato Juice .35

GOLDEN OMELET, FRIED TOMATOES—2.60
FRIED SPRING CHICKEN, SOUTHERN STYLE—2.60
BROILED RIB EYE STEAK, MUSHROOMS—2.85
(Vegetable or Salad, Potatoes, Bread, Butter and Beverage Included)

SALADS

B&O Salad Bowl ... 1.00 — Tuna Fish, Mayonnaise ... 1.25
Lettuce and Tomato ... .75 — Chicken, Mayonnaise ... 1.50
Special Salad Bowl with Julienne Ham and Chicken—1.75

SANDWICHES

Ham ... .75 — Club ... 1.75
Tuna Fish ... .80 — Ham and Egg ... 1.25
Chicken ... 1.00 — Chicken Salad ... 1.00
Fried Egg ... .65 — Cheese ... .65
Bacon and Tomato on Toast—.80

FRANKFURTERS (3), SAUERKRAUT
or
SEASONAL FISH, LEMON WEDGE
1.95
Whipped Potatoes — Combination Salad
Bread — Butter — Beverage

DESSERTS

Freshly Baked Pie ... .35 — Preserved Figs ... .35
a la Mode ... .60 — Cheese with Saltines ... .50
Ice Cream ... .30 — Half Grapefruit ... .40

BEVERAGES

Coffee, Pot ... .35 — Sanka, Pot ... 35
Tea, Pot ... 35 — Indiv. Milk or Buttermilk ... .25

A charge of 50¢ per person will be made for food service outside of dining car

Car in Charge of

J. B. Martin, Manager, Dining Car and Commissary Department, Baltimore & Ohio R.R., Baltimore 1, Maryland
7-8-E-10-65

B&O

BROADWAY LIMITED

sandwich menu

ALL SANDWICHES GARNISHED WITH PICKLE CHIPS AND TWO SLICES OF TOMATO
NO EXTRA CHARGE FOR TOASTED SANDWICHES
ALL SANDWICHES SERVED ON WHITE BREAD
RYE OR WHOLE WHEAT WILL BE SUBSTITUTED ON REQUEST

Cold Roast Beef . . . 2.35
Open Faced Chopped Steak with Melted Cheese on Toast . . . 1.70
Triple Decker Club . . . 2.35
Ham and Cheese *(American or Swiss Cheese)*, Lettuce . . . 1.45
Open Faced Sliced Tomato, Egg and Anchovy . . . 1.50
Cold Chicken *(White Meat)* with Lettuce & Mayonnaise . . . 1.85
Sliced Cold Chicken and Ham with Lettuce . . . 2.10
Swiss Cheese, Sliced Egg, Lettuce, Tomato . . . 1.45
Imported Sardine . . . 1.60
Ham with Lettuce . . . 1.10

RUSSIAN OR MAYONNAISE DRESSING SERVED ON REQUEST

20

PENNSYLVANIA RAILROAD

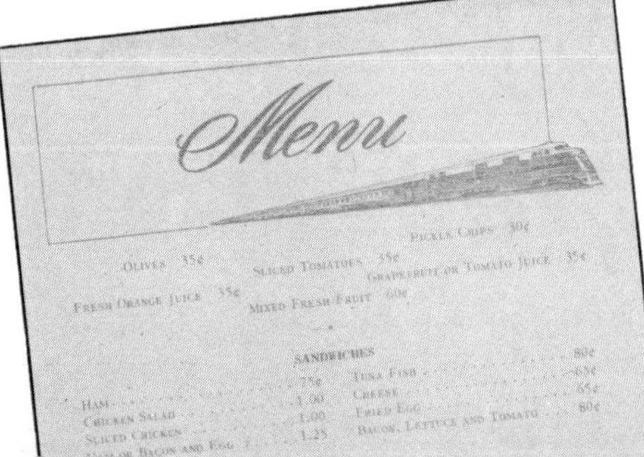

Menu

Pickle Chips 30¢
Olives 35¢ — Sliced Tomatoes 35¢ — Grapefruit or Tomato Juice 35¢
Fresh Orange Juice 35¢ — Mixed Fresh Fruit 60¢

SANDWICHES

Ham ... 75¢ — Tuna Fish ... 80¢
Chicken Salad ... 1.00 — Cheese ... 65¢
Sliced Chicken ... 1.00 — Fried Egg ... 65¢
... of Bacon and Egg ... 1.25 — Bacon, Lettuce and Tomato ... 80¢